WRITING TO THE KING

In the century before Chaucer a new language of political critique emerged. In political verse of the period, composed in Anglo-Latin, Anglo-Norman, and Middle English, poets write as if addressing the king himself, drawing on their sense of the rights granted by Magna Carta. These apparent appeals to the sovereign increase with the development of parliament in the late thirteenth century and the emergence of the common petition, and become prominent, in an increasingly sophisticated literature, during the political crises of the early fourteenth century. However, very little of this writing was truly directed to the king. As David Matthews shows, the form of address was a rhetorical stance revealing much about the position from which writers were composing, the audiences they wished to reach, and their construction of political and national subjects.

DAVID MATTHEWS is Senior Lecturer in Middle English Literature and Culture at the University of Manchester.

CAMBRIDGE STUDIES IN MEDIEVAL LITERATURE

GENERAL EDITOR
Alastair Minnis, *Yale University*

EDITORIAL BOARD
Zygmunt G. Barański, *University of Cambridge*
Christopher C. Baswell, *University of California, Los Angeles*
John Burrow, *University of Bristol*
Mary Carruthers, *New York University*
Rita Copeland, *University of Pennsylvania*
Simon Gaunt, *King's College, London*
Steven Kruger, *City University of New York*
Nigel Palmer, *University of Oxford*
Winthrop Wetherbee, *Cornell University*
Jocelyn Wogan-Browne, *University of York*

This series of critical books seeks to cover the whole area of literature written in the major medieval languages – the main European vernaculars, and medieval Latin and Greek – during the period c.1100–1500. Its chief aim is to publish and stimulate fresh scholarship and criticism on medieval literature, special emphasis being placed on understanding major works of poetry, prose, and drama in relation to the contemporary culture and learning which fostered them.

Recent titles in the series
Laura Ashe *Fiction and History in England, 1066–1200*
Mary Carruthers *The Book of Memory: A Study of Memory in Medieval Culture*
J. A. Burrow *The Poetry of Praise*
Andrew Cole *Literature and Heresy in the Age of Chaucer*
Suzanne M. Yeager *Jerusalem in Medieval Narrative*
Nicole R. Rice *Lay Piety and Religious Discipline in Middle English Literature*
D. H. Green *Women and Marriage in German Medieval Romance*
Peter Godman *Paradoxes of Conscience in the High Middle Ages: Abelard, Heloise and the Archpoet*
Edwin D. Craun *Ethics and Power in Medieval English Reformist Writing*
David Matthews *Writing to the King: Nation, Kingship, and Literature in England, 1250–1350*

A complete list of titles in the series can be found at the end of the volume.

WRITING TO THE KING

Nation, Kingship, and Literature in England, 1250–1350

DAVID MATTHEWS

 CAMBRIDGE
UNIVERSITY PRESS

CAMBRIDGE UNIVERSITY PRESS
Cambridge, New York, Melbourne, Madrid, Cape Town, Singapore,
São Paulo, Delhi, Dubai, Tokyo

Cambridge University Press
The Edinburgh Building, Cambridge CB2 8RU, UK

Published in the United States of America by Cambridge University Press, New York

www.cambridge.org
Information on this title: www.cambridge.org/9780521111379

© David Matthews 2010

First published 2010

Printed in the United Kingdom at the University Press, Cambridge

A catalogue record for this publication is available from the British Library

Library of Congress Cataloguing in Publication data
Matthews, David, 1963–
Writing to the king : nation, kingship, and literature in England, 1250–1350 /
David Matthews.
p.   cm. – (Cambridge studies in medieval literature ; 77)
Includes bibliographical references and index.
ISBN 978-0-521-11137-9 (hardback)
1. Political poetry, English (Middle)–History and criticism.   2. Politics and
literature–England–History–To 1500.   3. Literature and history–England–
History–To 1500.   4. Letter writing in literature.   5. Kings and rulers in literature.
6. Great Britain–Politics and government–1066–1485–Historiography.
I. Title.   II. Series.
PR317.P6M38 2010
821′.1093581–dc22
2009052530

ISBN 978-0-521-11137-9 Hardback

To my mother, Jeanne Matthews
with profound gratitude for all that she has made possible

Contents

Preface

I began this book at the end and came to its topic obliquely. I first read Laurence Minot's poetry in Joseph Ritson's 1795 edition in connection with another project and was perplexed at the relative neglect of the lively work of a poet active during Chaucer's youth.[1] Thinking about this, I was led to another antiquarian work, Thomas Wright's *Political Songs of England*, first published in 1839, reissued by Peter Coss in facsimile in 1996 and still a valuable anthology.[2] It furnished a great deal of the material discussed here and pointed me towards much else. Hence, although this book will appear to be a straightforward work of medieval *studies*, it is informed by and grew out of earlier work on antiquarian medievalist scholarship and the early shaping of the discipline. Some regard this as medieval*ism*; this book reflects my larger contention that the study of medieval literature should go alongside considerations of how that literature and its study have been constructed.

At its simplest, the book began as an attempt to do more with the genre, or genres, of political verse in England in the period before Minot's presumed death date of 1352, stopping short of the revolution in English writing which then took place in the second half of the fourteenth century. The political verses inhabit a grey zone between historical source material and literary writing. Thomas Wright's own assumption was that they were sources for the social historian. To a degree, however, he also saw them as expressions of the voice of the people and some later inquiry into them has been motivated by a desire to recover such voices. Alternatively, many of these political verses can be seen as quite skilful *creations* of voice, ventriloquisings of various possible speaking positions, probably composed by clerics. In that regard, they could be viewed as having something in common with the similarly (if immensely more sophisticatedly) ventriloquial *Canterbury Tales* or *Piers Plowman*.

The main focus of this book is the century before 1350; I do not ultimately attempt to make all the possible links forward to Ricardian writing. In this respect, the book responds to the tendency in Middle English studies of the past two decades to broaden the discipline's horizons. One of my concerns in this book is to help bring the century before Chaucer back into view, just as the half-century *after* Chaucer has been, in recent criticism, so brilliantly explored. It is no exaggeration to say that we have seen a renaissance in studies of fifteenth-century England in the past decade.[3] Beneficial though this has been to a more inclusive and arguably accurate sense of what Middle English literature is, it has also lent itself to a refashioning of literary history which links Chaucer ever more firmly forward to Wyatt and the sixteenth century, at the cost of detaching him and his contemporaries from their predecessors.[4] The re-establishing of the fifteenth-century writers is new; the downplaying of the period before 1350, with its consequent tacit re-placing of Chaucer as Father of English Poetry, simply restates assumptions prevalent from the sixteenth century onwards.

My aim here is to counter the increasing tendency to assume that it is only with the birth of Chaucer that Middle English becomes interesting. Firmly linking the thirteenth century and the early fourteenth with the period after 1350 may not provide an easily negotiated, curriculum-friendly period. But it might just give a truer sense of the development of late medieval English literature. In reading the 'pre-Ricardian' writing discussed in this book, I have found again and again concerns in it that *do* anticipate the later and better-known work – and in such a way as to revise some recent critical paradigms. It would be surprising if it did not. Much of the literature in question, after all, is what would have been available to the young Chaucer, Gower, and Langland before they began to write and absorb the lessons of continental literature.

I embark on this project with an introduction which discusses the idea of 'writing to the king'. Here, I juxtapose the literary materials with the common petition, in order to show how the motif of 'writing to the king' – literally possible via the petition – is routinely deployed in literary writings. This suggests that 'documentary culture', as discussed by Emily Steiner in particular, was not confined to Ricardian writing but (not surprisingly) goes back to the period of the beginnings of parliament.[5]

The introduction also considers writing that flows in the other direction, from king to people: the well-known letters addressed by Henry III to his subjects in 1258, written in English. In closing the introduction, I consider the implications of this unusual move, not to be repeated until the fifteenth century, and look at the claims and counter-claims that have been made about nationalism in the Middle Ages, in order to conclude that although they may well not describe any *existing* form of political community in England, the letters are an attempt to wish political harmony into being by imagining it.

There is little surviving political verse in *English* before the Barons' Wars in the 1260s. Chapter 1 is largely devoted to discussion of such Latin verse as *The Song of Lewes*, found in London, British Library, Harley MS 978, and it considers the implications, for a sense of Englishness, of such clerkly and Latinate productions. The survival of one English poem, however – 'The Song Against the King of Almaigne' – does suggest that a lively English tradition of political satire and advice was also in existence. Chapter 2 examines the abusive Anglo-Norman and English verses of Langtoft's *Chronicle*, which provide a commentary on the invasion of Scotland by Edward I in 1296. These I consider in relation to recent arguments for the emergence of an English national self-consciousness from the late thirteenth century.

Chapter 3 examines poems from the very end of the reign of Edward I through to Edward III's entry into personal rule in 1330. While examples of Anglo-Norman verse are still found in this period, there was now a growing tradition of complaint, satire and advice in English. Such poems as 'The Execution of Sir Simon Fraser', the Anglo-Norman 'Outlaw's Song of Trailbaston', two versions of the 'Elegy on the Death of Edward I', and Adam Davy's dream visions of Edward II are juxtaposed with chronicle materials in this chapter in order to examine their meditations on kingship and justice in the context of troubled handovers of power between 1307 and 1330. Chapter 4 also considers the reigns of the first three Edwards but focuses in particular on the 1340s and the major crisis confronting Edward III at the beginning of that decade. It looks at complaint writings, such as William of Pagula's *Speculum Regis Edwardi III* and English poems: the 'Song of the Husbandman', 'Against the King's Taxes', *The Simonie*, 'King Edward and the Shepherd'.

Chapter 5 then considers views of the 1330s and 1340s from which this sense of crisis is entirely absent. Praising his king and positing a unity between king and nation, Laurence Minot constructs an aggressive English nationhood. Finally, in the conclusion, I will consider the implications of this study for the reading of later fourteenth-century literature.

It is a very happy task to acknowledge those who helped me in the writing of this book, which took place through many changes. It was begun in the Rare Books room of the British Library, to the staff of which I am deeply indebted; I am also grateful to the University of Newcastle for two periods of research leave in which the early work was done.

I continued work in the Bibliothèque Nationale de France; my thanks are due to the staff of reading room U in particular, to all at the Collège Franco-Britannique (especially my neighbour, Penou-Achille Somé), and to the De Landtsheer family. I gratefully acknowledge early conversations about what I might be doing, before I had any sense of the book's shape, with Gordon McMullan and Andy Gordon. My thinking about the discipline of Middle English studies, and how I might fit my work into it, has benefited enormously from separate but sometimes overlapping conversations with three acute scholars, Stephen Knight, Ruth Evans, and Larry Scanlon, who often have a better idea of what I am trying to do than I have myself.

Richard Osberg and Tom James participated with me in a session on Laurence Minot at the Leeds International Medieval Congress in 2001 which proved to be particularly stimulating – I am grateful to all who were present for the discussion. I thank also Stephanie Trigg and Ruth Evans for their tough but sympathetic readings of the Minot material, to Jill Rudd for letting me teach it to undergraduates, and Tom Goodman for letting me talk about it at the New Chaucer Society Congress in 2004. I also wish to record my thanks to the editors of *Viator*, in which some material in chapter 5 first appeared, in volume 38 (2007). Other material from the book has been aired at the Middle English seminar at the University of Manchester (I am grateful to Murray Pittock for this seminar's revival in recent years), and in the School of English at the University of Leeds, in which I thank Alfred Hiatt, and Catherine Batt and Oliver Pickering for their help with the elegy on Edward I. Eric Stanley issued an invitation which gave me an opportunity to air some thoughts about Simon Fraser, and Richard Firth Green, at the resultant session, helped my thinking along.

In the final stages, I was hugely helped by a stint at Harvard University as Morton W. Bloomfield visiting scholar, where the time afforded and the resources of the Widener Library let me all but complete the book; my particular thanks go to Daniel Donoghue, James Simpson, Nicholas Watson, and Amy Appleford for that enormously pleasurable period. The unique research facility run by Rohan Mead in Melbourne gave me the space to write a final chapter.

The book constantly brought me up against my own limitations in fields beyond English literature. I am tremendously grateful to Tony Edwards and Julia Boffey for their freely given advice and help in the world of manuscripts and their contexts; Mark Ormrod generously responded to queries about fourteenth-century history; Ros Brown-Grant and Daron

Burrows gave invaluable help in Anglo-Norman. In all these matters, remaining errors and opinions stubbornly adhered to are my own.

I, and the book I kept promising, arrived at the University of Manchester in 2006. I am grateful to all my new colleagues in English and American Studies for the environment they have provided. Elsewhere at Manchester, I owe my thanks to Steve Rigby, who was an invaluable interlocutor on matters of fourteenth-century history and read a complete draft, saving me from numerous difficulties; to Adrian Armstrong and Anna Dezeuze, who invited me to speak at their seminars; and to Steve Milner, whose comments were greatly appreciated. Fergus Wilde at Chetham's Library was generous with his compendious knowledge of Langtoft. To David Alderson and Laura Doan, Heads of English while I was completing this project, I am very grateful for numerous small but vital bits of help. Kate Ash took time out of her own doctoral studies to work as an editorial assistant on my other commitments, giving me back valuable time; I am very grateful to her, and to Graham Ward of the School of Arts, Histories and Cultures for making that possible. In early stages at Manchester, John Anderson was an enthusiast for the project and helped me on the translation from the St Albans chronicle on the first page; it is a great sadness that he did not live to see the book completed.

At Cambridge University Press, I am very grateful to Linda Bree and her team for calmly shepherding the book through at all stages, for an anonymous reader's report which helped me reshape the central sections, and to Geraldine Stoneham for her meticulous editing.

Finally, my greatest debt is to Anke Bernau, who did not type the manuscript, nor do the index, but made everything worthwhile.

Abbreviations

AND	*The Anglo-Norman Dictionary**
Aspin, *ANPS*	Isabel Aspin (ed.), *Anglo-Norman Political Songs* (Oxford: Anglo-Norman Text Society, 1953)
Brie, *Brut*	Friedrich W. D. Brie (ed.), *The Brut or the Chronicles of England*, Part 1, EETS o.s. 131 (Oxford University Press, 1906)
CUL	Cambridge University Library
EETS	Early English Text Society
EHR	*English Historical Review*
Manual	J. Burke Severs and Albert E. Hartung (gen. eds.), *A Manual of the Writings in Middle English, 1050–1500*, 11 vols. (New Haven, Conn.: Connecticut Academy of Arts and Sciences, 1967–2005)
MED	*Middle English Dictionary**
NIMEV	Julia Boffey and A. S. G. Edwards (eds.), *A New Index of Middle English Verse* (London: British Library, 2005)
o.s.	original series
ODNB	H. C. G. Matthew and Brian Harrison (eds.), *The Oxford Dictionary of National Biography* (Oxford University Press, 2004)*
RS	Rolls Series
TEAMS	The Consortium for the Teaching of the Middle Ages*
W.A. Wright, *Robert of Gloucester*	William Aldis Wright (ed.), *The Metrical Chronicle of Robert of Gloucester*, 2 vols., RS 86 (London: HMSO, 1887)

| Wright, *Langtoft* | Thomas Wright (ed.), *The Chronicle of Pierre de Langtoft*, 2 vols., RS 47 (London: Longmans, Green, Reader and Dyer, 1866–8) |
| Wright, *Political Songs* | Thomas Wright (ed. and trans.), *The Political Songs of England: From the Reign of John to that of Edward II* (London: Camden Society, 1839) |

Asterisked entries are used in their on-line versions: *The Anglo-Norman Dictionary* at www.anglo-norman.net; the *Middle English Dictionary* at http://quod.lib.umich.edu/m/med, and the *Oxford Dictionary of National Biography* at www.oxforddnb.com. In addition, all texts in the TEAMS Middle English Texts series are cited in their on-line versions, at www.lib.rochester.edu/camelot/teams/tmsmenu.htm.

Translations throughout are my own, except where otherwise indicated.

Introduction

As King Edward II celebrated the feast of Pentecost in 1317 in Westminster Hall with his magnates, a surprising visitor arrived:

A certain woman, dressed and equipped in the guise of an entertainer, mounted on a good horse bearing an entertainer's medallions, entered the said hall, circulated amongst the tables in the mode of an entertainer, ascended to the dais by the step, boldly approached the royal table, laid down a certain letter before the king, and, hauling on the bridle, having greeted the guests, without commotion or hindrance departed on the horse.

At which the great as well as the less, looking by turns at one another, and judging themselves to be scorned by such a deed of daring and female mockery, sharply rebuked the doorkeepers and stewards concerning that entry and exit. But they, thrown into perplexity, made a virtue of necessity, saying that it was not the practice of the king to deny access, on such a solemn feast-day, to any minstrel wishing to enter the palace.

At length the woman is sought out, captured, and put in prison; asked why she had acted thus, she boldly confessed that she had been instructed to do this by a certain knight, and had been hired for money.

The knight is taken and is brought before the King, summoned concerning the one sent before. Who boldly called for that same letter; of which the tenor was: that the lord king had less regard by way of gratuity for his knights who, in the time of his father, and with himself, had undergone various battles and dangers, and that others, who had not endured the burden and heat of the day with him, he amply enriched, beyond measure.

Because of which the said knight won thanks and promotion from the king, and he freed the said woman from prison.[1]

Concerning this story, which is told in one of the St Albans chronicles, J. R. Maddicott suggests that it 'is too circumstantial in its details to be false …'. Antonia Gransden seems also to accept it as true and comments that 'The purpose of the letter was to remind the king of his duty to his nobles.'[2]

I

As a modern reader it is difficult, however, not to be sceptical of a chronicle story which seems so resonant of another genre, one we think of as entirely fictive. In Arthurian romance, the surprising irruption into court on a major feast day of a disrespectful challenger or a woman with a request to make is a staple. The fact that the day should be specified as Pentecost aligns this story with *Sir Launfal, Ywain and Gawain* and Malory's *Tale of Sir Gareth.* There is even, in the phrase 'the woman is sought out' ['mulier quaeritur'], an embryonic romance quest and at the end of the story, a knight previously alienated from the courtly world is reintegrated into the Arthurian court.

Did the chronicler let some of his own less authorised reading seep into his account of history, or is it that romance influenced the actors in the story themselves? Either way, the romance influence does not penetrate very far, as the hint at the genre is quickly dispelled by a dramatic reversal of roles. In Arthurian romance, the challenges that come from outside are mysterious and otherworldly; knights who go out in fulfilment of the quests such challenges invite engage in rambling, random travels, trusting to their chivalry in negotiating the unknown. But in this story, knightly quest is swift and efficient, as women who horse about in court soon learn. The sequence of passive verbs which follows the phrase 'mulier quaeritur' produces a narrative economy of ruthless efficiency rather than the dilation of the quest. It is best represented in the Latin: 'mulier quaeritur, capitur, et carceri mancipatur … Miles capitur, coram Rege deducitur, super præmissis convenitur'. In Arthurian romance, the workings of the otherworld outside Camelot are mysterious to us. Here, the relations between centre and margins are reversed. We do not know *how* Edward's agents achieve their result, or even who they are, while we do learn all about the mechanism of the original challenge. The story ultimately dispels romance in favour of a narrative about the effective assertion of monarchical power. Coming from a chronicle that is characteristically pro-baronial, this seems a very comforting story from the point of view of Edward II. The disrespect shown to his court is swiftly dealt with and the king emerges as a paragon of Arthurian tolerance when the Knight of the Letter, as we might call him, is treated judiciously.

More closely examined, the text of the letter continues to unravel in Edward's favour. We are told that the tenor of the knight's letter is: 'that the lord king had less regard by way of gratuity for his knights who, in the time of his father, and with himself, had undergone various battles and dangers, and that others, who had not endured the burden and heat of the day with him, he amply enriched, beyond measure' ['quod

Dominus Rex milites suos, qui tempore patris sui et secum diversis bellis et periculis fecerant, minus curialiter respexit, et alios qui nec pondus diei vel æstus secum portarant, nimis abunde ditavit']. Edward's favouring of outsiders and newcomers was a common complaint of the time. Most notoriously, his cultivation of the Gascon knight Piers Gaveston had led to brutal retribution by the barons five years earlier. Edward reacted to Gaveston's death by finding new favourites, most prominently, the father and son both named Hugh Despenser. It was probably these two who were indicated by the letter, and perhaps other, lesser barons among the court party in 1317, such as Hugh Audley, Roger Amory, and William Montagu – all of whom could be accused of being arrivistes 'who had not endured the burden and heat of the day' ['nec pondus diei vel aestus'].

It is this phrase which is most interesting in the complaint. It is almost a direct quotation from Christ's parable of the labourers in the vineyard in the Gospel of Matthew. A householder hires men in the morning to work in his vineyard, promising them pay of a *denarius*; at later hours of the day he hires other workers but in the evening pays all who have worked in the vineyard the same amount. The first hired complain that those who came later have been paid the same as those who endured 'pondus diei et aestus' (Matthew 20.12). The good householder reproves them, saying that he will pay the last as the first. Jesus concludes, 'sic erunt novissimi primi et primi novissimi' (20.16).

The lesson of this text – that the last (strictly speaking, the newest, most recently arrived) shall be first and the first, last – runs entirely against what the Knight of the Letter is trying to achieve. His complaint is made on behalf of those who consider themselves the 'primi' against the 'novissimi'. Faced with this challenge, Edward II could have responded by positioning himself as the householder (and so by extension as Christ): he could have said that his preference for the newcomers was Christ-like even-handedness; that it was not for lesser men to question him, and that, finally, 'sic erunt novissimi primi et primi novissimi'. Instead, the knight is honoured for his timely reminder of the master-code of chivalry. The story's intertexts, sacred and profane, all direct attention to the great tolerance of Edward II.

Depicting an extravagant form of transmission, the story draws attention to the role of *writing* in political complaint and to the need to bring such writing to the attention of the king. From Magna Carta to the Provisions of Oxford and the 1311 Ordinances, from the Mise of Amiens to the Mise of Lewes – both royal and baronial parties sought to consolidate their gains by the use of documents. Documents 'were quite literally speech acts that were answered sometimes by other documents, sometimes by physical force', writes Tim William Machan in reference to the 1260s, 'so that the weapons of the Barons' War, unlike those of the Norman Conquest, were indeed as much words as pickaxes and swords'.[3] Michael Clanchy has charted the process by which documents assumed an importance in thirteenth-century England which they did not have in the eleventh. In the reign of Henry II an increasing formalisation of the law entailed a shift from custom to the use of writs and in consequence the proliferation of documents. Clanchy notes an incident during the reign in which the justiciar mocks a knight for mentioning his seal. But in the fourteenth century, ownership of a seal (with its implication of the basic use of documents) was commonplace.[4] 'Writing', he observes, 'proved to be a more powerful and intractable force than anyone had bargained for.'[5]

The early fourteenth-century story of the Knight of the Letter clearly assumes basic literacy. The knight calls for the letter he has sent as if it will protect him, just as one might call for a charter guaranteeing one's liberty. Between them, the king and the knight apparently agree on the content of the letter. But then nothing really happens. The king is shown in all his tolerance and forgiveness – but he issues no document. A political complainant, having made a documentary complaint, would have sought further documents as guarantees of liberties and laws and perhaps even the curtailment of royal power. Complainants knew the vital importance of the king's writ and, conversely, the importance of addressing him in writing. But in the ideal world of this story, writing wishes itself out of existence once it has achieved its aim.

Hence, although it is centrally concerned with writing, this story is ultimately sceptical of it. What makes it particularly interesting is the elaborate mechanism by which the letter is brought to Edward II's attention, as if to stress the great *difficulty* of reaching the king with a letter. The justice that is delivered by the end of the tale relies not so much on written law as on the re-establishment of a personal bond between knight and king. That bond is brought about not by the authority of writing but by appeal to a nostalgic sense of the way things were in the past, 'tempore patris sui'.

In fact by 1317 the practice of petitioning the king had become a well established feature of government and hence in one important sense, the idea of writing to the king was commonplace, even for those far from the centres of power. In the 1270s, Edward I invited his subjects to address local grievances to him in the form of petitions; by the 1290s the mechanism had become so popular that special clerks had to be devoted to its administration.[6] Around the same time the General Eyre collapsed under the pressure of its own appeal and popularity, and this may have contributed to the rise of the petition.[7] '[F]or the first time', Maddicott writes, 'the voice of the aggrieved and of the socially insignificant could be heard at the centre of government.' He suggests that in its early days the importance of parliament to individuals lay less in its impact on legislation and taxation than in 'the occasion which it offered for the redress of individual grievances through the presentation of petitions'.[8] At the same time the mechanism suited the monarch: 'One of the main problems of thirteenth-century kings', Alan Harding argues, 'was to control the fast-growing corps of officials who acted in their name, and in sending commissions to elicit complaints, whether against their own bailiffs or against the bailiffs of the nobility, they were serving their own interests at the same time as their subjects'.'[9]

Petitioning grew in importance in the first half of the fourteenth century.[10] Through the mechanism, a person or, more likely, a community of people, literally wrote a letter to the king. The surviving documents, and there are dozens of them from the early fourteenth century, almost all begin with the same formula. In 1305, 120 of 133 extant petitions presented begin 'A nostre segnur le roy'.[11] Later, when the volume of correspondence was such that the king could not possibly review all of them, letters nevertheless retained the form of address to the king. The perception that parliament existed in part for the redress of private grievances was a powerful one and the king's role in such redress was taken for granted.

In this very real sense, then, writing to the king was not unusual, but simply another facet of the burgeoning late medieval English bureaucracy. The idea of having recourse to the king, therefore, did not necessarily rely on an idea of his mystical and divinely appointed presence. Steven Justice, writing about more celebrated events, has argued that the well-known faith of the 1381 rebels in the king was not the result of naivety, but in fact an attempt 'to appropriate the gentry's local administration to [the rebels'] own purposes'. Justice suggests that 'the rebels' "trust" in the king derived less from the mysterious and mythicizing distance of the king's person than from the extraordinary accessibility of his name at law'.[12] The rebels were using their knowledge of the availability of the king's name, exploiting such real practices of government as the petition.

Nevertheless, whether in 1381 or earlier, it must have been difficult to separate the idea of the king as, on the one hand, a practically available resource in law from, on the other, his 'mysterious and mythicizing distance'. When a shire community drafted its letter it would have done so according to certain legal expectations and formulae. But it was, in the end, *the king* to whom the villagers were writing: a man they would only ever encounter, if at all, at the centre of elaborate ritual. It must have been difficult to distinguish between the king's two bodies – his physical self and his mystical presence. The common topos of 'evil counsel' arises a result: the belief that it is not the king himself who is to blame for the disorders of the time, but those around him, the mediating level of lesser mortals who could and did fail to govern wisely. The king would put things to rights – the topos of evil counsel usually maintains – if he only knew of the abuses. As the author of the Auchinleck *Simonie*, a bitter complaint poem of Edward II's reign, writes: 'Ac if the king hit wiste, I trowe he wolde be wroth, / Hou the pore beth i-piled, and hu the silver goth.'¹³

'Evil counsel' can appear naive in its faith that the king cannot be touched by the corruption which affects his officials. But it is a logical aspect of any system which relies on a notion of sacral kingship. The king must be the final court of appeal (or at least the penultimate court of appeal before God himself). If the king is not above criticism then nothing is; the system would be wholly corrupt, and without redress or hope. Given such a documentary regime, some literary texts attribute an exaggerated power to royal documents. W. M. Ormrod discusses the case of the outlaw ballad, *Adam Bell, Clim of the Clough and William Cloudesley*, in which an ordinary letter is brandished by the outlaws as a ruse to enter Carlisle. They guess correctly that the porter cannot read, but that he will accept the supposed royal authority of the letter which they tell him has the king's seal on it. (Later, less conveniently, the same outlaws are placed in jeopardy when they are before the king and messengers arrive with letters detailing the carnage the outlaws have perpetrated in Carlisle.)¹⁴ Ormrod finds a more pointed example in the ballad of *Robin Hood and the Monk*. Robin Hood is imprisoned as a result of the actions of a monk. Little John steals from this monk a letter he has written to the king complaining about Robin's activities. Taking the letter to the king, Little John obtains from the king a writ to the Sheriff of Nottingham requiring the sheriff to deliver Robin into Little John's hands. The monk's letter, Ormrod points out, is 'recognizable as a petition' and it 'provides the justification for the issue of the writ of privy seal' – the letter given by the king to Little John.¹⁵

Nevertheless, political verses of the period (and particularly those of the complaint genre) often exhibit scepticism about the effectiveness of writing. 'Ne lerray ke ne vus die ne vaut ore escripture' as the poem 'Vulneratur Karitas' has it: 'I will not refrain from telling you that a written document is worthless now.' This poem, probably from the 1260s, consists of alternating stanzas in Latin and Anglo-Norman, in which the latter translates the former. 'In praesenti tempore non valet scriptura', the Latin, more crisply, puts it, in a poem which laments the general state of political and social disorder:

> Vulneratur karitas, amor egrotatur,
> Regnat et perfidia, livor generatur,
> Fraus primatum optinet, pax subpeditatur,
> Fides vincta carcere nimis desolatur.
> Amur gist en maladie, charité est nafré,
> Ore regne tricherie, hayne est engendré,
> Boidie ad seignurie, pes est mise suz pé,
> Fei n'ad ki lui guie, en prisun est lié.

[Love lies sick, affection is wounded, now faithlessness reigns, hate is engendered, fraud exercises lordship, peace is trodden under foot, trustworthiness has none to guide her, she is fettered in prison.][16]

'Vulneratur Karitas' is found in London, British Library, Harley MS 746, a manuscript which gathers together material on the laws of England and contains copies of the Statute of Marlborough (1267) and the first Statute of Westminster (1275).[17] The poem is the last of the manuscript's original contents, presumably included because of its reflections on the disorder that immediately followed the fall of Simon de Montfort at the battle of Evesham, and which the Statute of Marlborough was designed to address. The alternating of the poem's Latin and French stanzas projects a certain linguistic mastery on the part of the composer; it shows that he knows the languages of power at the same time as he condescends to those who are not *clerici* and have no Latin (while completely ignoring those who have only English). The poem is sceptical about documents, but only in a way that is not possible to take entirely seriously, given that it is included in a manuscript among the very documents on which it comments and thereby takes on documentary status itself.

This developed sense of documentary culture is not confined to the literate strata capable of appreciating 'Vulneratur Karitas'. Justice has suggested, of the 1381 rebels, that they 'aimed not to destroy the documentary culture of feudal tenure and royal government, but to re-create it'. Paul Freedman, while 'not completely accept[ing] this assessment of literacy as the crux of rebellion', gives examples from before 1381 which suggest 'the peasants' knowledge of law, belief in its efficacy, and a continuity between actions at law and local organized opposition ...'[18] Early fourteenth-century political verse, similarly, often rails against documentary culture, but only in a context in which it is clear that the verse is *reliant* on that culture and indeed *wants* writing. In the poem entitled by Wright 'On the King's Breaking His Confirmation of the Magna Charta', the poet plays on the impermanency of wax:

> La chartre [est] fet de cyre,
> Jeo l'enteink et bien le crey,
> It was holde to neih þe fire,
> And is molten al awey.[19]

[The charter {is} made of wax, I understand it and well believe it.]

In one of its two manuscript versions this poem is headed 'De Provisione Oxonie', as if it were a comment on the Provisions of Oxford enforced by the barons on Henry III in 1258. As it stands the poem cannot date from that time and Isabel Aspin argues that it was probably composed in 1306–7, in the last days of the 'struggle for the charters' as Edward I's reign drew to a close. The rubric referring to the 1258 Provisions seems to look back over the long period of strife, which it now sees as coming to nothing:

> Ore ne say mes que dire,
> Tout i va a tripolay,
> Hundred, chapitel, court an shire,
> Al hit goþ a devel wey.[20]

[Now I no longer know what to say, all goes out of joint, hundred, chapter, court and shire, it all goes the way of the devil.]

This state of affairs is provoked by the poet's sense of the failure of key documents since the 1258 Provisions. The poem, macaronic like 'Vulneratur Karitas', alternates Anglo-Norman and Middle English, implying a less learned audience. But the English is not the lowest possible common denominator; it does not translate the Anglo-Norman as the Anglo-Norman, in 'Vulneratur Karitas', translates the Latin. Instead, it supplements the French; linguistic competence is always at issue in macaronic poetry and this is a code-shifting poem which implies that the reader or hearer has at least enough Anglo-Norman to muddle through. Alternatively, the Anglophone reader or hearer can participate in it, at least in part, though not without constantly being reminded of the importance of access to the language of power. Macaronic play, in a trilingual culture in which linguistic knowledge was unevenly distributed, signals not so much the will to even-handed clarity, as the ostensive use of literate authority.

At around the same time, the Anglo-Norman 'Outlaw's Song of Trailbaston', found in London, British Library, Harley MS 2253, presents the voice of a speaker who represents himself as having been a soldier in Edward I's wars: 'J'ai servi my sire le roy en pees e en guere, / En Flaundres, Escoce, en Gascoyne sa terre.'[21] But now, because of the depredations of the commission of trailbaston ('trop est doteuse la commune loy' [line 56]) he lives in the forest as an outlaw. He concludes the poem by inviting others to join him in his rural retirement and withdrawal from the social world: 'venez a moy, / Al vert bois de Belregard, la n'y a nul ploy / Forque beste savage e jolyf umbroy …' [come to me, in the green forest of Belregard, where there is no annoyance but only wild animals and beautiful shade …] (lines 53–5). The speaker alludes to the likely ineffectiveness of his own composition: 'Cest rym fust fet al bois … / Escrit estoit en perchemyn pur mout remembrer / E gitté en haut chemyn qe um le dust trover' [This rhyme was made in the wood … it was written on a parchment to keep it the more in remembrance, and thrown on the highroad that people should find it] (lines 97–100).

Evidently, complaints about the ineffectiveness of writing made in writing cannot be taken entirely at face value. We cannot read of a poet's despair at his unread poem without knowing that his poem has already been read. The expression of these doubts points rather to the *pervasiveness* of written instruments in the politics of the period, in a motif similar to a modesty topos, in which a poet confidently fulfils the task he has set himself even as he expresses his complete inadequacy to do so. These poems speak of the difficulty of finding an audience, a sentiment which of course can only be appreciated by the audience that has been found.

Although the speakers of such poems represent themselves as coming from lower social levels than the Knight of the Letter, they share with his story the assumption that ultimately all authority flows from the king and the implication that written texts do something different in his presence. Because these poets, unlike the knight, cannot seek a resumption of privilege close to the king under renewed feudal bonds, they remain more obviously invested in a culture of the document. As a result, many of the poems discussed here are small but explicit examples of what has recently been termed a 'documentary poetics'. In her book *Documentary Culture and the Making of Medieval English Literature*, Emily Steiner notes that the literature of the period 1350–1420 'abounds in documentary terms and metaphors, tales of miraculous charters, and fictive (spurious or literary) pardons, manumissions, feoffments, patents, testaments, and safe-conducts'.[22] In the context of the massive increase in documentation in the fourteenth century, Steiner proposes:

> it is at the intersection between documentary culture and late medieval literature that we encounter distinctly medieval – and even, perhaps, distinctly English – relationships between the institutional and the expressive, the material and the textual, the literate and the literary, and Latin and the vernacular. I call this intersection a documentary poetics … (p. 10)

Writing to the King is also about a documentary poetics. But this book rejects the idea that such a poetics is found only, or even especially, in the Ricardian writers and their immediate successors. Steiner's important book is thoroughly convincing about the links between documentary culture and later fourteenth-century writing. But there is no real justification for the *terminus a quo* of 1350. In general, recent criticism makes too much of late medieval literary self-reflexivity. Steiner herself speaks of 'strange intersections between documentary practice and literary form' (p. 143). But in a culture in which literacy was particularly concentrated in a massive and expanding bureaucracy, what could be *less* surprising than that much of the literature is saturated with bureaucratic/legalistic discourse? As Matthew Giancarlo writes, thinking about the relationship between literature and parliament, 'the question … is not, why would artists be influenced by all of this?, but rather, how could they *not* be influenced, given the ubiquity and intensity of these parliamentary matters in both intellectual and political life?'[23] A broad view is taken by Wendy Scase in *Literature and Complaint in England, 1272–1553*, which demonstrates the crucial links between petitions, plaints, and literary writing. Scase locates the key period not in the middle of the reign of Edward III, but in that of Edward I, making the gradual rise of parliament of key importance.[24]

There is no point in denying the proliferation of documentary culture in the writing of the later fourteenth century, but at the same time no need to collude in the institutional politics which in recent years has authorised a concerted attempt to enshrine the period after 1350 as offering the only Middle English worth our regard.[25] The literature of the century *before* 1350 – though there is less of it and though it is more obviously struggling for a means of vernacular self-expression – is not only thoroughly entwined with documentary culture but is also far more formally innovative than has often been acknowledged. It is quite clear that verse was *not*, for these writers, solely and simply a convenient means to express their protest. Many of them were deeply interested in poetics. The

'Elegy on the Death of Edward I' discussed here in chapter 3 is, as Geert de Wilde notes, composed in the pseudobalade form with an *ababbcbc* rhyme scheme, and 'it is – by far – the earliest attestation' of this form in Middle English verse.[26] 'The Execution of Sir Simon Fraser' found in Harley 2253, discussed in the same chapter, concludes each stanza with a bob followed by three trimeters, rhyming *abba* in an effect anticipating the bob-and-wheel of *Sir Gawain and the Green Knight*. In chapter 5 I discuss Laurence Minot – possibly the most maligned poet of the fourteenth century – who was another innovator, mixing tetrameters and long lines, end-rhyme and alliteration, and experimenting with stanza-linking.

The last third of the fourteenth century is certainly remarkable for the fact that Chaucer, Langland, Gower, and the Gawain-poet were writing in it. It would be strange if we were not interested in what they read and absorbed before they started writing. One aim of *Writing to the King* is simply to elaborate on Janet Coleman's contention 'that it is less the traditional French/Latin satire of the twelfth–thirteenth centuries that stands directly behind the Ricardian success, than the topical verse journalism of the political and social commentary poems – like *The Simonie* – of the early to middle fourteenth century'.[27]

DISCIPLINE, TACTICS, VOICE

Where do such poems come from? How and why are they preserved?

The English Prose *Brut* claims that in summer 1327, as treaty negotiations proceeded between English and Scots in York, the Scots made 'a bille þat was fastenede oppon þe cherche dores of Seint Peres toward Stangate': 'Longe berde hertles, peyntede Hode witles, Gay cote graceles, makeþ Engl[i]ssheman þriftles'.[28] The English, the chronicler explains, were dressed in coats and decorated hoods and were bearded. Hence, the *Brut* and the wording of the scurrilous verse leave us to think that a Scotsman associated with the negotiations, either openly or in secret, made his sentiments known by posting a 'bille' or 'Scripture' suggesting that though the English might have the ostentatious wealth, the latest fashions, they are, nevertheless, thriftless.

Whether this was a bitter reflection or triumphalism on the part of the unknown Scot – and hence what kind of 'thrift' is referred to – is difficult to say because in fact there were no such negotiations in York at the specified time.[29] The chronicle correctly records that in July 1327 English forces under the *de facto* ruler Roger Mortimer stopped in York on their way to the (certainly thriftless) Stanhope Park campaign against the Scots. There had been some negotiations in the lead-up to the campaign, but these were broken off in June – which is why an English army had been raised. The *Brut*'s addition, that 'þe Scottes comen þider vnto þe Kyng forto make pees and accorde, but þe accordement bituene ha*m* laste but a litel while', is then possibly a conflation of the English troops' stay at York in 1327 (notable for a riot between English archers and Hainault mercenaries, which the chronicle records) and Anglo-Scottish negotiations that did take place in York, but not until February of the following year, which led to the Treaty of Northampton.[30]

If the chronicler was making this conflation for the sake of narrative economy, then the 'bille' he records is a gesture of Scottish triumph over the infamous (to the English) *turpis pax* brought by the Treaty.[31] Its point is not any poetic merit as what we might call, after Michel de Certeau, its 'makeshift creativity' in seizing a fleeting opportunity. It is an example of what Certeau calls tactics formed on the wing, the spur of the moment, exploiting a gap in the nets of discipline.[32] Posted on a church door, it mocks the more official kinds of pronouncements which were proper to such places; its point was less what it said than the place, and the offensive manner, in which it said it. Indeed, the 'cherche dores of Seint Peres toward Stangate' were a very significant place: the doors of York Minster, facing one of the city's main streets.

There are several occasions on which the Prose *Brut* records verses on the events it details. This may be because the compilers happened to have such material to hand and thought it worth inclusion either as authority or curiosity. But it may be that, as V. J. Scattergood suggests, the *Brut*'s compilers 'used popular verses as source material'. He notes that more generally 'it was not uncommon for verses to be rewritten as prose for incorporation in chronicles'.[33] In the 1327 example, the inclusion of a verse critical of the English was probably part of the chronicle's critique of Mortimer, who, a few pages later, is accused of having betrayed the English campaign to the Scots. Hence the supposed Scottish triumph is somewhat contained; in Mortimer, the chronicle and its readers have an enemy in common with the Scots.

Regardless of what its intention and effect were, this broadside is no more than medieval graffiti, and I am not suggesting that such relatively sophisticated poems as the 'Outlaw's Song of Trailbaston' or 'Vulneratur Karitas' ever had this sort of public existence. But I am proposing that a tradition of public critique can be inferred from the graffito and one or two other pieces of evidence – a little earlier than is usually thought – and that the longer poems can be regarded as the more literate end of such critique. Justice notes that the rebel letters of 1381 had received 'publication' as broadsides, known as *escrowez* or *schedulae*.[34] He adds that with a couple of minor exceptions, few examples of such broadsides are known to have existed before the late fourteenth century. The example from the *Brut* I have just mentioned stands as one exception, however, as does another instance Justice himself raises. May McKisack records how, when Mortimer and Queen Isabella invaded England in 1326, Edward II attempted to rally support by having a papal bull denouncing invaders read out at St Paul's Cross. Londoners did not respond to Edward, who fled the city. Later, a copy of a self-justifying letter by Isabella was posted in Cheapside, with further copies appearing in the windows of houses. The reading of a Latin document (with explanations in French?) at St Paul's Cross must have been a relatively familiar occurrence. Edward's use of a papal bull was a highly literate strategy but also in a way another example of 'makeshift creativity' – he had the bull to hand because it had been obtained for use against the Scots.[35] Isabella's letter, copied and displayed, is evidently the documentary riposte to the bull.

From the relatively harmless broadside on the doors of York Minster to Isabella's propaganda, there is every suggestion that 'documentary warfare' took place long before the late fourteenth century, for which we have more evidence. It is in this climate that political poetry might have flourished, and in some cases might have been composed by the same people, or the same kinds of people, who read out papal bulls or copied letters for public display. As chapter 3 will argue, 'The Execution of Sir Simon Fraser' in Harley 2253 can be regarded as an early form of pamphlet, and chapter 2 discusses fragments of verse in Pierre de Langtoft's chronicle which possibly record contemporary poetic political abuse from the wars in Scotland. There is evidence, then, for the life of political fragments which was in all likelihood more extensive than the usual focus on the late fourteenth century would lead us to believe. Clearly, there was an assumption that such diverse poems as 'The Execution of Sir Simon Fraser', the 'Song of the Husbandman' or the 'Outlaw's Song of Trailbaston' merited display, publication or, in some other form, circulation. Hence they were preserved, probably in writing, for two or three decades until they ended up in manuscripts that happen to have come down to us. Many more, it seems safe to assume, did not.

I have suggested that the York graffito was an example of tactics in Certeau's sense. *Tactics* are distinguished by Certeau from *strategy*, which is the more official and overarching form of discipline against which tactics act.[36] The action of Edward II, the crowned king, in causing the reading of a papal bull at St Paul's Cross, would appear to be strategic; Isabella's riposte by distribution of a letter, tactical. There are grey areas; as I have already suggested, there is something makeshift and tactical about Edward's use of a bull procured for other purposes – there was no possibility in the time he had, of course, of obtaining a new bull specific to his needs. He was trying to persuade the City of London that the pope had already ruled against Isabella's invasion, and failed.

In general the political verses have the appearance of tactical manoeuvres. Even when, as is sometimes the case, they seem completely aligned with hegemonic interests, there is a sense that they are opportunist. At some point early in Edward II's reign, for example, Adam Davy, the self-described marshal at Stratford, east of London, composed a dream vision about the king. Using his admittedly limited talent for versifying in Middle English, he seized the moment by laying claim to divinely inspired and highly flattering visions of Edward. At the same time he insisted he was not doing this for 'meed'. It is difficult not to suspect that that is precisely why he was writing.

It may be because of this tactical and sometimes 'underground' character that the verses are often oblique and difficult. When Adam Davy describes Edward being attacked by two knights who are unable to harm him, the figures are perhaps to be understood as standing for France and Scotland. When he goes on to say that four streams of light issue from the king's ears and cover England, the somewhat bizarre image is apparently a positive one. Adam Davy appears to think it is, and perhaps even thinks that Edward II will see it as positive. But why? Why encode his praise of Edward's rule in this obscure imagery when what he is apparently trying to make is a *popular* move in praise of the king? Such works, Peter Coss suggests, 'seem to draw upon a whole vocabulary of saws, proverbs and the like which is largely irrecoverable by us and which helps to explain some of their elusive quality'.[37]

Adam Davy was writing in *praise* of the king; whatever his obscurities, they do not seem to have been meant to veil the intent of an author who in fact takes pains to identify himself and tell his readers where he may be found. Many political verses, by contrast, engaged in a form of encoding apparently designed to protect the author from detection and harm. Judith Ferster suggests that the characteristic anonymity of much late medieval writing may simply testify to the dangers inherent in writing. Langland, she notes, does not 'dare' interpret his own fable of the belling of the cat in the prologue to *Piers Plowman* but invites readers to do so: 'Although there are public issues to be discussed, poets often point to their inability to join in.'[38]

The problem with the view that sees writers as veiling their critiques for fear of authority is that this veiling is in plain view. When Langland says he does not dare interpret his own fable, he could hardly draw more attention to the fact that there is something to be decoded. This is not the action of someone who wishes his meaning to be divined only among the likeminded: a code, evidently, is often designed to do something other than conceal. Its function is often, in fact, artfully to point out that there is something hidden out in the open (Poe's celebrated story, 'The Purloined Letter', reminds us of the effectiveness of this strategy). The French argot known as *verlan*, for example, involves the reversal of syllables to create new words. The name is self-referential as it is a made-up word which itself contains the key to the code, consisting as it does of the reversed syllables of *l'envers*. Spoken in rapid patter, *verlan* no doubt can act as a concealing code. But more often, given that everyone knows its basic principle, its use is ostensive, signalling membership of a group. In any language, children revel in using phrases their parents cannot understand; but if the encoding is *completely* effective, so obscure as to pass without being noted, then that effect is lost.

The medieval political verses often operate in this way. They have an investment in creating the illusion of coded secrecy. The 'Lament of Edward II', discussed in chapter 4, is a poem purportedly in the voice of the deposed king, who refers to his own poem as reaching an addressee: 'Va t'en chaunson ignelement / A la Bise'.[39] 'La Bise' is anagrammatically Isabel, Edward's queen who had just helped to depose him. The easily penetrated code suggests an intimacy of address, a private dimension to the poem as if it really were a correspondence between Edward and Isabella. But this is a political poem, not a private correspondence, and one very unlikely to have been written by Edward himself. It is more likely an argument made by the real author on behalf of the deposed king's successor, Edward III. Its codedness allows readers to feel that they are looking in on something private, when in fact it is a piece of political propaganda presumably intended to be widely disseminated.

Although there are records of political versifiers losing their lives for scurrilous verses,[40] anonymity (the norm, in any case, for Middle English before 1350) is not primarily because of the need to hide, but because of a certain kind of position-taking. In one of the more extensive poems, the 'Song of the Husbandman', for example, the composer is somebody who assumes a persona that was near at hand to him, though not his own.

His poem of complaint is in sympathy with those who suffer on the land. In order to make a complaint against what appears to be a monolithic system of discipline, this poet adopts a peasant persona. In doing so he appears the more effectively to give voice to the complaint by locating it among those who are most affected by the strategy of taxation – but by doing it in a literate manner, he complains from within the same discursive world as those who would do the taxing. This too, I would argue, is one of 'the clandestine forms taken by the dispersed, tactical, and makeshift creativity of groups or individuals already caught in the nets of "discipline"', as Certeau puts it.[41] A poem is composed, and, presumably, circulates; it eventually finds its way into a large manuscript compilation; its appearance in literate record suggests a certain level of exposure – of success, in short, in bringing to wider attention the miseries of an over-taxed life on the land. The author does this without drawing attention to himself, certainly, and thereby exposing himself to potential retribution. But that is perhaps incidental. There are codes, I suggest, which do not so much encode as allow readers to enjoy the feeling of having decoded. Their function is not to hide, but to reveal, and to draw attention to that revealing.

Who then were the authors? Coss suggests that 'the relationship of these works to popular, and indeed to oral, culture is a complex one'.[42] Like other critics, he agrees that the authors were probably clerics of one or another kind. It has been generally accepted, since G. R. Owst first made the argument in 1933, that there is a strong relationship between these political poems and sermons.[43] Maddicott has even suggested names of known preachers who might have been involved in composition of political verses and proposes that penitentiaries, licensed to hear confessions, might have had a special insight into the condition of the poor. But Coss pertinently asks whether literate knights or lay lawyers could also have been involved.[44] As I will discuss more fully in relation to individual poems, there seems no reason to reject such possibilities.

What is almost universally agreed is that the *apparent* speakers of many of these verses – men on the land – are never the *actual* speakers. To be *behind* the plough was almost automatically a disqualification from being able to write *about* ploughing. '[E]ven in our own age', Stephen Knight points out, 'there have been few successful writers who were simultaneously manual workers, and in the medieval period it is highly improbable that anyone who wrote at all also laboured manually, though clearly a number of clerics originally came from that social grouping.'[45] Those poems purportedly representing the voice of the labouring poor,

Knight argues, are actually examples of 'Labour clericized' – clerical ventriloquisings of the peasant. A partial exception is made for the 'Song of the Husbandman', which Knight classes as 'one rare text which speaks throughout in something very much like the voice of labour' making it 'a rare phenomenon in the fourteenth century, a realization of the labouring consciousness and voice from some intellectual and social distance'.[46] Even so, Knight cannot push home the full argument about this poem, which can only be 'something *very much like* the voice of labour'. The labourer's voice remains elusive.

The problem might be in the doomed search for the popular voice, which arises more from the ambitions of twentieth-century left-wing criticism than the actualities of the poems. A more important question is *why* clerical authorship should always be held against the poems and as compromising their notional authenticity. As I will make clear in the course of this study, ventriloquising is central to many of these poems, as their frequent use of apostrophe suggests. Though they might not be authentic instances of certain kinds of political voice, they attempt to enable political speech by their use of pronouns and vocal positions. Leo Spitzer's idea of the 'lyric ego', particularly as further developed by Judson Boyce Allen, is pertinent here. Developing a distinction between the 'poetic' and 'empirical' 'I' in medieval verse, Spitzer discusses cases of medieval 'plagiarism', in which the plagiarist unashamedly takes over the pre-existing 'I' of the work plagiarised.[47] The former notion of a fictive 'I' is built on by Allen to suggest that 'medieval lyric … in most cases utters the position of a definite but unspecified ego whose position the audience is invited to occupy'. In such conditions the first- and second-person pronouns 'exist as ideal or universal to each member of the audience's own particularity and invite him to perfect or universalize himself by occupying that language as his own'.[48] In his turn, Steven Justice adapts this idea to remark on the way in which the pseudonymous character of the rebel letters in 1381 makes their 'authorship programmatically unlocatable' – with a similar effect of universalisation.[49]

To be considered *political* interventions, then, these poems should not have to fulfil criteria of authenticity in relation to authorship. But George Kane, opposing R. H. Robbins and others who have regarded the poems as motivated by political protest, argues strongly against seeing the poems as political at all. 'Some misreading', he suggests, 'seems to have been induced by a political disposition. The poems are in fact a highly miscellaneous body of writings.' There is no protest or dissent in the poems, Kane argues, concluding that the only 'common element' in them is a 'concern about the inadequacy of human conduct, the consequent malfunctioning of the social order, the loss of hope'.[50]

There is no doubt of either the miscellaneity or, frequently, the political conservatism of the poems and it may be that, in a *soixante-huitard* spirit, some critics have over-invested in the poems' political character. It is certainly wrong to suggest that the poets were proposing a new order (though neither Robbins nor anyone else actually says that). But it is equally pointless to say that these poems are not political. They are *about* political situations and political problems. They might be short on political answers but it is precisely that lack which they are attempting to deal with. The most radical answer was revolt and that can be glimpsed in the poems: 'Si Dieu ne prenge garde, je quy qe sourdra guere', as the 'outlaw' in the Trailbaston poem has it: 'if God does not prevent it, I believe war will flare up'.[51]

This book is about the forms of political critique that are available in such conditions. 'The weak', writes Certeau, 'must continually turn to their own ends forces alien to them.'[52] The political verses are frequently, as I have suggested, *tactics*. They are opportunist, almost guerrilla moments of political abuse and advice on the part of those with little real power and in this regard a form of antidiscipline, the visible remnants from the Middle Ages of 'the clandestine forms', to repeat words of Certeau's already quoted, 'taken by the dispersed, tactical, and makeshift creativity of groups or individuals already caught in the nets of "discipline"'.

HENRY III AND THE 'LOANDES FOLK': NATION

One facet of this tactical activity, so far undiscussed, is the shift towards the vernacular. While the literature of the baronial wars, as Maddicott has noted, is substantial, it is mostly in Latin.[53] It is only later, and then at first in fugitive form, that the vernacular takes its place until, by the end of the reign of Edward II, it has become the norm. Indeed the use of the vernacular, in some contexts, could be regarded as tactical in itself.

I suggested above that the increasing numbers of the political poems in English coincided with the rise of the petition and the general growth of bureaucracy in the late thirteenth and early fourteenth centuries. It would be wrong to make too much of this. In the first place, there might have been many more of these poems than we now have, altering the picture of a proliferation of such verses alongside the rise of parliament. We have a good record of Anglo-Latin poems about the Barons' Wars of the 1260s and almost nothing in English. But it seems reasonable to assume that there *was* material in Middle English, even if hardly any of it has survived. I do not want to argue for a simple, functional relationship between complaint verse and the petition. But they *are* aspects of the same thing. They point to a rise in self-consciousness about political process and the sense that a form of participation in that process, however limited, is available to ordinary people: people below the level of the knighthood, living in the shires. Such poems as those I have briefly discussed here are overtly sceptical towards the conditions that make them possible; they question the effectiveness of the charters, of writing itself. But in the same moment they do so, as I have suggested, they testify to their own rootedness in a culture of the document and to the inevitability of recourse to documentation.

This culture of the document is linked not just to regional political concerns but to a much larger framework: that of the nation. I want to approach this first by trying to hear from the king. The letter issued to the people of Huntingdonshire in October 1258, in confirmation of the reforming document known as the Provisions of Oxford, straightforwardly offers itself as being in the voice of King Henry III:

Henri, thur3 Godes fultume King on Engleneloande, Lhoauerd on Yrloande, Duk on Normandi, on Aquitaine, and Eorl on Aniow, send igretinge to alle hise holde, ilærde and ileawede, on Huntendoneschire.

It continues as a confident assertion of the rights of the 'loandes folk on vre kuneriche':

Þæt witen 3e wel alle þæt we willen and vnnen þæt, þæt vre rædesmen alle, oþer þe moare dæl of heom, þæt beoþ ichosen þur3 us and þur3 þæt loandes folk on vre kuneriche, habbeþ idon and shullen don in þe worþnesse of Gode and on vre treowþe, for þe freme of þe loande þur3 þe besi3te of þan toforeniseide redesmen, beo stedefæst and ilestinde in alle þinge a buten ænde. And we hoaten alle vre treowe in þe treowþe þæt heo vs o3en, þæt heo stedefæstliche healden and swerien to healden and to werien þo isetnesses þæt beon imakede and beon to makien, þur3 þan toforeniseide rædesmen, oþer þur3 þe moare dæl of heom, alswo alse hit is biforen iseid; and þæt æhc oþer helpe þæt for to done bi þan ilche oþe a3enes alle men ri3t for to done and to foangen. And noan ne nime of loande ne of e3te wherþur3 þis besi3te mu3e beon ilet oþer iwersed on onie wise. And 3if oni oþer onie cumen her on3enes, we willen and hoaten þæt alle vre treowe heom healden deadliche ifoan.

It concludes by telling its hearers and readers what they could already see, that this is a letter patent, witnessed by several of the magnates:

And for þæt we willen þæt þis beo stedefæst and lestinde, we senden 3ew þis writ open, iseined wiþ vre seel, to halden amanges 3ew ine hord. Witnesse vsseluen æt Lundene þane eʒtetenþe day on þe monþe of Octobre, in þe two and fowertiʒþe ʒeare of ure cruninge. And þis wes idon ætforen vre isworene redes-men, Boneface Archebischop on Kanterburi, Walter of Cantelow, Bischop on Wirechestre, Simon of Muntfort, Eorl on Leirchestre, Richard of Clare, Eorl on Glowchestre and on Hurtford, Roger Bigod, Eorl on Northfolke and Marescal on Engleneloande, Perres of Sauueye, Willelm of Fort, Eorl on Aubemarle, Iohan of Plesseiz, Eorl on Warewik, Iohan Geffrees sune, Perres of Muntfort, Richard of Grey, Roger of Mortemer, Iames of Aldithele, and ætforen oþre inoʒe.

And al on þo ilche worden is isend into æurihce oþre shcire ouer al þære kuneriche on Engleneloande, and ek in-tel Irelonde.[54]

This appears to be, then, a straightforward example of the opposite to what I discussed above; a letter from the king, to his subjects. There is no allusion to difficulties of transmission here. The letter was composed, witnessed, sealed, and sent to the shires, where it was read, and heard, and witnessed again.

Nothing is so simple as the letter makes it appear. Though royal docu-ments in English exist from the reign of the Conqueror, by Henry III's time English was never used in them. The vernacular would not become common in such documents before the fifteenth century, making this let-ter, which also exists in a French version and was perhaps additionally pro-claimed in a Latin version of which no record survives, extremely unusual. Nineteenth-century scholars often saw it as the beginning of English – but it was also seen, contradictorily, as the *end* of English.[55] The proclama-tion is, of course, neither. It is a chance survival, a fleeting glimpse of the development of the vernacular. As the document itself makes clear, copies were sent to all the shires but only the Huntingdonshire version and one other sent to Oxford have survived. Perhaps there were other royal docu-ments in English, but there cannot have been many. The use of English in Henry's letters is remarkable, in the context of the baronial strug-gle against the king which had shortly before reached one of its defin-ing moments with Henry's agreement to the Provisions of Oxford and a radical curbing of monarchical power. At a time when the baronial rebels were accused by their opponents of wanting to extirpate 'all who could not speak English', the use of English proposes a moment of harmony and political unity guaranteed by the possibility of direct address: the monarch speaking in unequivocal terms his people will understand.[56]

As such, Henry's letters have recently attracted attention as mark-ing a national role for the vernacular. Clanchy makes the limited claim that these letters represent the 'precocious beginning' of London stand-ard English.[57] Thorlac Turville-Petre goes much further in linking them directly to medieval English nationalism and seeing them as anticipating 'the nationalist associations of the English language' which he regards as appearing more fully in the 1290s.[58] The use of English in the letters is, in this view, programmatic. It is a deliberate attempt to enlist the 'loandes folk' (interpreted as the whole people of England) and it looks forward to such appeals to English as that made by Edward I in the 1290s when he warned that England's enemies wanted to blot out the language.[59]

In a trenchant critique of this position, however, Tim William Machan has rejected the possibility that Henry's letters can speak for any kind of nationalist position. Machan acknowledges that in their Englishness they 'are aberrations in medieval English documentary practice'. But standardised national vernaculars – Machan goes on to argue – historically have not been brought into existence 'by a single political or literary gesture'.[60] English in the thirteenth century cannot be considered parallel to some of the nationalist linguistic efforts of the nineteenth century, such as the deliberate fashioning of Nynorsk in Norway or Elias Lönnrot's bolstering of modern Finnish in the collection of folktales, *Kalevala*. English, Machan argues, 'lacked the status to mediate English ethnicity, cultural identity, or political resistance, whereby composition in it could constitute the kind of ideological statement that Lönnrot's compilation of *Kalevala* did'.[61]

Machan acknowledges the importance in thirteenth-century England of an orchestrated fear of foreigners and reminds us that such a fear had been a feature of English thought since the Conquest. But to posit nationalism at the time, he suggests, would be anachronistic. Machan sees Henry's letters as certainly issuing from the king himself (albeit in English directly translated from an original French composition). Henry was skilfully mobilising the 'foreigner question' of the day to further his own power. But for him, 'these documents were merely stratagems containing provisional sentiments and not policy statements'.[62] Furthermore, the letters were aimed specifically by Henry at the baronage, not the people at large. 'Loandes folk' translates 'la commune' in the original Anglo-Norman and *commune* at this time is more likely to mean the community of barons rather than the community of the realm in the widest sense, Machan argues. Hence, 'the letters negotiated not the rights or character of the realm of England but the relative responsibilities and privileges of the monarch, the barons, and the sheriffs who administered their wishes'. Henry does use 'a loosely constructed sense of Englishness' in the letters,[63] but 'this is a strategy much different from an attempt to declare and appeal to nationalism by evoking a national language and addressing the country at large'. Instead, Henry's stratagem 'embodies a significance for English that is much more amorphous and much less consequential than one that would render English an authoritative language, ennobling vernacular, or medium of resistance'. The letters are weapons on the 'documentary battlefields' of the war with the barons, a war in which, as has already been observed, the weapons 'were indeed as much words as pick-axes and swords'.[64]

Machan is surely right to resist the idea that a single linguistic act or moment, particularly in the thirteenth century, could create a new linguistic status for and belief about English. Thirteenth-century England, as he observes, did not have an equivalent of the Académie française to create linguistic norms.[65] The spelling reforms recently applied to the German language with only equivocal success also highlight the difficulty of successfully imposing language standards, even within a modern centralised state.

And yet, the fact remains that the 1258 letters are in English. Can that unusual Englishness be explained by a subtle plan on Henry's part, as Machan has it, to take some of the cachet of English to himself? Without subscribing to the nineteenth-century idea of Henry's letters as marking any kind of crucial origin, I want to argue here that the increasing use of the vernacular can and should be linked to nationalist thinking in the thirteenth and fourteenth centuries – though it will be necessary to qualify what exactly can be meant by nationalist imaginings in the Middle Ages.

Even if medieval English cannot be paralleled with such programmatic uses of vernaculars as those in nineteenth-century Finland or Norway, it is not possible to escape the fact that language had an intimate relation to the way people thought about their social relations, their relation to the land they lived in – and to its colonisers. The thirteenth-century chronicle attributed to Robert of Gloucester was well aware of that in its depiction of the aftermath of the Conquest:

> & þe normans ne couþe speke þo · bote hor owe speche ·
> & speke french as hii dude atom & hor children dude also teche ·
> So þat heiemen of þis lond · þat of hor blod come ·
> Holdeþ alle þulke speche · þat hii of hom nome ·
> Vor bote a man conne frenss · me telþ of him lute ·
> Ac lowe men holdeþ to engliss · & to hor owe speche ȝute ·
> Ich wene þer ne beþ in al þe world · contreyes none ·
> þat ne holdeþ to hor owe speche · bote engelond one ·
> Ac wel me wot uor to conne · boþe wel it is ·
> Vor þe more þat a mon can · þe more wurþe he is ·[66]

These words, only an aside in Robert of Gloucester's narrative of the Conquest and the accession of William I, begin with a slight sense of regret for the way in which English is underprivileged because of a colonisers' language. But the passage quickly turns to approbation for anyone who knows English and another language or languages. The fact, of course, that the chronicle is in English at all is striking; its Englishness is here turned to account in a moment of quiet defiance which anticipates the fuller claims for the language later to be made by Robert Mannyng.[67] Nearly two and a half centuries after the Conquest, then, a memory is retained of a linguistic division which was also a colonial and ethnic division. In recent years scholars have paid increasing attention to such expressions and whereas once it was a commonplace that nationalism was incompatible with the Middle Ages, there is now a growing consensus on the presence of national feeling in medieval England.

Traditional definitions of nationhood take a set of empirical criteria based on the modern nation state, which are then found to be lacking in medieval states. Anthony D. Smith, for example, does see a cultural and linguistic fusion occurring in fourteenth-century England that differentiates it from earlier centuries. But for Smith, '[a] nation can … be defined as *a named human population sharing an historic territory, common myths and historical memories, a mass, public culture, a common economy and common legal rights and duties for all members*'.[68] Applying these criteria, Smith observes that he is not claiming 'that by the fourteenth century an English nation had come into existence, only that some of the processes that help to form nations had become discernible' (p. 56). The lack of a common public education or common legal rights, the absence of economic unity and the fact that borders remained in dispute all, in Smith's view, mean that there can be no English nation in the fourteenth century.

The problem with this approach is that it is always self-fulfilling if one set of criteria is deduced from a modern nation and then, inevitably, found to be lacking in a prior historical community. Smith's formulation relies on a notion familiar to medievalists, the Middle Ages as the childhood of modernity. Here, the fourteenth century is the cradle of a nationalism that will only grow to adulthood in modernity. By contrast, seeking to avoid the centrality of empirical criteria, Benedict Anderson influentially suggested that a nation 'is an imagined political community – and imagined as both inherently limited and sovereign'. Anderson's emphasis on an *imagined* community results from his view that 'the members of even the smallest nation will never know most of their fellow-members, meet them, or even hear of them, yet in the minds of each lives the image of their communion'. The nation 'is imagined as *sovereign* because the concept was born in an age in which Enlightenment and Revolution were destroying the legitimacy of the divinely-ordained, hierarchical dynastic realm'. And 'it is imagined as a *community*, because, regardless of the actual inequality and exploitation that may prevail in each, the nation is always conceived as a deep, horizontal comradeship'.[69]

In envisioning nations as inherently constructed and to a degree artificial Anderson does not, however, depart from the long-standing position that nationhood is a modern phenomenon, arising first in the late eighteenth century: 'in Western Europe the eighteenth century marks not only the dawn of the age of nationalism but the dusk of religious modes of thought' (p. 11). In the past, medievalists too have espoused the 'modernist' position, typically taking the view that universal religion excludes the more local ideology of nationalism. Medieval culture has been typically understood in terms of 'the communal mind', as Hans Kohn put it in 1944, of which 'nationalism, in the sense understood today, did not form any essential part'. He continues:

Of course, there was a primitive and natural feeling of community of language or homeland, especially in the latter part of the Middle Ages, and of tribal cohesion in the earlier part. But the decentralization and differentiation within those bodies which were later to form the future nations in no way allowed the growth of that political and emotional integration which is the basis of modern nationalism.[70]

Writing of such theories, Kathleen Davis says: 'the medieval period is necessarily prior to the idea of the nation and at the same time is the homogeneous material out of and against which the modern nation imagines itself. The sine qua non of all these premises is a totalizable Middle Ages that serves as an unconstructed origin of prehistory to the modern nation.' The view criticised by Davis offers a teleology in which nationalism can only ever be what we have now. In turn this position enables any apparently obvious expressions of national sentiment in medieval writing to be dismissed as only the harbingers of something to be more fully realised after the Enlightenment. Davis makes it clear that she does not propose 'that the medieval nation is the same as the modern nation'. Nevertheless, 'imagining national identity is not restricted to one set of historically specific conditions such as print culture, democracy, capitalism, and secularization'.[71] The problem remains, as Boyd C. Shafer describes it, of distinguishing when early glimmerings of nationalism actually become the thing itself.[72]

It is significant that much of the scepticism towards the idea of medieval nationalism arose during or shortly after the Second World War. The patriotic romanticism of the nineteenth century was replaced at that time by a deep scepticism about nationalism, which perhaps lies behind the words, for example, of the Czech-born Hans Kohn, writing in 1944. In an article published in 1947, Barnaby C. Keeney accepted a limited case for late medieval nationalism but nevertheless made it sound like a disease when he wrote about 'the symptoms of nationalism … evident in England at the turn of the fourteenth century'. He found that 'the fanatical intensity of twentieth century nationalism' was not to be seen in the fourteenth – though 'a step toward modern nationalism was made at the turn of the fourteenth century'.[73] (As I will argue in the final chapter, such fanatical national intensity is precisely what is found in the verse of Laurence Minot.)

Yet there have always been dissenting voices. 'Towards the end of the Middle Ages, then', Johan Huizinga writes, 'the forces of patriotism and nationalism were winning more and more ground in Church and state alike, and no less so in popular life and culture.'[74] Marc Bloch discusses the role of language in shaping nationalities in the case of medieval France and Germany.[75] Ernst Kantorowicz notes the relatively common late medieval idea of the *patria*, not as a local region but as meaning 'fatherland' in a broad sense, while Gaines Post, elaborating on Kantorowicz's suggestion, examines the ways in which the canon law of the twelfth and thirteenth centuries negotiated the relation of individual states to the idea of empire. Post concludes that there was a substantial body of opinion that held up the idea of *patria* (in the full rather than local sense) as a key element of an individual's identity.[76]

These hints towards a wider understanding of medieval nationhood have recently been developed more fully, particularly in the English case.[77] Turville-Petre, for example, suggests in his study of early fourteenth-century texts that 'it is the similarities between medieval and modern expressions of national identity that are fundamental, and the differences are peripheral' – though he makes no further argument against the modernist position.[78] Similarly, Anderson's key contention, that national communities are *imagined*, can be read against his own stated intentions as a useful way of thinking about medieval communities. Susan Reynolds, writing about Europe generally, has in effect put a persuasive Andersonian position.

National character is that which is attributed to any group thought of as a nation: the nation itself is the product of its members' belief that it exists. In medieval terms, it was the fact of being a kingdom (or some lesser, but effective, unit of government) and of sharing a single law and government which promoted a sense of solidarity among its subjects and made them describe themselves as a people – irrespective of any relationship that we can now trace between the medieval 'people' and its kingdom on the one hand and the modern 'nation' and its state on the other.[79]

The important thing is not the discovery of something we could regard as an empirically verifiable nation in the Middle Ages. Indeed, it is crucial to avoid the assumption that such a thing can or ought to be found. Medievalists working in this field need to think carefully about what it is they are doing when investigating nationhood. We must not lapse into nineteenth-century nationalist romanticism and the celebratory possibilities that arise when nationhood is seen as a form of destiny.[80] In this book, it is not my purpose to celebrate the emergence of nationhood in the medieval or any other period; I am interested in 'nation as artifact', as Kathy Lavezzo has recently put it.[81]

Few historians today would lapse into a celebratory patriotism. It was nevertheless only in 1953 that Sir Maurice Powicke wrote of the thirteenth century, with a detectable trace of pride, 'We are watching England become more aware of itself.'[82] More recently – and certainly in a more hardheaded way – it has become relatively common to see assertions by historians of England of a strident national self-confidence in the thirteenth and fourteenth centuries. The title of G. L. Harriss's volume in the new Oxford History of England, *Shaping the Nation: England, 1360–1461*, could hardly be more explicit.[83] Of the thirteenth century, R. R. Davies states in *The First English Empire* that there is no doubt 'the English political community became more self-consciously, stridently, and even aggressively English in its posture', reiterating the point when he says that English attitudes to the British Isles were shaped by 'a strident and self-confident Englishness'.[84]

It is important to see that we are not, *pace* Powicke, watching England become more aware of itself. 'England', in Powicke's phrase, is a personification. It is not mere nit-picking to say that a nation cannot become aware of itself: to personify it suggests that the nation was always there and it is our task simply to watch it burgeon. But in the course of this book I also argue with Davies' position: in most important ways the emergent national consciousness of the thirteenth century is not self-confident at all. It is *strident* only because it has to be demonstrated, repeatedly and loudly. And that is the case precisely because it has no convincingly demonstrable empirical foundation. Medieval

English nationalism is based, much of the time, on fear: fear of the other, whether the Scots or the French, a fear which was periodically whipped up by monarchs and such lesser folk as Laurence Minot who looked to exploit it.[85]

In this context I would like to return briefly to Henry III's letters. When they were first discussed in the nineteenth century it was assumed that Henry himself could not have written them as they represent his political defeat by the Provisions of Oxford. The true authorship, it was thought, must have been baronial, and they most likely issued from the chief rebel and architect of the Provisions, 'Simon of Muntfort, Eorl on Leirchestre', whose name sits so significantly just after the ecclesiastics in the list of witnesses. But more recent judgements situate the authorship with or near Henry. Clanchy sees the letters as Henry's though actually written by the clerk Robert of Fulham.[86] In a somewhat different argument, Machan regards them, as we have seen, as expressing Henry's will in a particularly subtle way.[87]

If they do express Henry's will, they do so in a language he almost certainly did not speak. If they express Montfort's, the same is true: it is unlikely that the Frenchman Montfort ever became fluent in English. And to the extent that the letters appear to issue orders and guarantees, they are again not what they appear. Henry III, on the resumption of his power in 1259, wasted no time in repudiating the Provisions of Oxford. So the letters – whoever wrote them – appear to fail to do the main thing they set out to do.

The letters, I suggest, are trying to do something unexceptional in the context. They are trying to wish political harmony into being. They do so by their inclusive address to an incipient nation. It is true that in the English letters, 'loandes folk' translates a word, *commune*, which at the time did not usually refer to the people at large. This has been taken to suggest that the letters were *not* apprehended as a national document. In Middle English 'folk' nevertheless – even if it represents a misconstrual of the Anglo-Norman – *could* simply mean 'the people' at this date.[88] But translation tells only part of the story. When these letters were brandished in the marketplaces, the seals exhibited as a guarantor of their truth, their address to the 'loandes folk' read aloud – what did ordinary English-speaking people understand by that? The fact that 'loandes folk' was designed to translate *commune* would not have been evident in the moment of dissemination; in translation, the original phrase does not limit and determine the possible connotations of the translated phrase. The letters obviously *ask* to be understood as an address in the broadest sense and it follows that 'loandes folk' was understood as addressing ordinary people in town and country.[89] The letters invite a sense of community by the address they make. They are about the appropriateness of writing in the vernacular as a way of proposing that there is a politically unified entity in England, defined by its speaking of the vernacular. *But* they are also about the manipulation of discourse, and specifically vernacular discourse. Henry did not write the letters and did not want them written; they *were* constrained from him by rebellious barons. The harmony they propose was to a large extent illusory. That illusory character, however, does not undermine their role in trying to create a sense of national community. The community was also illusory, imagined. The crucial thing about the letters is that they are performative. They are one element in an effort to bring something into being, to enact it by discourse.

In this instance the manipulation of Henry's voice did not endure long. Within a short time, the king fought back against the reformers and another document, the Treaty of Paris (1259), enabled his resumption of power. Crisis could only follow.

CHAPTER I

Defending Anglia

THE PROBLEM OF *CUMELINGS*

On the day of the battle of Evesham in 1265 a chronicler thirty miles away in Gloucester witnessed a great storm and darkening of the sky. He made a comparison with the darkened skies at the Crucifixion and chose this moment to identify himself as 'roberd / Þat verst þis boc made & was wel sore aferd'.[1] For Robert of Gloucester (as we know him), an evident supporter of Simon de Montfort, it was indeed a dark day, when Montfort and his followers were slaughtered, and Montfort's body savagely dismembered. That the chronicler should name himself at this point, thousands of lines into his work, suggests the event's particular importance to him; it perhaps does more than that, indicating that it is these events which stand as the chronicle's originating trauma. Having dealt with it, the chronicler concludes shortly afterwards, with the Lord Edward's departure on crusade and the end of Henry III's reign.

Several centuries and nearly 12,000 lines before that, the chronicle begins fictively with that exemplary narrative of invasion and conquest, foreignness and indigeneity, the story of the Trojan named Brut and his settlement of Britain. This story begins by announcing an encomium to the land: 'Engelond his a wel god lond · ich wene ech londe best · ' (1). What immediately follows, however, is a description not of England, but of Britain:

> þe see geþ him al aboute · he stond as in an yle ·
> …
> Fram souþe to norþ he is long · ei3te hondred Mile ·
> & tuo hundred mile brod · fram est to west to wende ·
> Amidde þe lond as hit be · & no3t as bi þe on ende · (3–8)

The redactor of this part of the chronicle was simply paraphrasing and conflating the accounts of Britain in two well-known twelfth-century works, Geoffrey of Monmouth's *Historia Regum Britannie* and Henry of

Huntingdon's *Historia Anglorum*. At the equivalent points in their own narratives, as Thorlac Turville-Petre points out, both Geoffrey and Henry refer to *Britain*.[2] Henry is aware of the complications of nomenclature, as he refers to 'the most celebrated of islands, formerly called Albion, later Britain, and now England ...' ['insularum nobilissima cui quondam Albion nomen fuit, postea uero Britannia, nunc autem Anglia'].[3] But there is no appreciation of these nuances in the 'Gloucester Chronicle.' Although he follows Geoffrey and Henry, the Gloucester redactor converts Britain into England at a single stroke. The earlier writers both say that *Britain* is 800 miles long and 200 miles wide; the Gloucester redactor copies the figures but assigns them to *England*. Where Henry of Huntingdon writes that the Orkneys are north of Britain (12), the Gloucester author, paraphrasing, says that 'þe gret yle of orkeneye [lies] bi yonde scotlonde' (32). Because of the way he has previously described England, 'scotlonde' must be understood as part of an island named England.

The 'Gloucester Chronicle' does not use the term Albion and 500 lines go by before 'Britain' receives a mention. After Brut and his confederate Corineus settle in their new island they divide it between themselves, Corineus taking Cornwall:

> Brut huld him to engelond · he ne dorste him naȝt pleine ·
> & after brut his owe name · he clupede hit brutaine ·
> Brutons me clupede alle men · þat were in engelonde ·
> As me clupede hom longe suþþe · vor te nou late ich vnder stonde ·
>
> (504–7)

Later, when Julius Caesar enters the narrative at line 1037, the author will commonly refer to *Brutaine*. But the land which Brut had earlier discovered is unequivocally 'Engelond', and it is that name which inaugurates this long narrative.

As the Brut-legend in this chronicle is probably older than the later sections claimed by Robert, and by a different author, there is no certainty that the Anglicised Brut narrative was composed in direct reaction to the politics of the 1290s and Edward I's claim to overlordship of Scotland. Nevertheless, to a compiler in the 1290s, the Brut material which unfolds from the encomiastic description of England would have suggested itself as highly acceptable reading. It is not simply the ease with which Scotland is absorbed into England. Even before they arrive in England/Britain, Brut and Corineus rout the king of Gascony in battle, laying waste to the land and then raising castles in the region of Tours, all of which would have appeared attractive in 1294 when Edward I went to war with France over the question of homage for his Duchy of Aquitaine.[4]

In Geoffrey's account of these events the Gascon king Goffarius, looking on Brut's camp before battle, urges his men on to destroy the Trojans: "'How sad my destiny is! These ignoble exiles [*ignobiles exules*] have pitched their camp in my kingdom. Arm yourselves, and charge through their serried ranks! In a short time we shall seize hold of these weaklings [*semimares*] as if they were sheep and carry them captive through our kingdom."'[5] In the 'Gloucester Chronicle', Brut's camp has become a castle; the passage is otherwise closely paraphrased:

> þo he sei þe grete walles · castles as it were ·
> Ou3 he sede þe gret despit · þat i se to me here ·
> þat þis vile cumelinges · castles leteþ rere ·
> Vpe min londe baldeliche · as me vor to afere ·
> Ne doþ hii me ssame inou · hou mi3te hii do me more ·
> Bote ich be þer of awreke · ich ssal deie wel sore ·
> Vor godes loue stalwarde men · armieþ 3ow vaste ·
> To sle þis proute cumelinges · & hor castles adoun caste · (422–9)

Geoffrey's Goffarius calls the Trojans 'ignobiles exules' and 'semimares'. The latter term, somewhat euphemistically translated by Thorpe as 'weaklings', means castrates or eunuchs. In the 'Gloucester Chronicle' one term stands for both expressions: the word *cumeling*. The intent remains the same – Goffar (as the 'Gloucester Chronicle' calls him) wishes to paint the Trojans as unworthy adversaries who should be put to ignominious flight. But the emphasis is different. The Middle English word *cumeling*, derived from Anglo-Saxon **cymeling*, has the sense of 'foreigner', 'outsider' and translates the Latin *alienigenae*. It can also connote a convert from another religion and appears in records denoting a stray animal that joins a herd.[6] Putting this word in Goffar's mouth, the 'Gloucester Chronicle' could hardly be giving a stronger sense that the Trojans do not belong.

Goffar's exhortations are ineffective. The men of Gascony are destroyed and Brut and Corineus continue on their way to Britain. There (despite an earlier prophecy which told Brut the land would be empty) they find a few giants whom they put to flight. Even then this 'empty' land has more surprises when the giant Gogmagog, with twenty of his fellows, attacks Brut. The implication is that the giants, being monstrous, count for nothing; the prophecy of emptiness is not contradicted by the presence of such subhuman beings. Their presence does mean, however, that the occupation of the land not yet called Britain is violent.

These unmistakable motifs of colonisation and conquest in the Brut narrative have recently been taken up by several critics who view them through a postcolonial lens.[7] My interest in this passage here is less in the motif of colonisation and more in its inverse, that of the resistance to outsiders. It is in the deployment of *this* idea that the Brut narrative, for all its extravagant fictiveness, functions extremely well as the foundation of the later narrative of the reign of Henry III by Robert of Gloucester. It foreshadows some of Robert's themes, thereby integrating Galfridian history with his eyewitness narrative of the Barons' Wars. The use of the Brut narrative in the 'Gloucester Chronicle' is a way of 'making native' the Brut story (not for the first time, of course), which looks ahead to the great issue of thirteenth-century politics: the foreigner question or what we might call the problem of *cumelings*.

A VINEYARD WITHOUT WALLS: THE CHRONICLERS AND THE FOREIGNERS

Chroniclers consistently complain of Henry III's promotion of *cumelings*. Although, as Michael Clanchy writes, such complaints were not new, the context was.[8] Claire Valente notes that King John brought foreigners into official positions 'at the very time when the barons, due to loss of their own overseas lands, were defining themselves as English and men from overseas as foreigners'.[9] Foreignness was, in other words, becoming more visible as a category in the thirteenth century, as Englishness was being more fully imagined by and for the magnates. Henry III drew particular attention to it by promoting two sets of foreign relatives: the Savoyard kin of his wife, Eleanor of Provence, and his own half-brothers, sons of his mother Isabella, the Poitevins of the house of Lusignan.[10] One marker of anti-foreign feeling is the way in which it is registered in official documents: the confirmation in 1263 of the 1258 Provisions of Oxford, for example, makes explicit reference to the removal of foreigners from positions of power.[11]

Henry's promotion of foreigners is a consistent theme of the *Chronica Majora*, by the period's pre-eminent chronicler, Matthew Paris. Broadly, Matthew's complaints are twofold: in the secular sphere, the king's foreign relatives are promoted at the expense of English men, while in the English church, foreigners are brought in to fill important offices. One of Matthew's more colourful examples (in this instance taken from his St Albans predecessor Roger of Wendover) concerns the arrest of the justiciar Hubert de Burgh in 1232. Burgh is led to a blacksmith to be fettered but the smith recognises the captive and refuses to do as he is asked, saying, 'Is this not that same most faithful and magnanimous Hubert who has so many times taken England back from the devastation of foreigners [*eripuit Angliam a vastatione alienigarum*], and restored England to the English [*restituit Angliam Angliae*]?'[12]

A few years later, in 1238, Henry III's sister Eleanor was married in secret to a prominent Frenchman at court, Simon de Montfort. This quickly led to a revolt on the part of the king's brother, Richard of Cornwall,[13] and Matthew Paris, who certainly had personal access to Richard, records him as making both the general complaint that the king had enriched his wife's foreign relatives with lands, and that the marriage of his sister had ensured fresh impoverishment. Furthermore, the king, Richard continued, had allowed benefices to be seized on as *spolia* and distributed among foreigners [*alienigenis*]. He has made England, Richard concluded, like a vineyard without walls, plundered by all who pass.[14]

The following year, Matthew records how the king violently [*vehementer*] oppressed the church of Winchester, forcing the appointment of a foreigner [*alienigenam*] as prior. What is interesting about this appointment is that the man in question is described as being of the *natione Britonem*; his name, as other sources suggest, was Andrew. Yet he is obviously regarded as being as alien as anyone from France. Once appointed, the new prior 'laid aside the fear of God, subverting all and perverting all and squandering the wealth of the church' ['omnia subvertit, omnes pervertit; et thesaurum ecclesiæ dilapidando'].[15] The monks, in response, sent a mission to Rome where they received the right of free election from the pope: no 'foreign person, hateful to the whole realm' ['alienigenam personam et invisam universitati regni'] should be elected through the king's will.[16]

In Robert of Gloucester's account of the same period, the emphasis is initially on the 'good old laws' of the past. England, Robert reminds his readers, was an occupied country when Henry came to the throne. But when the French were cast out and the land was brought to 'god pays' the nobles turned their thoughts to the restoration of 'þe olde lawes' (10634–5). They speak with the king, Robert explains:

> Vor to abbe as we sede er · þe gode olde lawe ·
> þe king made is chartre · & grantede it wel vawe* ·   *happily*
> þe gode lawes of forest · & oþere þat wule* were ·   *formerly*
>   (10638–40)

Despite this happy outcome, later – in Robert's opinion because he had married and had an heir – Henry turned to other counsel, '& of þe riȝtes of holichurche · & of þe gode olde lawe · / þat he adde of is chartre ymad · he him gan wiþ drawe' (10890–1). Henry's withdrawal leads to political chaos, the 'mest wo' of Henry's day, as Robert calls it (10986).

Nevertheless, in describing that woe, Robert shifts the emphasis from what he has presented as a constitutional concern with law and takes a stance informed by what he casts as the politics of race. Because of the king's foreign half-brothers and his foreign queen, Robert says, many French people were brought to England who held Englishmen to be of no account ('of englisse men · me tolde as riȝt nouȝt' [10993]). Henry lets each one of these newcomers act as a king, Robert complains, and they take poor men's goods (10994–5). Anyone who objects receives the response, 'we beþ kinges' (10998). As a result, barons, earls, and bishops, seeing that these men wish to cast native Englishmen ('þe kunde eng-lissemen') out of the land, take counsel and, at Oxford, bring the king to make a 'porueance' (11007), in which he promises to make amends. Henry agrees to send the French away from England and 'to graunti gode lawes · & þe olde chartre al so · / þat so ofte was igraunted er · & so ofte vndo ·' (11018–19).

It is of course the crisis of the mid-1250s that Robert is narrating here and its outcome in the adoption of a 'porueance', the Provisions of Oxford, in 1258. He goes on to describe the solemn ceremony in which the Provisions were sealed. For Robert, solutions are to be found in documents and the laws they enshrine, sanctioned by antiquity. But before long, King Henry is thinking about how he might undo the 'porueance'. Robert, comment-ing on this, once again shifts away from his concern with law and order and finds another foreigner to blame: it was as much the queen's idea as Henry's (11051–2). Hence in Robert of Gloucester's contemporary account of the beginnings of the Barons' War, the good old laws quickly turn out to be synonymous with a concern for the promotion of Englishmen at the expense of *cumelings* – though that term does not reappear in this part of the chronicle. Robert's concern, no less than that of Matthew Paris, is with the *universitas regni* and the community of the English. The first word of the chronicle is 'Engelond' and that is still the concern in 1258.

THE BATTLE OF LEWES AND THE LITERATURE OF VICTORY

In April 1261 Pope Alexander IV absolved Henry of his oath to maintain the Provisions and as the king went about retrieving his rights Simon de Montfort, still regarded as a leader of the baronial opposition, left the country.[17] In April 1263 Montfort was recalled by anti-royalist nobles, amid fresh demands for the restoration of the Provisions. Renewed ten-sion was not resolved by the Mise of Amiens early in 1264, in which Louis

IX arbitrated and found overwhelmingly in favour of Henry.[18] Montfort could not accept it, and the opposed forces came to battle at Lewes in May. Although Montfort commanded the lesser force, the day went against the royalists.[19] At the end of it Henry III and his heir, the Lord Edward, were trapped in a priory and forced into negotiations which ended with their captivity. The period of Montfort's complete ascendancy had begun.

This brief period of struggle and triumph produced a substantial body of political verse; it is '[t]he one crisis', J. R. Maddicott writes, 'which has left an enduring literary legacy'.[20] He is referring chiefly to the several accomplished Latin poems which were composed at or near the time of the events, which tend to reflect the point of view of the Montfortian reformers. Of these, the most substantial is *The Song of Lewes*, found in a single copy in London, British Library, Harley MS 978.

There are indications, however, that there was also a *vernacular* poetic reaction to events. The sole complete survival in Middle English from the period is the poem edited by Thomas Wright as 'Song Against the King of Almaigne', but now also known, confusingly, as *The Song of Lewes*. It represents, as John Scattergood notes, 'the earliest surviving English *sir-ventes*'.[21] This poem has a refrain and appears to be an actual song – one of the few in Wright's collection that truly merits the title. It is preserved in London, British Library, Harley MS 2253 (*c.*1330) but the original was presumably composed soon after the Battle of Lewes. Wright's title is accurate and I will use it in order to avoid confusion of the English poem in Harley 2253 with the Latin poem in Harley 978 (which I will continue to call *The Song of Lewes*).

The 'King of Almaigne' was Henry III's brother, Richard, earl of Cornwall, elected king of Germany, and aspirant to the imperial throne. At the battle of Lewes he fled and took refuge in a windmill, where he was captured by the Montfortians.[22] He would spend the following year in captivity, playing no role in events until after the battle of Evesham. Wealthy and powerful, Richard of Cornwall had vacillated between the baronial and royal causes and political verses make it clear that as a result he had a reputation for untrustworthiness. In the scurrilous French poem, 'Song of the Peace with England', which Wright thought likely to have been composed after the Mise of Amiens early in 1264, Richard is punningly called 'Trichart' – deceiver or trickster.[23] The 'Song Against the King of Almaigne' makes the same wordplay in its refrain: 'Richard, thah thou be euer trichard, / trichen shalt thou never more.'[24] Perhaps the earlier French poem was known to the writer, but it may be that the rhyme 'Richard/trichard' had common currency, because the English poem clearly plays on the idea that now he is a captive, Richard's deceiving days are over.

The poem unfolds as a mixture of occasionally bitter invective along with more gentle mockery for Richard and others. Richard is accused of spending 'al is tresour opon swyvyng' and is satirised as having mistaken the windmill in which he sought refuge for a castle. There are four such stanzas of mockery of Richard before two more stanzas of invective against Earl Warenne and Hugh Bigod: barons who, like Richard, had wavered between royalist and Montfortian causes before fighting for Henry at Lewes.[25] The final stanza criticises the Lord Edward:

> Be the luef, be the loht,* sire Edward,   *whether you wish it or not*
> Thou shalt ride sporeles o thy lyard*   *a white or grey horse, perhaps with*
>   *implication that it is a poor one*
>
> Al the ryhte way to Dovere ward;
> Shalt thou never more breke fore-ward,
> ant that reweth sore:
>   Edward, thou dudest ase a shreward,
> forsoke thyn emes lore.
> Richard, [thah thou be euer trichard,
> trichen shalt thou never more.][26]

All of this suggests a composition date well before the royalist recovery at Evesham a little more than a year later, as the poet speaks as if all the royalist forces are defeated and implies that Warenne and Bigod are still in the self-imposed exile which they chose after fleeing Lewes. The poet's lines about Edward also suggest composition before Edward escaped Montfort's custody in May 1265 and joined the returned Warenne, Bigod, and others. 'The King of Almaigne', then, seems to be a confident production from the baronial side; given that it is in English, it was perhaps composed by a lesser member of one of the baronial retinues, obviously by someone who regards Montfort in a positive light. Hilmar Sperber sees the poem as the cultural counterpart to the military victory and as 'ideological revenge'.[27]

The mockery in the poem of Richard's misfortune in being captured in a windmill is echoed in the Melrose Chronicle's account of Lewes, which records that as evening drew on after the battle the Montfortian barons surrounded the mill, crying out: 'Come down, you bad miller! [*pessime molendinarie*] Come out at once, mill-master! [*molendini magister*]'.[28] The humiliated earl had no alternative but to submit. The brief account dramatically highlights the reversals of the day for the royalist side. Richard of Cornwall, the wealthiest noble of his day, aspirant to the imperial throne, is mocked as a miller – a class of labourer despised even by his fellows.

This is one of the moments in the chronicles which highlight problems of language and translation. The barons present before the mill presumably did *not* actually call Richard *molendinarius*, but spoke to him in Anglo-Norman or possibly English. But whether they called him *molendinarius, moliner,* or *millere*, they were abusing one of the most powerful men in the country and they were doing so because they knew they had him beaten. Richard is very lightly encoded as a miller in words that are aimed at him and meant for instant decoding. Similarly, the composer and hearers of the 'Song Against the King of Almaigne' make little attempt to conceal their sentiments, presumably feeling, in the time of victory, that there was nothing to be lost by abusing Richard and the Lord Edward. What is at stake, when such abuse is made? Did such abuse ever reach the ears of the Lord Edward? Was the use of English alone a safe enough code?

To chroniclers, these moments of linguistic opacity are usually not noteworthy or even visible. As Matthew Paris's story of the patriotic blacksmith suggests, all characters in Latin chronicles speak like well-educated monks, in Latin and often using biblical references. The story of the blacksmith simply smoothes away any linguistic difficulties and shows how the smith, who must have been English-speaking, is more closely allied to the earl of Kent and justiciar, Hubert de Burgh (whose mother tongue was probably Anglo-Norman), than he is to foreign-born despoilers of England. The earl of Kent and the blacksmith are both English and that, Matthew Paris implies, is what matters. Divisions created by social rank are less important than those of national origin. The opposition here would appear to be a simple one based on nationality and birth.

In reality, such divisions were far from straightforward in the thirteenth century. The career of Simon de Montfort alone, the hero of the verse of the 1260s, shows this. In a world in which members of the English royal dynasty are consistently and bitterly criticised, Montfort is often lionised for taking up the cause of ordinary Englishmen against a king who promotes foreigners. But of course Montfort was himself a Frenchman born and bred. In the legacy of political verse in which his career is described, this apparent contradiction must be elided altogether. It is not so much that Montfort is excused his French origin; it is simply forgotten.[29]

The Latin *Song of Lewes* in Harley 978, for example, embodies the contradictions posed by the fact that the hero is a Frenchman while the villain, the Lord Edward, is the heir to the English throne. This poem

of nearly 1,000 lines was composed, perhaps by a Franciscan, soon after
the Montfortian victory at Lewes.[30] It is resolutely pro-baronial, focusing
its anger on Edward in particular, and on foreign councillors. With one
minor exception, no one is named except Montfort and Edward, who are
heavily contrasted. There is implied criticism of Henry III but the poet
avoids speaking too directly of or to Henry, couching most of the criticism as general advice on kingship. Nevertheless the poem leaves 'little
doubt as to God's intervention in repressing wicked kingship by backing
Simon de Montfort and his allies'.[31]

The Song of Lewes begins with the poet adjuring his own pen to write
quickly, in emphasis of the literate character of the work. The implication
is that he writes in the immediate aftermath of the battle, when 'The proud
people are fallen, the faithful are glad.'[32] 'Now England breathes again',
the poet comments, 'hoping for liberty' (9). He then gives an account of
the battle, in which the emphasis is less on accurate description of events
(though he does seem to know what happened) than on the description
of the moral rightness of the result. Although Montfort had the inferior
forces both numerically and in terms of their training, he won: right was
the winner against might. The poet then makes an extended comparison
of Montfort and the Lord Edward.

The second half of the poem shades from critique of a specific reign
into a meditation on kingship itself. The consistent note here is that true
kingship and good rule are based on the rule of law. In this section the
poet is knowledgeable, if completely conventional. The source of his
theory of kingship might ultimately be, as C. L. Kingsford suggested,
Policraticus and 'Bracton', but what he reduces into often skilful Latin
verse is a generally accepted theory of kingship based on law.[33] The king,
the poet argues of Henry III, wished to be entirely free:

> Rex cum suis uoluit ita liber esse.
> Et sic esse debuit, fuitque necesse,
> Aut esse desineret rex priuatus iure
> Regis, nisi faceret quicquid uellet; cure
> Non esse magnatibus regni, quos preferret
> Suis comitatibus, uel quibus conferret
> Castrorum custodiam, uel quem exhibere
> Populo iusticiam uellet; & habere
> Regni cancellarium, thesauriumque
> Suum ad arbitrium uoluit quemcunque
> Et consiliarios de quacunque gente,
> Et ministros uarios se precipiente;
> Non intromittentibus se de factis regis

Anglie baronibus, uim habente legis
Principis imperio; & quod imperaret
Suomet arbitrio singulos ligaret. (489–504)

[The king with his party wished to be thus free, and urged that he ought to be so, and was of necessity, or that deprived of a king's right he would cease to be king, unless he should do whatever he might wish; that the magnates of the realm had not to heed, whom he set over his own counties, or on whom he conferred the wardenship of castles, or whom he would have to show justice to his people; and he would have as chancellor and treasurer of his realm anyone soever at his own will, and counsellors of whatever nation, and various ministers at his own discretion; without the barons of England interfering in the king's act, as 'the command of the prince has the force of law'; and that what he might command of his own will would bind each.]

What is at issue here is the limits of kingship itself: the same questions that provoked Magna Carta, and which would be rehearsed again in the struggle for the charters in Edward I's reign and then by the Ordainers in Edward II's. The poet underlines his theme by addressing Edward, the future king:

O edwarde! fieri uis rex sine lege;
Vere forent miseri recti tali rege!
Nam quid lege rectius qua cuncta reguntur?
Et quid iure uerius quo res discernuntur?
Si regnum desideras, leges uenerare:
Vias dabit asperas leges impugnare,
Asperas & inuias, que te non perducent;
Leges custodias, ut lucerna lucent. (451–8)

[O Edward! thou dost wish to become king without law; verily they would be wretched who were ruled by such a king! For what is more right than law, whereby all things are ruled? And what is more true than justice, whereby matters are decided? If thou desirest the kingdom, reverence the laws; the attacking of the law will give rough roads, rough and impassable roads, which will not lead thee through; if thou dost guard the laws, they shine as a lamp.]

The opening lines addressed to Edward, with their play on *rex* and *lex*, clearly recall words in 'Bracton', probably written only a few years before: 'Non est enim rex ubi dominatur voluntas et non lex' ['for there is no *rex* where will rules rather than *lex*'].[34] The poem's legal concerns are balanced by what is taken as a self-evident truth: the law is ultimately sanctioned by God and derives from God. The implications of breaking it are commensurately serious. 'Every king is ruled by the laws he makes', the poet writes. 'King Saul is rejected because he broke the laws; and

David is related to have been punished as soon as he acted contrary to the law' (445–8). By implication, it is impossible for a king to claim that he is above the law because of the divine sanction by which he rules; the law itself is divinely sanctioned. As the poet reminds:

> Vnus solus dicitur & est rex reuera,
> Per quem mundus regitur maiestate mera,
> Non egens auxilio quo possit regnare,
> Set neque consilio qui nequid errare. (641–4)

[One alone is called, and is King in truth, through Whom the world is ruled by pure majesty; Who needs not assistance whereby He may be able to reign, nay nor counsel, Who cannot err.]

God, the poet continues, grants rule to his people under him; they are able to fail and to err (645–8). A king must understand that he is the servant of God (701). Yet a king is not, thereby, entirely unfree and deprived of agency.

> Set quis uere fuerit rex, est liber uere
> Si se recte rexerit regnumque; licere
> Sibi sciat omnia que regno regendo
> Sunt conueniencia, set non destruendo. (693–6)

[But whoever is truly king is truly free, if he rule himself and his kingdom rightly; let him know that all things are lawful for him which are fitted for ruling the kingdom, but not for destroying it.]

This passage illuminates medieval *realpolitik*. The kingly freedom it describes is a freedom which is best not used. The king is free, this poem is in effect saying, so long as he does not flex his muscles and use that freedom. But, in English political theory, he must *have* that power, as Cary Nederman notes: 'English thinkers insist that the king must exceed in power all others in his realm, having neither superior nor peer.'[35] To put it in Giorgio Agamben's terms, '[t]he paradox of sovereignty consists in the fact that the sovereign is, at the same time, outside and inside the juridical order'.[36] But the possession of power he cannot actually use is potentially a politically unstable situation for any monarch, one against which such kings as Henry III and Edward II constantly railed. Yet others, notably Edward I and even more decisively, Edward III, showed how kings *were* at times able to carry the population with their decisions, ruling with relative autocracy through not much more than their own political skill and charisma. They were able to do this – as later chapters will discuss – in part through skilful manipulation of patriotism.

Claire Valente sees in *The Song of Lewes* support for her idea that the barons were not opposed to personal rule as such; they simply thought that such power was too big for any one king. 'Henry III's opponents and subjects certainly thought the king's rule had flaws', she suggests, 'but they did not see royal government as necessarily or inherently or primarily oppressive so much as in need of guidance'.[37] But this is to miss the point that opponents appear to attack the inadequacy of personal rule because they are reluctant to attack the king's person overtly. The attack on personal rule in *The Song of Lewes* is really a very careful, elaborately coded attack on Henry III himself and his inadequacies – in the context of a system which had no way to replace a monarch other than by another monarch (and that does not seem to have been contemplated). In fact the poem embodies a contradiction: to give the impression of an attack on personal rule as such rather than the rule of a given king, a political commentator must say that personal rule is itself inadequate, and in addition that no king is adequate to it.

Weaker kings than Edward I were routinely accused of destroying the kingdom when they attempted to rule directly and forcefully. It is the nation itself that is at stake when an unwise king rules and it is in defence of the realm that such adversaries of the king as Hubert de Burgh and Simon de Montfort are operating – at least according to those who write about them. This concern with the community of the realm is evident in *The Song of Lewes*. As is often the case in the thirteenth century, it is not entirely clear how broadly the phrase *communitas regni* is to be understood. It can refer narrowly to the magnates, though there are moments in this poem when it seems the broader sense is intended. When the poet says, 'Therefore let the community of the realm take counsel, and let that be decreed which is the opinion of the commonalty, to whom their own laws are most known' ['Igitur communitas regni consulatur, / Et quid uniuersitas senciat, sciatur, / Cui leges proprie maxime sunt note'] (765–7) the term perhaps embraces only the magnates.[38] This seems even more likely in the following passage:

Ex hijs potest colligi, quod communitatem
Tangit quales eligi ad utilitatem
Regni recte debeant; qui uelint & sciant
Et prodesse ualeant, tales regis fiant
Et consiliarij & coadiutores… (778–82)

[From this it can be gathered that the kind of men, who ought rightly to be chosen for the service of the kingdom, touches the community; namely those who have the will and knowledge and power to be of profit, let such men be made counsellors and coadjutors of the king.]

Such passages suggest a 'communitas regni' that is restricted to the traditional governing classes. But elsewhere the poet's sympathies are wider. 'For the oppression of the people [*plebs*] pleases not God, nay rather does the compassion whereby the people [*plebs*] may have leisure for God' (613–14). In such sententious passages as these, the idea of *communitas* seems to broaden out in the poem and extend below the magnate level.

There is one respect, however, in which *communitas* is radically restricted in *The Song of Lewes*. The poem's chief concerns are, as has been seen, with the king's subjection to God and to the law. To these ideas can be added a third preoccupation: an embryonic sense of nation and its role in kingship. The author of *The Song of Lewes* was deeply interested in Englishness and what such a concept might mean. Like Robert of Gloucester, the poet of *Lewes* slides from kingship and the law to race; what was contested at Lewes was not just good kingship, but Englishness itself.

This is first expressed through a fear that would later be more famously mobilised in the time of Edward I. There are those, the poet says, whose aim is 'to blot out the name of the English' ['anglorum delere / Nomen ...'] (281–2). Like Matthew Paris, Robert of Gloucester and many another, those he has in mind are influential foreigners in England:

> Hinc alienigenas discant aduocare
> Angli, si per aduenas nolunt exulare.
> Nam qui suam gloriam uolunt ampliare,
> Suamque memoriam uellent semper stare,
> Sue gentis plurimos sibi sociare,
> Et mox inter maximos student collocare;
> Itaque confusio crescit incolarum,
> Crescit indignacio, crescit cor amarum... (285–92)

[Hence may the English learn to call in foreigners, if they wish to be exiled by strangers; for they who wish to increase their own glory, and would wish their memory to stand for ever, are eager to associate many of their own nation with themselves, and soon to place them amongst the greatest; so the confusion of the natives increases, indignation increases, bitterness of heart increases ...]

The king, continues the poet, ought to use escheats and wards to reward his own people ['suos']. If he rewards those of no account, who have arrived with nothing (by implication, foreigners) then they will supplant his natural subjects ['viros naturales'];[39] these foreigners study to turn the heart of the prince from his own people ['Principis avertere cor a suis student'] (304–5).

The poet began with a reference, in the wake of the battle, to the 'gens elata' and the 'fideles' – the proud ones cast down by the battle and the faithful who now rejoice. Now *Anglia* breathes again, the poet continues, hoping for liberty. In *Anglia*, what such a poem imagines, then, is an uncomplicated idea of England – the kind of England envisioned in Matthew Paris's tale of the patriotic blacksmith – in which Englishness is a simple matter of birth. But in fact, as these poems tend to reveal, Englishness is deeply complicated: '[t]he myth of racial purity could be used as a test of national identity when it suited', Turville-Petre has observed, 'although it was a test that no one in England was in a position to pass'.[40] In this poem, the best of Englishmen is actually a Frenchman; the most perfidious man is the heir to the English throne; some among the 'gens elata' who have fallen are English yet are excluded, all of which implies that only the 'fideles' are truly English. 'Englishness' becomes a personal quality of character.

The argument is not unique to this poet. Another poem on the same struggle is found inserted in a contemporary chronicle on the Barons' Wars by William Rishanger. It was entitled by Wright 'Song upon the Divisions Among the Barons' and is also known, from its opening lines, as 'Plange plorans'. Rishanger places it soon after the Mise of Amiens. It is clearly another Montfortian poem, urging the baronial party to hold together (apparently in the face of the unfavourable judgement given in the Mise) and lamenting the destruction of the land, which is first per-sonified and addressed. 'Lament, weeping, O England, full now with anguish; in sadness you see sorrowful things, languishing in sorrow.'[41] The address to *Anglia* quickly leads on to a lament on the general state of affairs:

> Sic respublica perit, terra desolatur;
> Invalescit extera gens et sublimatur;
> Vilescit vir incola, et subpeditatur:
> Sustinet injurias, non est qui loquatur. (18)

[Thus the state vanishes and the land is laid waste; the foreigner grows power-ful and is raised up; the native man becomes worthless and is trodden under foot: he sustains injuries, but there is no one who will speak out. (122)]

Apart from such general laments, the poem uses apostrophe, the char-acteristic technique of political verse. The address in the opening line sets the tone of a poem largely in the vocative mode. This is exhibited in the shift to an address to the earl of Gloucester, warning him to remain steadfast. (Gilbert de Clare, a major supporter of Montfort's among the nobles, defected from his cause in the months after Lewes and went back to Henry.) The next address is to Montfort himself, then to the earl of

Norfolk, Roger Bigod, enjoining him to maintain his oath (presumably to the Provisions). The final address is to the magnates in general:

> O vos magni proceres, qui vos obligastis
> Observare firmiter illud quod jurastis!
> Terræ si sit utile quod excogitastis,
> Juvet illud citius id quod ordinastis. (19)

[O you great nobles who bound yourselves to observe firmly that which you swore; if what you imagined be profitable to the land, let that which you have ordained aid it immediately (123).]

The poet then links the magnates to the land, which in turn is identified with the *respublica* and the *vir incola*. The address to Montfort himself is brief but telling; it refers to him as a man powerful and strong [*vir potens et fortis*]. 'Fight now for the fatherland' ['Pungna nunc pro patria'] the poet urges; 'defend the state and your own fortune' ['Rem defende pupplicam resque tuæ sortis'] (19).[42]

Like the *Lewes*-poet, the author of 'Plange plorans' must overlook Montfort's birth in asking him to fight for the *patria*. Behind the political theory about the need for kingship to be bound by law and religion is a simpler and more pragmatic mobilisation of concepts of race and nation – concepts which would have had much less impact prior to the thirteenth century given that the French landholdings of English nobles complicated the issue of foreignness. Such poets ostensibly argue that good kingship is a matter of rule by a law which is God-given. But at the same time they argue that good politics is a matter of the promotion of the *vir incola*.

This political position is then further complicated in such texts as the *The Song of Lewes* by the evident fact that it is possible to have a good foreigner as well as a bad Englishman. The Lord Edward, the native-born Englishman, is the enemy in *The Song of Lewes* while the French-born Simon de Montfort is that poem's ideal man. This occurs in part because although it is very easy for writers from Matthew Paris to Robert of Gloucester to construct an opposition between foreigners and Englishmen, they do not in fact have a very developed sense of what Englishness is. This is scarcely surprising in the thirteenth-century context of a mixed racial heritage and a complex linguistic situation. While Robert of Gloucester writes in English, the author of *The Song of Lewes* implies an audience, addressing England and the English and speaking of the *communitas regni* – but doing so in sophisticated Latin verse which the vast majority of English people could never have appreciated. Kingsford speculated that the poet's use of alliteration might reflect an interest in native English verse-forms (xxxiv–xxxv). If that were the case, the adaptation of native versification is nevertheless done in such a way that hardly anyone who still appreciated English alliterative verse could have understood the *Lewes*-poet's use of it. The implication is that a literate, educated few have a consensus on what Englishness is that is untroubled by any reference to the bulk of the English people – unlikely patriotic speeches put in the mouths of blacksmiths notwithstanding.

By comparison with the clerkly Latin material, such a poem as the *sirventes* on Richard of Cornwall in the 'Song Against the King of Almaigne' looks naive and simple. Where *The Song of Lewes* uses sophisticated rhyme patterns, the English relies heavily on the rhyming wordplay 'Richard/ trichard'. The English poem has nothing to offer by way of political theory, only broad and general – if not unfounded – accusations against Richard as lecherous and grasping. The poet's vocabulary is vernacular, the tone colloquial, its humour founded on bathos and basic inversions. The poet says, for example, that Richard imagined 'the sayles were mangonel / to helpe Wyndesore',[43] recasting the earl as a fool who sees siege engines where there are only windmill sails. Richard's capture by the barons turns an earl into a miller, and even the oaths attributed to the poem's one positive character fall somewhat short of the heroic. Montfort swears 'bi ys chyn' that he will deal with the Earl Warenne and 'bi hys cop',[44] or head, to take care of Bigod. These oaths suggest a simple bodily guarantee – the same kind of synecdochic reassurance offered by an oath made on a saint's body part. In all these ways the poem tempers bitter mockery with a note of comic simplicity.

Yet for all their differences there is a great deal that links the Middle English poem with the more sophisticated Latin texts. The author was probably more learned than might at first appear and his poem cannot simply be taken as the naive, vernacular shadow of the more learned productions. He was clearly conversant with events: he knew about the movements of various nobles and in specifying a figure of £30,000 he probably indicates that he knew about the sum of money which according to chroniclers, Richard was offered by the Montfortians before Lewes in an attempt to buy peace.[45] The French terms *trichard* and *lyard* make their earliest recorded appearances in Middle English, suggesting that this is not a naive writer imprisoned by his use of English but someone who was at least bilingual.

Most importantly, the Middle English poem shares with the Latin poems the vocative mode. It appears to address a set of defeated enemies, beginning with Richard of Cornwall and ending with the Lord Edward, forcefully suggesting that Edward should hasten to Dover and leave the country. In reality, of course, this is an example of political poetry's typical *pseudo*-apostrophe: in purportedly addressing the defeated enemy, the poem is really addressing a community closer at hand. That community, in the case of the English poem, is nebulous. But it is one constituted along lines of bitter anger against spendthrift nobles and, of course, by its preference for vernacular song. It is not really Edward who is addressed here, but other Englishmen who think like the poet. Moreover, anyone who sings the song is performatively participating in it: to occupy the position offered by the 'lyric ego' is also to abuse Edward.

The answer to the question of what was at stake in the reciting of such a poem receives a partial answer here. There was little risk that Edward would somehow hear the sentiments expressed in the poem and punish the composer or performer. Performers may have felt residually protected by the linguistic Englishness of the scandalous material they sang. But the prime function of such a collective address to an enemy (as political ralliers and football crowds the world over know) is to unite a group of people wearing, as it were, the same colours, against a figure of dislike or hatred. In doing that, the English poem makes no *explicit* appeal to an English community. It does not need to. That message is carried by its form and its language of composition. It is the *Latin* poems that make the more explicit appeals against foreigners and for an English *communitas regni*.

Tim Machan observes that the bulk of the contemporary criticism of Henry III and his patronage of foreigners, such as that found in Matthew Paris and *The Song of Lewes*, is written in Latin or French, languages which 'could little further any specifically English national consciousness, both because most inhabitants of England were not conversant with them and because by the thirteenth century French as well as Latin had pan-European implications'.[46] Nevertheless, as is clear from the single survival, there *was* English material on these themes, and it suggests that the concerns of the Latinate material did extend to the exclusively Anglophone sphere.

In all this material, we might feel that we are watching England become more aware of itself. But the vision of Englishness in these poems is more complicated than that phrase suggests. The Lord Edward, future English king, is given a resounding send-off; the Frenchman Montfort is acclaimed as popular hero. Englishness is a quite specific quality having little to do with birth.

THE REBEL'S BODY

Whoever the author of 'The King of Almaigne' was, he seems to have been able to imagine a land with an exiled king and non-divinely appointed replacement. This would indeed be radical change. But Montfort's rule lasted a little more than a year. His personal acquisitiveness contributed to his making some very familiar mistakes. 'Like any "bad" king', Maddicott points out, 'Montfort had concentrated patronage too narrowly and so divided his court.' And as Henry himself had done in 1258, 'Montfort had allowed his court to become divided by faction.'[47] The defection of the earl of Gloucester from the Montfortian cause was a major blow, destabilising the March with Wales. When the Lord Edward escaped from Montfort's custody in May 1265, key towns in the March quickly fell to him. After two months of manoeuvrings, the royalists and Montfortians met for the last time at Evesham on 4 August 1265.[48]

Could it have been any other way? What if, we might counterfactually ask, Montfort had ruled like a good king, or at least one with the skills of an Edward I or Edward III? Could he have ensured his political survival? Even had he ruled more cannily, there would still have been a vacuum at the centre of royal government. Although it was a political system that throve on criticism of monarchs, it was also one which could not function without them: much as the English system resisted the extremes of divine monarchy seen on the continent, that divinely anointed figure on the throne was still a necessity. As Powicke insists, Montfort himself and his allies 'were and could only be royalists. Their political thought and intentions were bounded by their ideas of kingship, its rights and its duties.'[49] When barons rebelled they did so, Valente remarks, not 'to overthrow their kings so much as to control or influence them'.[50] Such misfortunes as the loss of the earl of Gloucester to the Montfortian cause should perhaps be regarded not as symptoms, but as inevitabilities.

It was for these reasons that Montfort kept both King Henry and the Lord Edward with him, even during his final campaign against the rebellious Marcher lords. Conversely, the escape of Edward was a great blow to Montfort's authority. In the closing stages of the Battle of Evesham, Simon de Montfort and his closest associates fought in a circle around their captive, King Henry III. There they were cut down by the forces of Edward, 'in an episode of noble bloodletting unprecedented since the Conquest'.[51] When Montfort was killed his body was hacked to pieces. 'Sic sic truncatus, sic omnino spoliatus / Et sic castratus summos patitur cruciatus', wrote a poet in London, British Library, Cotton MS Otho

D.viii. 'Alas, dismembered, spoiled in every way', as A. G. Rigg renders the lines, 'Truncated and castrated where he lay.'[52] The head was cut off and sent to the Mortimer castle at Wigmore. Appalled, like most of the chroniclers, Robert of Gloucester called the slaughter indiscriminate and referred to the event as 'þe morþre of einesham · uor bataile non it nas ·' (11736).

The treatment meted out to Montfort and his followers seems to have been thought fitting by the royalist party for men deemed traitors. Valente notes that other rebels who escaped the slaughter and were captured were neither tried for treason nor executed. Henry III, she argues, 'was still unable to condemn rebels formally as traitors'.[53] In the thirteenth century rebellion, even against the king, had not yet been included in the definition of treason. This would await the expanded definition which developed in the fourteenth century. Hence, Valente suggests, the slaughter of Montfort and his allies might have been deliberate, in order to solve the legal problems. A recently discovered narrative of the battle supports the idea that Montfort was specifically targeted, as it recounts the formation by Edward of a 'death squad' whose role it was to murder the rebel earl.[54]

But were such legal niceties in the minds of those who hacked at the bodies of the fallen rebel leader, his sons and associates? It is easy to imagine that as they reached the bitter conclusion to years of baronial struggle, the royalists simply reacted with savagery born of relief and revenge: basic emotions which chivalry and the law were designed to restrain, but which, from time to time, were bound to be expressed. Katherine Royer notes that although the dismemberment of traitors seems to have begun in Henry's reign, it was only in that of Edward I that it became 'a more regular feature of English justice'. She finds Montfort's dismemberment unsurprising in a context in which 'the body of a defeated enemy had long been part of the spoils of war, and its dismemberment a traditional practice'.[55] All the royalist hatred was focused on this moment and on the bodies of the rebels. At the same time, it is true, this was the simplest way of confirming that Simon de Montfort was, indeed, a traitor. This way, he would never be able to answer the charge. The English poet of the 'Song Against the King of Almaigne' sought a simple guarantee in imagining Montfort swearing by his head to stop Hugh Bigod; the royalists too react to Simon's body, cutting off that head. The traitor's body is dismembered and rendered abject.

In the same moment of abjection, however, as several chronicles and poems record, the basis of the earl's future veneration was revealed. As he was cut to pieces, Robert of Gloucester reports, his limbs 'ne bledde noȝt me sede · & þe harde here was · is lich þe next wede · ' (11734–5). The revealing of the hair shirt begins the revelation of the martyr behind the dismembered traitor. In the Anglo-Norman poem, 'Lament for Simon de Montfort', the same events are related:

> Pres de son cors,
> Le bon tresors,
> Une heyre troverent.

[Near to his body, that great treasure, they found a hair shirt.][56]

This poem is another which has the look of a song, as it consists principally of short lines of four to six syllables, each stanza accompanied by a six-line refrain. The composer begins by announcing 'Chanter m'estoit', and says that he weeps in making the poem. But he feels compelled to write about 'nostre duz baronage' (6), who for the sake of peace let their bodies be hacked to pieces and dismembered to save England ['Se lesserent … / Lur cors trencher / E demenbrer / Pur salver Engletere'] (9–12). The poet compares Montfort with Thomas à Becket, even giving him a distinctly Christly look when he proposes that by his death he won victory ['par sa mort / Le cuens Mountfort / Conquist la victorie'] (37–9).

Simon de Montfort's remains were buried by the monks at Evesham and the dead earl became an unofficial saint, the subject of private worship. As a martyr, Montfort could no longer be held to account and it seems to have been even easier to make him into an Englishman. In London, British Library, Cotton MS Vespasian A.vi, there is a record of a series of miracles achieved by Montfort's intercession, at the end of which is a poem about Montfort's martyrdom, which calls him 'Protector gentis Angliæ'.[57] In the antiphon accompanying an office in his memory, Montfort is acclaimed: 'O decus milicie / gentium anglorum', while in another Latin lament, he is compared to Achilles, as one who fights for the fatherland ['Qui pugnat pro patria'].[58] This, as Frederic Maitland says, 'is the Montfort of popular hagiology, who wears a hair shirt, treads in the footsteps of Becket, and fights for the ideas of Grosseteste'.[59] The bodies of abjected traitors have a way of staging returns, to the embarrassment of those who try to expunge their memory.

It is true that the Latin poems examined here probably circulated in written form among the learned and consequently had only limited appeal. They speak, broadly, of *Anglia* and various kinds of *communitas* within *Anglia* but they do so in a way that only a tiny minority could have understood. Nevertheless the existence of the Middle English poem on Richard of Cornwall, together with fragments of other vernacular compositions, suggests that there *was* a vernacular arm to this form of polemic. If the English composer of 'Song Against the King of Almaigne' was, as I have argued conversant with Anglo-Norman, then what he was doing was trying to ensure circulation of some basic anti-royalist ideas at the vernacular level, drawing on his learning and his understanding of current affairs which was based on his own knowledge of the barons' principal language. His composition may have been a true song and so may, in its appearance in Harley 2253, represent a chance survival from a once-widespread genre.

None of this is to suggest that there is a general sense of a specifically English *communitas* operating at this date. As we have seen, political theories are clearly very malleable when it is thought necessary to expel the most prominent of Englishmen (such as Edward) while retaining the French Montfort in the ranks of loyal Englishmen. It is not possible to accept Powicke's formulation, that in this period 'we are watching England become more aware of itself'. We are instead witnessing a process in which a small group of learned people, linked to a rebellious group of nobles, are theorising something – an *Anglia* for everyone – which can be put back into the mouths (for example) of such figures as Matthew Paris's eloquent smith. *Anglia*, as defended by Matthew Paris and the poets, is not England. Not quite. *Anglia* is Latinate, bookish, a construction of the clerks. *England* – something implied in the English poem on Lewes but not named – will emerge more fully later on.

Some of the poems examined here were deeply sceptical of the future Edward I. In 1270, the struggles of the Barons' Wars behind him and already receding into memory, Edward left England and went on crusade. Powicke regarded the crusade as expiation for the civil strife, 'the expression of a general desire to forget the past'. When Henry III died in 1272 with Edward still in the Holy Land, the 'quiet, undisputed, and almost instantaneous succession of an absent prince to the English throne was a proof of the unity of the realm and a landmark in the history of the monarchy'.[60] Prestwich notes that Edward travelled back from crusade in a 'leisurely' fashion (not reaching England until August 1274) and was able to attend to matters in Gascony on his way at length, as 'the news he had received from England had not suggested that there was any urgent need for his presence'. Chroniclers did not treat of Edward's return in any great detail.[61]

One royalist versifier was moved to state that the king of England's 'flourishing deeds' compelled him to write, 'for it is shameful to let famous actions pass in silence'.[62] Edward, the poet declares, 'shines like a new Richard'. 'Sic gemino flore Britones titulantur honore, / Bella per Eaduuardi similis et probitate Ricardi' (128). [Thus the Britons have a double claim to honour, by the wars of Edward equally and by the valour of Richard.] These words are the hackneyed expression of a well-known topos, that of hope for a new reign. In 1307 Edward II would be acclaimed in similar terms (as will be discussed in chapter 3), though he would go on to disappoint such hopes utterly. Edward I, of course, fared much better. Among other things, for him the foreigner question would not be a difficulty. This was partly, no doubt, because he had seen enough of his father's bad example and learned from it. Partly also, the problem simply arose less often, because England, after the 1259 Treaty of Paris, was becoming more cut off from France.

However, it is also important to see that the foreigner problem was never really a problem. Foreignness was a convenient and obvious thing to attack when there was widespread discontentment with the king. The example of the foreigner Montfort and his widespread acceptance is not an anomaly. It clearly shows that it was not foreign birth that truly mattered. It was what foreigners did once they were in England that counted. If foreigners' actions – such as those of the Poitevins or, supposedly, of Queen Eleanor – appeared to work against an idea of what was appropriate for England, then their foreignness was held against them. As Prestwich notes, 'dislike of the Poitevins cannot … be analysed in simple chauvinist terms. Dislike of them was more because of the patronage they received, and the way in which they behaved, than because of their origins in Poitou.'[63] Otherwise, English identity was sufficiently inchoate and labile as to be able easily to absorb the foreign-born.

In the 1290s, Edward – once the villain, as we have seen, in the 1260s – was able to mobilise specifically pro-*English* sentiment, aligning himself with his subjects' increasingly coherent expressions of vernacular politics. The perception of fresh threats, this time from nearer at hand, provoked new efforts to define *Anglia*, or, as it would now more frequently and more appropriately be known, *England*.

CHAPTER 2

Attacking Scotland: Edward I and the 1290s

TEACHING BRITISH TO THE ROMANS

Reclining on the dais with his nobles and knights after a great feast at Pentecost, the king is visited by a delegation from Rome, twelve men bearing olive branches in token of a peaceful mission. They deliver a letter which, read aloud, causes outrage in the court. Lucius Hiberius, who is variously, according to the source in which this story is read, procurator, senator, or emperor of Rome, denounces Arthur's conquest of Gaul and his failure to pay tribute to Rome, owed since the conquest of Britain by Julius Caesar. Lucius demands Arthur's presence in Rome, bearing the tribute. Like any good sovereign, Arthur immediately calls a council with his magnates in order to decide on a course of action. Cador, duke of Cornwall, speaks first, cautioning against the vice of idleness and welcoming the arrival of the letter with its promise of warlike action. Arthur then argues that the conquest of Britain by Caesar was unlawful and that no tribute is owed. The king of Scotland responds in support. It is agreed that Arthur will summon all his vassals and lead an invasion of Rome. Rome shall pay tribute to Britain, rather than the other way around.

This story ultimately goes back to the early twelfth-century version by Geoffrey of Monmouth in his *Historia Regum Britannie*, but it was retold through the centuries by all of Geoffrey's imitators. Each time, of course, it receives a new inflection. Wace introduces a countering note to Cador's words by having Gawain respond to him in favour of peace. La3amon then retains this detail from Wace, but makes Gawain's response a vehemently angry one. Other alterations more obviously respond to an adaptor's historical situation. La3amon, writing from his embattled position as an English voice in a French-Angevin culture, has Cador say that if the Romans come to Britain, 'we 3am solle teche Brutisshe spech(e)'.[1] As a euphemism for the inflicting of military defeat, 'teaching the Romans how to talk British' adds a note of 'British' vernacular defiance in the face of Latinity which allegorically reverses the actual situation, in Laȝamon's time, of the English vernacular in relation to French.

The version in the chronicle attributed to Robert of Gloucester has its own nuance. When the king of Scotland begins his speech it is made clear (as it is not in earlier versions) that Arthur had *made* him king. It is not certain that the Brut-section of the 'Gloucester Chronicle' was composed at the same time as Robert of Gloucester's own narrative of the reign of Henry III (as was discussed in the previous chapter). There is no *necessary* connection between Arthur's creation of a king of Scotland and Edward I's settling on John Balliol in 1291 as king of Scots. But it is not difficult to believe that the Gloucester-redactor tailored the story in minor ways in the 1290s to produce this detail of a king of Britain who *creates* the king of Scotland, in implicit endorsement of Edward's actions in the Great Cause, his arbitration on the disputed Scottish succession.

If the Gloucester-redactor was adapting an older version of Brut history, he was doing so in a context in which comparisons of Edward with Arthur were commonplace. The Galfridian Arthur's imperialist achievements, especially in the context of the British Isles, had their obvious appeal to Plantagenet kings with ambitions to rule over England, Wales, Scotland, and Ireland. While modern accounts of the extent of his personal interest in the Arthur story have perhaps been exaggerated, Edward I's opportunist use of the legend for political purposes is not in doubt.[2] Contemporary chroniclers were well aware of the possibilities offered by comparisons with Arthur. The late thirteenth-century chronicler Pierre Langtoft is one who consistently invokes Arthur to make comparisons with Edward. In one of the better-known passages of his Anglo-Norman chronicle, Langtoft refers to a prophecy by Merlin of the union of England and Scotland, and notes (somewhat optimistically) that this has now been fulfilled by Edward, who alone unites these lands: 'Arthur ne avayt unkes si plainement les fez' [Arthur never so plainly held the fiefs].[3]

There is much in the narrative of Arthur's Roman campaign that would appeal to an expansionist king. In the chronicle of Robert of Gloucester, Cador, like a skilled warm-up man, sets the scene for deliberations on war against Rome with his speech against idleness, which leads men only to dice, play, and lose strength through dalliance with women. Arthur then, as part of the build-up to his attack on Rome, denies the legitimacy of the tribute payable to Rome. Caesar, he points out, first exacted this tribute with 'strengþe', 'outrage', and 'vnriȝt' at a time when there was strife between the ancestors of the Britons. But, Arthur continues, 'þing þat is mid strengþe inome · hou miȝte it be mid riȝte · / Vor he naþ reson non · bote robberie & mi3te ·'.[4] So far his point is straightforward: we British do not pay tribute because it was unlawfully exacted in the first place.

This argument was originally given to Arthur in Geoffrey of Monmouth's version and followed by Geoffrey's imitators. At this point, Geoffrey and his followers then involve Arthur in a remarkable volte-face. In the 'Gloucester Chronicle', the king states, 'mid as god reson mowe we · of hom esse ywis · / Bere he þanne þe truage · þat bineþe is ·' (4043–4). 'With as good reason', he says; but as he has just explained, that is no reason: something taken by strength is not taken at all. Rhetorically, Arthur ought to be occupying the moral high ground by saying that Britain does not exact tribute, just as Rome should not. Instead, he continues:

> Vor Iuli & oþere emperours · hii seggeþ come þer to ·
> Þat emperours were of rome · ich may segge al so ·
> Þat min auncetres of þe lond · wule* wonne rome ·   *once*
> As bely* þe noble king · þat 3e abbeþ yhurd ylome ·   *Belin, a legendary*
>   *Briton*
>
> & constantin eleyne sone · 3e witeþ wel rome nom ·
> & suþþe maximian · þat of hor beyre blod* ich com·   *the blood of both*
> Min auncetres hii were alle þre · & kinges of þis londe ·
> & wonne þe aumperye of rome · & boþe adde an honde ·
> Of france & of oþer londes · þat we wonne mid vre mi3te ·
> We mowe segge þat we nabbeþ · to ansuerye no3t mid ri3te ·
> Wanne hii vorsoke is & uorslewede · & to none defense ne come ·
> Þo we þoru chiualerie · out of hor poer is nome · (4045–56)

Belin and Constantine, both of them Arthur's forebears, *won* the empire of Rome and thereby subjugated France and other lands 'mid vre [the Britons'] mi3te'. Consequently, as their heir, Arthur is as entitled to levy tribute from Rome as Rome is from Britain. Given that Arthur has just said that the levying of tribute by conquest is illegitimate, the argument ought to be self-cancelling; by contrast, Geoffrey and his successors all regard it as self-*authorising*. While Geoffrey's successors might alter details here and there – allowing Gawain, for example, to advance an argument in favour of peace – none of them seems the least concerned with the contradiction Geoffrey's Arthur elaborates.[5] For Geoffrey's followers, it is acceptable that Arthur calls on the invented past in this way to authorise the Arthurian present.[6]

PIERRE DE LANGTOFT AND ROBERT OF GLOUCESTER

The two verse chronicles by Pierre Langtoft and Robert of Gloucester are in obvious ways very different from each other. Langtoft writes in

Anglo-Norman, using the characteristically French *laisse*; Robert of Gloucester, the English writer, composes loosely alexandrine couplets. Yet in another sense they are mirror images of each other. In their ponderous verse forms, each created what appear to have been popular works, surviving in twenty and fourteen extant manuscripts respectively.[7] Each grafts on to Brut-history an eyewitness account of the thirteenth-century present: the reign of Henry III in Robert's case, that of Edward I in Langtoft's. Both authors appear to have been writing in the 1290s (Langtoft either continuing, or continued by others, into the early fourteenth century). Working on opposite sides of the country, they were presumably unaware of each other's work, but their similarities are not purely accidental. At the end of the thirteenth century a new desire was evident to link up legendary, Brut-history with the English present; its continuing influence is witnessed in a range of fourteenth-century works, including the translation in the 1330s by Robert Mannyng of Langtoft's chronicle, Thomas Castleford's *Boke of Brut*, the various versions of the prose *Short Metrical Chronicle* (a digest of Brut history) and the astonishingly prodigious tradition of the English Prose *Brut* chronicle.[8]

Langtoft and Robert of Gloucester stand at the head of this renewed tradition. Their chronicles raise what can seem to modern eyes a pressing question: Why, when a chronicler has much to say about the king in his own time, including valuable eyewitness testimony, does he preface it with thousands of lines of pseudo-history paraphrased from another source? The answer lies in the attitude to history found in the chronicles themselves. As we have just seen, King Arthur regards old history as warrant for his present acts; so too the contemporary Plantagenet monarchs, in the eyes of the chroniclers, are enhanced rather than diminished by their association with such ancient history. As R. R. Davies notes, 'in a past-oriented and a past-validating society, claims to empire and supremacy, as to all other forms of power, had ultimately to be located in the past'.[9] Arthur and those who write Arthur assume that the past, and the conquests of the past, legitimate the practices of the present, insisting on this (as in the Roman case above) to the point of self-contradiction.

In March 1291, Edward I made a very similar appeal to history, looking to the British past to legitimate his own claims to overlordship of the kingdom of Scotland. The Great Cause arose because of the crisis in the Scottish succession that resulted from the deaths of Alexander III in 1286 and of his heir the Fair Maid of Norway in 1290.[10] Called upon to arbitrate among the several claimants to the throne, Edward, who had recently subjugated the Welsh, used the occasion to establish himself as feudal overlord in Scotland. He refused to hear the case unless his feudal overlordship was recognised, not because this was 'a mere legal fiction that would allow him to hear the case, but a right that he was anxious to establish and exercise, by obtaining seisin of Scotland'.[11] Edward caused letters to be sent out to English monasteries ordering a record search, presumably having already had the rolls at Westminster investigated.[12] If it could be demonstrated that in the past the English monarch had had overlordship, then that should be the case in the present.

Edward duly installed John Balliol (a candidate with a very good claim) as a client king and received his homage. This apparent English success was followed, however, by a period of crisis in 1294–8 involving, first, war with France over the question of English rights in Gascony, then a Welsh rebellion. In March 1296, a Scottish raid across the Tweed on the town of Pressen brought immediate English retaliation, opening Anglo-Scottish hostilities. Through these years of warfare, the king's need for funds was unending, which led directly to his forced concession in parliament of the *confirmatio cartarum* in 1297 and eventually of the *articuli super cartas* in 1300. Celebrated though Edward's wars were by many at the time, the king never surmounted these various crises and the problems they posed for his reign and the kingdom.

Amid all the difficulties, however, Edward's handling of the Scottish situation in 1296 appeared entirely decisive. In response to Balliol's act of rebellion against his client status, Edward besieged Berwick and reduced it, before an English army under Earl Warenne of Surrey defeated the Scots in the field at Dunbar in late April. Routed, Balliol was forced to abdicate. As he had earlier done with Welsh symbols of royalty, Edward removed the Scottish regalia, including the Stone of Destiny, from Scone to Westminster, 'ma[king] it visually clear that the other kingships in Britain had been eradicated by, or absorbed in, the English kingship'.[13] From the English point of view, then, 1296 could be viewed as a splendid high-point in the reign of a martial king, rather than, as it quickly turned out to be, a transitory success.

For Pierre Langtoft, these events are both central and, paradoxically, tangential. Central, in that he clearly had a great deal of first-hand material to use and devoted considerable space to a narration of 1296. Tangential, in that Langtoft gives readers to understand that it is in fact *France*, and the reconquest of Edward's Gascon inheritance, that he would rather be writing about. Rebellious Britons, whether in Wales or Scotland, are a distraction from what he seems to regard as a more chivalrous undertaking: warfare with the French king. But because the Scots and Welsh will not submit, Langtoft, like his king, is forced to devote

much space to them. In this context, and given the tendency of his narrative to emphasise Edward's fulfilment of Merlin's prophecy of the unification of Britain under one monarch, the apparent success of the 1296
campaign is very important to the chronicle. In turn, it is in the course
of this narrative that Langtoft inserts the single most discussed aspect of
what is otherwise a rather under-noticed work. Without prior announcement, Langtoft laces his story with eight tail-rhyme verses in a mixture
of English and Anglo-Norman, markedly breaking with his usual mono-
rhyme *laisse*.[14] A little further on a ninth poem appears, detailing the
death of William Wallace.

Thea Summerfield summarises the formal characteristics of these
poems. They are:

invariably in tail-rhyme …: three short lines of two stresses each with a varying number of unstressed syllables, rhyming a-a-b/ c-c-b/ d-d-e/ f-f-e. They vary
considerably in length; the English songs are never longer than four stanzas,
while the Anglo-Norman songs fall into two groups: short songs of two or at
most three stanzas (nos. 1, 3, 9) and extremely long songs, of 16, 10 and 12 stanzas
respectively (nos. 6, 7 and 8). Whereas, as the numbers given them here indicate,
the short Anglo-Norman songs occur at irregular intervals, very much like their
counterparts in English, the long songs appear in a cluster, separated from one
another by one *laisse* only.[15]

Summerfield also distinguishes between the 'earthy' nature of the English
poems, and the more dignified tone of the Anglo-Norman, which she
regards as consistent with the discourse of the *laisse*.

These odd verse performances are not seen elsewhere in the chronicle
and alone serve to highlight the narrative of 1296. Their status has always
been in dispute; Thomas Wright edited them in his *Political Songs* but
only in an appendix, as if unsure what to do with them. Their reception
ever since has been marked by quite opposed views of their purpose.

In the previous chapter, we saw problems of inclusion and exclusion,
and the labile strategies of learned writers in discussing a context in which
they wanted to uphold native men while at the same time leaving room
for a heroic alien. Lacking a legal mechanism by which to dispose of
Simon de Montfort, the future Edward I ensured his abjection through
humiliation, physical annihilation, and death, only to see the abjected
body stage a return as the focus of political anti-monarchical sentiment.
In this chapter, I will look at abjection in a very different form. Langtoft's
verses either record, imitate, or perform non-learned and apparently popular voices, in order to stage the difference between the abject subjects of
abuse and the English themselves. Where Montfort was the foreign-born

honorary Englishman in the first chapter, in the 1290s an even more equivocal figure, John Balliol, focuses the problems inherent in the proto-nation-building which is taking place in the Langtoft poems.

For Langtoft, the Great Cause passes as an unremarkable matter which he describes in an anodyne version: for lack of an heir, there is 'grand contencioun' in Scotland; the land is surrendered to Edward 'en proteccioun' and 'sanz dissensioun' (190:12, 26–7; 260, 272–3). The decision in favour of Balliol is given by several judges, with whom Edward simply concurs. Then, in a variation from the usual metrical pattern, Balliol's homage to Edward is emphasised by being given in prose (pp. 192–4; p. 257).

The chronicler has a far greater commitment to his narrative of 1296, which he opens with a curse for the Welsh, whose rebellion distracts Edward from the regaining of his French possessions. His account of the Scottish campaign picks up rhetorically from that curse:

> Escoce sait maudite de la mere Dé,
> Et parfound ad deable Gales enfoundré!
> En l'un ne l'autre fu unkes verité. (220:12–14; 619–21)

[May Scotland be cursed by the mother of God and may Wales be sunk deep to the devil! In neither was there ever truth.]

Just as there was never *verité* in Wales and Scotland, there is a sense that the *true* subject of this narrative should be the conflict between Edward, flower of chivalry, and his equally chivalrous rival, Philip IV of France. Instead, it must concern itself with the doings of a barely civilised people. Langtoft accuses Balliol, 'Li fol ray de Escoce', of seeking the pope's sanction to reign over Scotland in his own right. Balliol suggests that (like Arthur in Britain) he 'Dayt de ly [Scotland] tenyr par antiquité' and claims that Edward (like Julius Caesar) 'par poer et poesté / Li fist fere homage encountre volunté' (220:19; 222:3, 4–5; 626, 634–6). Pope Celestine concurs and Balliol throws off English overlordship. It is at this point that the first of the tail-rhymed 'political songs' appears, continuing seamlessly in both rhyme and syntax from the preceding part of the *laisse* (given here as the first two lines):

> Pur le grant honur ke Eduuard le sené
> Fist à Jon Bayllof, tel est la bounté
>   Dount li rays Eduuard
>   Du ray Jon musard

> Est rewerdoné.
> De Escoce soyt cum pot;
> Parfurnyr nus estot
>   La geste avaunt parlé.

(222:14–21; 645–52)

[For the great honour with Edward the wise did to John Balliol, such is the good-
ness with which King Edward is rewarded by King John the fool. Of Scotland,
be it as it may; we must continue the *geste* spoken of before.]

To break into tail-rhyme trimeters at this point after several thousand
alexandrine lines is obviously a major departure. The presentation of
Balliol's homage in prose 350 lines earlier perhaps could be regarded as an
indication of the poet's willingness to make significant formal shifts. But
the homage was clearly marked as 'Forma homagii Johannis Baliolensis'
(19:220; 257); there is by contrast no explanation for the shift out of the
laisse offered by the tail-rhyme, nor any sense of what, if anything, is being
quoted. This brief formal interruption writes itself off as unimportant by
ending with a call for a resumption of the 'geste avaunt parlé'. There is little to suggest that this is anything other than the same discursive register
of the *laisse* – the same narrative voice – in which the poet himself alters
his own meter with a formally variant wake-up to the reader or hearer.
Like the prose record of Balliol's homage, the poem functions as a pause
which highlights something Langtoft regards as essential knowledge: the
difference between the English Edward's noble conduct, and the under-
handed reward for that conduct he receives from the treacherous John
Balliol.

Despite the rapid resumption of the alexandrine *laisse*, this poem turns
out to be more than simply a momentary formal variation. Retrospectively,
it can be seen to function as the introduction to seven further poems,
all of them in tail-rhyme, but of varying lengths and linguistic regis-
ters. With the exception of a poem about the execution of Wallace, these
poems are all about the Berwick–Dunbar campaign of 1296. Hence the
short Poem 1 lacks any introductory comment because it is itself the formally variant introduction to a section of his narrative which the poet
wishes to highlight.

The second tail-rhyme poem appears 150 lines later, and institutes a
more dramatic formal break. It follows on a section in which Langtoft
details Edward's response to Balliol's insurrection: he holds a muster at
Newcastle in March and advances on Berwick, which he conquers 'par
espé' and causes to be encircled by a 'fosse large e lee' (234:19–20; 806–
7).[16] At this point the second tail-rhyme poem appears, specifically because

Edward's fortifications are said to be built, 'En reprovaunt le Escot, ke ad
de ly chaunté / Et par mokerye en Englays rymeyé' ['In reproof of the
Scot, who had sung about him, and by way of mockery, made rhymes in
English'] (234:21–2; 808–9):

> Pykit him,
> An diket hym,
>   On scoren sayd he;
> He dikes, he pikes,
> On lenche als hym likes,
>   Hu best may be.
> Skaterd be the Scottes,
> Hoderd in thar hottes,
>   Never thay ne the.*   *may they never prosper*
> Ryth if I rede,
> Thai tumbed in Twede,
>   Thet woned by the se.
>
>   (234:25–8, 236:1–14; 810–21)[17]

Although there is no direct announcement of the metrical variation here,
there *is* on this occasion a narrative justification for the change of meter
and with it, the introduction for the first time of the English language.
The Scots had mocked Edward in verse; the implication is that the English
words that follow are those which the Scots rhymed, in that language, 'par
mokerye'. 'Pykit him, / An diket hym' – let him pike and ditch as he likes.
We are invited to see this as a fragment of *Scottish* mockery.[18] In the third
line of the poem, the pronoun is plural and must refer to the Scots; this
is clearer in manuscripts other than the one used by Wright, which give
the verb in the plural form 'saiden'.[19] While the pronoun clearly attributes
the words to the Scots, however, it just as clearly shows that the poem is
not what Langtoft appears to have implied it would be: the *actual* rhyme
'en Englays' composed by the Scots. As the poem unfolds, it becomes
obvious that the voice can only be regarded as an *English* one, saying that
now Edward ditches and pikes, 'On lenche als hym likes'. Edward's building works might have been momentarily mocked but this activity is now
turned triumphantly in Edward's favour, as the second half of the poem,
with its abuse of the hapless, defeated Scots, goes on to make clear.

   While the first poem was a metrical departure it remained within the
same register as the narrative voice of Langtoft's poem. Syntactically,
Poem 1 was not a break but a continuation, in a different meter, of the
poet's sentence. But Poem 2 is dialogic: the first voice is the represented
point of view or sentiments from the Scottish side; the second is the
reasserted voice of the anti-Scottish poet, appropriating these possible or

imagined Scottish sentiments to reaffirm Edward's superiority, but doing so in a language other than that of the poet's official, narrative discourse. Perhaps underlining this, there does appear to be a formal shift in the middle of the poem, as the first stanza emphasises internal rhyme, the second alliteration.[20]

The narrative then continues with an account of raiding in the north of England by Scots, described as 'xl. mil felouns', under the earls of Mar, Ross, and Menteith (236:18; 825).[21] Having carried out destruction the Scottish earls take refuge in the castle of Dunbar north of Berwick (whose absent lord, Patrick, was actually a liegeman of Edward I). An English army then invests the castle and the besieged Scots send a knight named Sir Richard Siward to treat with them. Siward promises that the castle will be given up in three days once a messenger is sent to Balliol. But Siward acts treacherously; this messenger is instructed to tell Balliol to come and fight. His words to the king of Scots are given as direct speech: 'Sir rays, vos barouns demorent en dur esplayt; / En le chastel de Dumbar, en chauns les chascait' ['Sir king, your barons remain in a parlous situation in the castle of Dunbar, driven from the field'] (242: 4–5; 884–5). The speech to Balliol continues, occupying in all twenty-one lines of the *laisse*, rhyming on *-ait*. Then there is an unannounced shift into Poem 3:

> De nos enemys,
>   Kant serount pris,
>   Mercy nul en ait. (244:3–5; 905–7)

[On our enemies – when they shall be taken – let no one have mercy.]

These words clearly suggest that the messenger is still speaking and the third line's final 'ait' firmly integrates the poem with the preceding *laisse*. No explanation is given for the shift into tail-rhyme but the effect is perhaps roughly comparable to what happens in an Icelandic saga when a character's direct speech in prose gives way to an elaborate verse which we understand to have been improvised by him. The very end of the messenger's speech is in this regard peculiar, however. Two six-line stanzas of tail-rhyme in Anglo-Norman give way to a concluding stanza in English:

> On grene
> That kynered kene
>   Gadered als gayt;
> I wene
> On summe it es sene,
>   Whare the byt bayt.
>   (244: 15–20; 917–22; *NIMEV* 2686)

[On the green, that sharp race are gathered like goats; I believe that on certain of them it will be seen, where the bit punishes.]

Like all the tail-rhymes, this one concludes the *laisse* so that visually at least – and perhaps aurally also – the English rhyme-words *gayt* and *bayt* appear to continue the Anglo-Norman rhyme in *-ait* of both *laisse* and tail-rhyme.[22] The English lines seem, then, intended to constitute part of the messenger's speech, though Thiolier, presumably on the basis of the shift to English, places a closing quotation mark at the end of the Anglo-Norman, which would imply that the English lines are narratorial comment.[23]

Battle is joined, the Scots are routed, the castle surrendered. This section of the narrative is marked by two further short, abusive English verses (Poems 4 and 5):

> The fote folk
> Put the Scottes in the polk,
>   And nackened thair nages.* *bared their buttocks*
> Bi waye
> Herd i never saye,
>   Of prester pages,* *lads more ready*
> To pyke
> The robes of the rike,
>   That in the felde felle.
> Thay token ay tulke;
> The roghe raggy sculke
>   Rug ham in helle.
>
> (248:5–16; 956–67; *NIMEV* 3352)[24]

> For Scottes
> Telle i for sottes,
>   And wrecches unwar;
> Unsele
> Dintes to dele
>   Tham drohu to Dumbar.
>
> (252:5–10; 999–1004; *NIMEV* 841)

After these elliptical verses the narrative continues with a description of the aftermath of the successful English campaign. The chronicler announces that Edward now holds Scotland 'enterement, / Cum Albanak [a legendary king] le avayt al comencement' (254:14–15; 1034–5). This concluding section is punctuated by three further poems, 6, 7, and 8, longer works mostly in Anglo-Norman.[25] The concluding stanzas of 7, however, are in English, and celebrate the removal of the Stone of Scone to London. With that – the poet concludes – just as Merlin prophesied the island is united: 'Ore sunt les insulanes trestuz assemblez, / Et Albanye rejoynte à les regaltez / Des quels li rays Eduuard est seygnur clamez' ['Now are the inhabitants of Britain all joined together, and Albany reunited to the royal domains of which Edward is proclaimed lord'] (264:22–4; 1167–9). There remains only France to be subdued. This conclusion occasions another verse, 8, entirely in Anglo-Norman, celebrating the defeat of Edward's hapless *enemys* and confirming Merlin's prophecy that 'Trays regiouns' should be gained by Edward (266:31; 1202).

The narrative then shifts to the negotiations which take place before Edward is able to take ship for Flanders to do war for Aquitaine (a land which, we learn, is held by the English king because Arthur gave it to Bedivere). The unification of Britain was necessary, but it was a diversion, because Britain should have been unified in the first place. As Fergus Wilde notes, Langtoft presents the Scottish wars 'not as an act of conquest, but as an act of re-unification, restoring an ancient English hegemony'.[26] This culminating point of the 1296 narrative helps to explain why – if, as seems to be the case, Langtoft is principally interested in the reign of Edward I – he bothered with the legendary Brut material at all. Edward is to be measured against the standards created by legend. In the writing of the history of the recent past, events are seen as the fulfilment of truths set out in legendary, Brut history.

WHOSE VOICE?

To this point, I have made the simple proposition that one obvious purpose of Langtoft's chronicle is an encomium to Edward I, his actions and policies. This praise is manifested in the poem's principal and official discourse, the Anglo-Norman alexandrine *laisse* appropriate to *gestes*, tales of heroic deed. But it is also manifested at other discursive levels – hence for example the reproduced homage in prose, made by Balliol to Edward. And it is represented in the tail-rhyme stanzas which, as we have seen, at times seem to be no more than an extension of the authorial voice, but at other times seem to introduce competing voices.[27]

There is a long tradition of identifying these voices as those of ordinary people. Editing the verses for the first time in 1839, Thomas Wright considered them as 'apparently taken from songs of the time'. He later reaffirmed the suggestion in his Rolls Series edition. Noting that in introducing the tail-rhymes Langtoft 'changes his own long lines into the same form of verse' (i.e., the rhymes in *laisse* and lyric), Wright stated: '[W]e might be led to suspect that they are all part of his own composition, and

not old songs taken from popular recitation. But the words with which
some of them are introduced leave little doubt as to their real character.'[28]
As evidence, Wright cited Poem 2 and the reference to rhymes 'en Englays'
which precedes it, and some lines preceding Poem 5, which he thought
suggested that a tradition of verbal mockery existed after the Scottish
defeat at Dunbar:

> En tel plait de karole lur jeu est terminez;
> [Parmi Engletere en totes les cuntrez,]
> De lur surquiderye à touz jours ert parlez,
> Taunt cum le secle dure lur fet les ad mokez. (252:1–4; 995–8)[29]

[In such a style of dance their game is ended; in all the regions throughout
England there will forever be talk of their presumption; their deed has turned
them to mockery as long as the world shall last.]

Wright's assumption is that the verse immediately following is an example of the kind of mockery to which the Scots in their 'surquiderye' have
exposed themselves, in support of his conclusion that the 'real character' of
the Langtoft poems is that of 'old songs taken from popular recitation'.

Wright was influential in establishing the idea of the popular political
'song'.[30] In 1952, R. M. Wilson still regarded the Langtoft poems as popular songs, though he believed a later poet might have embellished them,
giving to some a more 'literary tinge'. Langtoft was probably quoting from
this poet, Wilson thought, though it was possible he composed some of
the poems himself; they were origin English and Langtoft translated
them into Anglo-Norman, occasionally seeming to tire of the translation
and leaving sections of them in English.[31] M. Dominica Legge, across two
books, remained convinced that Langtoft had preserved English songs.[32]
Similarly taking them to be popular productions, Lionel Stones wrote in
1981 of the 'barrack-room flavour' of poems which 'show how Englishmen
in 1296 could think, talk, and sing about Berwick and Dunbar as their
descendants were to do, centuries later, about Jubbulpore, Ypres, and
Armentières'.[33] Only slightly more sceptically, R. H. Robbins thought
it 'more probable that Langtoft's scraps are the work of a professional
minstrel seeking to improve the morale of the English army'.[34] In 1989,
Jean Claude Thiolier referred to the poems as 'chansons politiques et sat-
iriques ... dont l'origine ne peut être qu'orale et populaire au sens large du
terme'.[35]

These hypotheses, more or less in favour of popular origin for the
poems, were followed by a critical backlash in which the presence of
the voice of the medieval common-man was denied. 'Langtoft wrote

these taunts in tail-rhyme stanzas in order to distinguish them from the dignified alexandrines of the body of the chronicle', Thorlac Turville-Petre argues; 'and he composed some lines in English in order to lend the songs an air of authenticity.'[36] Thea Summerfield implicitly agrees with Turville-Petre's claim that Langtoft was the author rather than collector of poems which she sees as thematically highly integrated with Langtoft's larger text. Like Wright but to the opposite purpose, Summerfield notes the usual integration of the *laisse* rhymes with those of the Anglo-Norman (and some of the Middle English) tail-rhymes which, as it is hardly likely to be coincidence, she takes to be further evidence that Langtoft himself composed the lyrics.[37]

From Wright to Thiolier, then, the verses were viewed as what we might think of as *poèmes trouvés*, works which pre-existed Langtoft's chronicle and which somehow came into his hands. More recently, they have been seen only as *imitative* of such poetry, but in fact composed by Langtoft himself: overall a shift away from a romantic nineteenth-century detection of the popular voice (a view surviving into the 1980s), to a more sceptical line which takes them to be no more than fabrications of that voice.

Reviewing these positions, it can certainly be seen that what Wright took to be evidence of the poems' prior existence is not as straightforward as he suggested. Langtoft nowhere unequivocally states that he took the poems from another source. He does make it *seem* that Poem 2 will record actual Scottish abuse of Edward I, composed 'en Englays' and 'Par mokerye'. But the poem as it stands is clearly *not* that abuse. Similarly, while Poem 5 is in Wright's view an example of the mockery to which, the poet has just said, the Scots will be subject 'Taunt cum le secle dure', it can just as easily be taken as Langtoft's own comment on the Scots' 'surquiderye', varied linguistically and metrically for emphasis. Wright implies that Langtoft acted rather like a nineteenth-century antiquarian, collecting scraps of poetry where he found them. Langtoft himself, however, by no means makes this clear.

Wright drew his conclusions, then, on the basis of evidence that is not there. But the sceptical position espoused by Turville-Petre and Summerfield resorts to a similar logic, basing itself more on the absence of indications to the contrary than on any positive evidence. It is not necessary to return to the romantic position in order to see that the sceptical position is neither very nuanced nor makes strong arguments *for* Langtoft's composition (as opposed to arguments *against* popular composition). Summerfield does point to one apparently telling piece of evidence in the fact that the rhymes of the poems tend to be integrated into the rhyme scheme of the *laisses* that precede them. This is clearly no accident and, as the poems conclude a *laisse* in each case, a high degree of formal integration is indicated. Hence, Summerfield concludes, it is likely that Langtoft wrote the tail-rhymes to go with the *laisses*.

In fact this evidence can just as easily be read to the opposite purpose – exactly as Wright did. If Langtoft came across a pre-existing poem, then all he needed to do to integrate it was to create a *laisse* to precede it, anticipating the tail-rhyme. It is arguably simpler, in fact, to compose a *laisse* on the basis of a tail-rhyme (requiring just a single rhyme) than to do the reverse (integrating a predetermined rhyme into a complicated stanza).

In justifiably clearing away romantic assumptions, Turville-Petre and Summerfield do not find any evidence to suggest that Langtoft did *not* gather these poems, or more likely parts of them or even simply the inspiration for them, from an outside source. And they do not explain why Langtoft used the poems in the narrative of 1296 and in describing the execution of Wallace, but nowhere else: just as if he had a limited archive of tail-rhyme verses with which to work. The vehemence with which Turville-Petre and Summerfield assert Langtoft's authorship echoes the vehemence with which, earlier, the popular voice was detected in these poems. The possible outside source for them was no doubt unlikely to have been ordinary members of Edward's armies – we can safely dispose of Stones's 'soldiers' songs'. But it does not stretch belief to see, behind the poems, more people like Langtoft himself: rabidly patriotic clerks, middle-ranking at best, whose instincts were awakened by the Great Cause and the strife with Scotland that followed. Nor is it impossible that the clerks who were associated with any army did indeed collect fragments of abuse that circulated during a campaign. But we do not even have to assume eyewitness-versifiers. This kind of triumphalist composition could have gone on safely south of the Tweed, among the bureaucrats back in York and Westminster who, along with balancing the accounts of the money spent, made up scraps of verse which were then passed around.

One final piece of evidence in this regard is that although 'Langtoft's verses' are spoken of as if they are an unvarying feature of the chronicle, in fact hardly any two manuscripts of the chronicle are alike: few of the manuscripts contain all of the poems and more than half contain *none* (see the appendix, table 2). The manuscripts that do have the poems always have Poems 2 and 5 (except the generally anomalous Cambridge, University Library MS G.I.1, which lacks Poem 5). The extra poem on Wallace's execution, 9, is found in five manuscripts. The relation between the manuscripts and their chronology poses extremely difficult questions which have never been unravelled with any confidence.[38] The only pattern which is supported by the state of the manuscripts is one of a cumulative but variable process of accretion and composition in which, certainly, some invention of 'popular' poems might have occurred, but which also could have resulted from the addition by later continuators of already existing compositions they knew about. Poem 7 in CUL G.I.1, for example, contains an extra stanza; that manuscript also adds Poem 8a, not attested elsewhere. All of this suggests an *ad hoc* process rather than one guided by an authorial hand, something more akin to what Paul Zumthor calls the 'mobilité essentielle du texte médiéval'.[39]

We have, then, inescapably polyvocal texts in the verses found in the Langtoft chronicle. In the first chapter, I pointed to the way in which clerkly writings about England resulted in Latinate constructions of *Anglia* and a non-native heroic 'Englishman'. As if conscious of the linguistic contradictions the English situation at the end of the thirteenth century raised, Langtoft writes of his own hero, Edward I, in his language, Anglo-Norman. At the same time, he has seized hold of some English fragments which help locate his narrative firmly on the English side of a border which, in the 1290s, has suddenly begun to matter as it had not done before: at the time of the outbreak of war, '[t]he border did not divide societies of a different language and character: it was, rather, an artificial political divide through a region where there were strong links across the river Tweed.[40] It is of course a basic strategy to blacken the name of an enemy. But something more important was going on in the case of Balliol and the literature about him, in ways on which I will expand.

JOHN BALLIOL'S SINISTER INTENTIONS

At the time he was elected king of Scots as a result of the Great Cause in 1291, John Balliol was scarcely distinguishable from other magnates of the English court. The family's name came from its estates in Bailleul-en-Vimeu in Picardy and its main seat in Britain was Barnard Castle in Durham. John Balliol's father – also John – was a typical Anglo-Norman magnate; he was probably named for the English King John and went on to become a trusted counsellor of Henry III. It was only his marriage to Devorguilla, daughter of the lord of Galloway, that brought Scottish interests and considerable wealth through her large inheritance. John and Devorguilla's son, the future king of Scots, was born, quite possibly in Picardy, *c.*1248–50. He held the family estates in Durham and Picardy, and married the daughter of Earl Warenne of Surrey. When the county of Ponthieu came to Edward I in 1279 (as a result of Queen Eleanor's inheritance), Balliol, whose Picard lands were in Ponthieu, had to do homage for them to Edward. During the 1280s, Balliol was frequently resident in Picardy and although he inherited his father's Scottish interests, he seems to have had little involvement in Scottish affairs before the death of Alexander III.[41]

John Balliol was as English, then, as other English magnates, which is to say essentially hybrid, with landed interests in France, England, and Scotland, feudal allegiance to the king in England and, no doubt, French as his mother tongue. It is telling that this figure, with his relatively slight involvement in Scottish politics, should be regarded by many Scottish magnates as a credible candidate for the throne of Scotland. The reason is that they, like Balliol, were hybrid figures themselves, speaking French and perhaps English, some of them holding land on the English side of the border, most of them connected by marriage or descent to the Anglo-Norman nobility.[42] The Great Cause concerned the best claim through descent, and was certainly not a search for the candidate with the best Scottish pedigree.

Things changed when Edward I politicised the border between England and Scotland, creating a situation in which, eventually, magnates would have to choose which side of it mattered more to them (much as Anglo-Norman magnates had had to choose between France and England in the mid-thirteenth century). After decades of peace between Scotland and England, Edward had suddenly made of the king of Scots a more subservient figure than his predecessors. Alexander III had done homage to Edward, of course, for his lands in England; doing homage for Scotland itself was a very different matter. This was the position in which Edward placed John Balliol.

By becoming king north of the border the hybrid Anglo-Norman noble Balliol was transformed into a version of the 'mimic man' described by Homi Bhabha. Mimicry is a form of 'colonial imitation' in which the colonised Other takes on the guise of, and imitates, the coloniser – just as, in British India, the Indian administrators were to be anglicised by their passage through an English-style schooling. What is thereby produced is a new elite, trained by the colonial power in language and culture to mimic their values. But the mimic man, Bhabha continues, 'is the effect of a *flawed* colonial mimesis, in which to be Anglicized is *emphatically* not to be English'. Mimicry is always ambivalent; it produces a slippage because the colonised imitator is 'almost the same, *but not quite*'. It is hence capable of producing menace: 'The ambivalence of colonial authority repeatedly turns from *mimicry* – a difference that is almost nothing but not quite – to *menace* – a difference that is almost total but not quite.'[43] Balliol, as king of Scots, became 'almost the same, *but not quite*'; giving his homage to Edward for the realm of Scotland, he immediately became the colonised Other. In that, his potential menace lay. His role was to be Edward's man in Scotland; the moment he resisted that role, he lost his claims on Englishness. As Robert Young puts it, elaborating on Bhabha's ideas, 'Mimicry at once enables power and produces the loss of agency. If control slips away from the colonizer, the requirement of mimicry means that the colonized, while complicit in the process, remains the unwitting and unconscious agent of menace – with a resulting paranoia on the part of the colonizer as he tries to guess the native's sinister intentions.'[44]

The fact that Balliol was acceptable as a candidate in Scotland suggests that what was most important for the magnate classes on either side of the border was their sense of *caste*, underpinned by the bonds of inter-marriage, land exchange, and feudal homage. What begins to emerge in writings of the time, by contrast, is a sense of *nation*. This allows a disentangling of the complexities of relations among a caste for a view simplified as 'us and them'. The Latin poem edited by Wright as 'Song on the Scottish Wars' consistently, and predictably, depicts the Scots as a barbarous race whose refusal to bow to their English overlords is taken as an insult. The poet relates how Balliol gave his homage to Edward but afterwards, 'he declined *frango, frangis, fregi*' – that is, the verb 'to break', in reference to the homage.[45] The Scots become in this poem the 'Tunicatus populus multus et immanis' ['The kilted people, numerous and monstrous'] (81); the 'Scotici versuti' ['cunning Scots'] (109); the 'barbara bruta gens et stulta' ['barbarous, brutal and foolish race'] (153). English defeat is always attributed to treachery (e.g., 139, 144–5). 'Angli velut angeli semper sunt victores', the poet concludes, using a familiar play on words: the English like angels are always conquerors. The Scots and Welsh, he continues, are inferior. The 'Scotici polluti' attack England, so Edward makes them slaves (262–8). Similarly, Wright edited a verse he entitled 'On the Deposition of Balliol', from London, British Library, Cotton MS Julius A.v (a manuscript also containing Langtoft's chronicle), a poem concerned with the boundedness of the Scottish nation: just as Troy was barren of maidens after war, the poet says, so will Scotland be of Scots ('Percussis bellis, sterilis fit Troja puellis; / Finitis motis, sic fiet Scotia Scotis.')[46] The clerkly author of this poem is concerned to invent a Scottish nation, only in order to imagine its destruction.

Like these Latin poems of the late thirteenth or early fourteenth century, one of the functions of Langtoft's chronicle is to take the unremarkable and familiar, if hybrid, figure of John Balliol and develop his menace by turning him into a mimic man. This runs through the main register of the chronicle itself, from the moment Langtoft dubs Balliol 'Li fol ray de Escoce'. The point is that Balliol must be denied legitimacy – even sanity – because in essentials he was *indistinguishable* from any other 'English' magnate. He must be made different. That same situation of fluid hybridity could be exploited in clerkly discourse of the 1260s in order to abuse the English Lord Edward at the same time as lauding Montfort, while decrying the promotion of foreigners. Now, it is turned to different account: being foreign is beginning to matter in a new way.

This function of the main discursive register of the chronicle is replicated in the lesser discourse of the political verses. The first of the poems, the apparently negligible Poem 1, introduces the theme, as we have already seen:

> Pur le grant honur ke Eduuard le sené
> Fist à Jon Bayllof, tel est la bounté
> > Dount li rays Eduuard
> > Du ray Jon musard
> > > Est rewerdoné.
> > De Escoce soyt cum pot;
> > Parfurnyr nus estot
> > > La geste avaunt parlé.

'Musard' is a term amplifying the accusation of *folie* which has just been made; notably, it rhymes with 'Edward', so that the English king's name is counterposed to a reductive nickname (meaning fool, rogue, or rascal) for his opposite number. Even in the moment that this casual abuse is made, the poet retreats from the trimetrical abusive formulae as if there was to be only a restricted break-out from the main register; there will now be a return to that register and the 'geste avaunt parlé'. When this form of verse returns, in Poem 2, it has fresh, murderous abuse for the Scots as a group, a proto-nation:

> > Skaterd be the Scottes,
> > Hoderd in thar hottes,
> > > Never thay ne the.
> > Ryth if I rede,
> > Thai tumbed in Twede,
> > > Thet woned by the se.

The Tweed has become symbolically important here; those waters in which the scattered Scots perish are the marker of their own difference, the border which Edward is seeking so thoroughly to secure.

Poem 3 then does something different, by presenting the speech of the perfidious Scottish messenger. Of course the 'treachery' consists in proposing to do to the English *exactly* what the English want to do to the Scots:

> Tut Engleterre
> Par ceste guere
>   Voyliez ke perdu sayt …
> (244:9–11; 912–13)

[By this war, resolve that all England shall be ruined …]

As we have seen above, this poem concludes with six lines of English:

> On grene
> That kynered kene
>   Gadered als gayt;
> I wene
> On summe it es sene,
>   Whare the byt bayt.
> (244:15–20; 917–22)

As has been noted, Wright attributed these words to the Scottish messenger but Thiolier regarded them as a resumption of the English voice. It is impossible to say which is correct; even the language shift to English does nothing to resolve whether these ought to be Scottish or English words, because the words are entirely appropriate to either side.

The sixth poem returns to French and Balliol, giving him a more famous epithet in the six lines of English which complete the poem:

> Pur veir quant Jon de Balliol
> Lessa sun liver à l'escol,
>   Desceu fu tremalement.
>   For boule bred in his bok,
> Wen he tint that he tok
>   Wiht the kingedome.
> For he haves overhipped,
> His tipet is tipped,
>   His tabard is tom.
> (258:7–15; 1084–9)

[For truth, when John de Balliol left his book at the school, he was very ill deceived; for the falsehood bred in his book, he lost what he took with the kingdom (?). For he has over-reached, his tippet is knocked askew, his tunic is empty.][47]

The nickname 'Toom Tabard' refers to the stripping from Balliol of his insignia of kingship, which was part of the humiliation forced on Scotland at the same time as the regalia were removed to Westminster. In one sense the removal of the insignia from Balliol ought also to have been the removal of the mark of his Otherness. What was left in the empty tunic was an English magnate. In fact of course there was no way back for Balliol – he is simply the reduced mimic man. Continuing to fulfil the paradigm I have suggested for him here, Balliol did not lose his capacity for menace at this point. Taken to England and eventually exiled from there, Balliol ultimately made his way back home to Picardy, creating the genuine fear in England by the end of the thirteenth century that his sinister intention was to regain his Scottish throne.

INVENTING HISTORY

In this closing section, I want to situate the poems in the larger chronicle, giving a sense of the purpose of that chronicle.

The author of the chronicle, Pierre de Langtoft, identifies himself quite clearly in it. We know him to have been a canon of the Augustinian priory at Bridlington. In turn, in manuscript *A* Langtoft states that a certain Scaffeld asked him to write the chronicle. The work frequently mentions in a favourable light Antony Bek, bishop of Durham and one of Edward I's closest counsellors until they fell out in the late 1290s. As a result Bek is usually taken as the ultimate patron, Langtoft the man charged with the duty of producing the work, and Scaffeld as intermediary.[48]

Although there is broad agreement on Bek's role, recent accounts of the chronicle offer quite different views of its construction. Legge's view is that Langtoft had revised over the years, becoming more disillusioned so that a 'bitterer and bitterer tone' is evident in manuscripts which carry the chronicle narrative to the end of Edward I's reign. Legge thinks its account of the prospects for Edward II's reign was equivocal.[49] Thiolier has also argued for a lengthy period of composition but in a very different fashion from Legge. His examination of the widely varying manuscripts leads him to hypothesise a first phase of writing by Langtoft, up to 1272. There was then a long break, before Langtoft resumed in 1294, eventually covering the reign of Edward I from 1272 to 1296. He then stopped again, finally taking up the narrative once more after the the death of Wallace in 1305. Thiolier sees Langtoft as close to Bek, and his writing as ceasing (the second time) during the period of Bek's distance from the king, with a resumption once Bek returned to favour. Additionally, there is in some manuscripts the work of an editor, someone close to the king but less close to Bek, who modifies Langtoft's work. This editor is a more francophile writer, better disposed to Llywelyn ap Gruffudd and above all concerned to decry the assassination of John Comyn.[50] Thiolier names the first work, of which he sees Langtoft as the principal author, 'rédaction I'. The more widely disseminated form of the chronicle, appearing in fourteen manuscripts, is 'rédaction II'. This was the version translated by Mannyng, but the one which owed least to Langtoft.

Soon after, however, Thea Summerfield dismissed this theory altogether. The principal manuscripts which in Thiolier's view represent 'rédaction I', 'E' and 'F', do not have the similarities that they ought to have. 'I see no reason whatsoever for regarding these two partial manuscripts as closer to Langtoft's original text', Summerfield writes, 'or superior to the large group of manuscripts which offer a version of the text which shows very few textual variations'. Neither does she see any substantiation for the theory of two long breaks in the writing of the chronicle. As she points out, in no manuscript does the chronicle end in 1272, the end-point of Thiolier's notional first phase of writing.[51] Summerfield's own view of the chronicle's writing is radically different from Thiolier's and Legge's. For her, the chronicle's purpose was very precise. She argues that in 1305 or early 1306, John de Sheffield ('Scaffeld'), the new sheriff of Northumberland, acting for Bek, asked Langtoft to compose the chronicle. Its addressees were to be Bek himself, Edward I (from whom he was at the time still estranged) and the king's heir Edward of Caernarfon. Its purpose was to stress the importance of reconciliation between king and bishop, so that the war against the Scots could continue successfully. Summerfield believes, additionally, that the part of the chronicle containing the political 'songs' could have been performed before Bek and the two Edwards, the most likely occasion being the knighting of young Edward in 1306, an event described in one of the closing passages of the chronicle itself.[52]

There are a number of problems, however, with this view of Langtoft's chronicle as having a narrowly defined purpose. First, it does not deal with the fact that the chronicle exists in twenty manuscripts which exhibit considerable textual variation. The wide dissemination this implies does not sit very well with the notion of a text written for a single purpose and presentation to a tight circle of the highest in the land. (In addition, as Wilde points out, the chronicle lacks a 'dedication of the sort almost invariably found in works presented to noble patrons'.)[53] Secondly, Summerfield's very late date for the chronicle (one necessary for her argument about the purpose of the chronicle, the reconciliation of Bek with Edward) means that she posits a very short period for its composition: a matter of a few months in c.1305–7 (with notional performance of one section of it at Pentecost 1306 and completion shortly after Edward I's death).[54] This presupposes very rapid composition of a work of upwards of 8,000 lines.[55] It also does not explain why in three manuscripts the narrative ends in 1296 – not impossible, of course, for a work completed in 1307, but not especially plausible, either.[56] There is also the question of *why* Bek should have been so concerned about reconciliation with Edward I in 1306. Edward was by then old and, as those close to him would have known, sick. It must have been clear by then to a political operator like Bek that it was Edward of Caernarfon who needed to be cultivated, not his father. In summary, the commissioning of a long chronicle with a view to rapid completion to catch the attention of a dying king is implausible, and certainly does not explain that chronicle's subsequent wide dissemination.[57]

In offering an alternative explanation, I want first to go back to the Great Cause in 1291, and Edward's well-known call to the monasteries for a record search, looking for justification of his claim to overlordship. The monastic houses had little time to work in and the recorded material returned in 1291 does not seem to have been very helpful. As Stones and Simpson write, 'when Edward asked the monasteries for assistance, they responded dutifully, but with no very great imagination'.[58] Edward, as we have seen, successfully went ahead with his claim to overlordship, establishing Balliol as a client king, subjecting Scotland in a way that later led to the conflict of 1296.

In 1291, although some of the houses did present legendary history in their returns, Edward seems not to have been particularly interested in Brut-history. No use was made of it; as Stones and Simpson note, his clerks 'may have been tempted to go further back than 901, using the legendary materials in Geoffrey of Monmouth which appeared in some of the monastic returns, [but] they did not do so'.[59] A decade later, however, Edward ordered a second search and this time he *was* prepared to introduce legendary material. Around the same time the Brut legend was exploited in a letter to the pope compiled for Edward, and included by the clerk Andrew de Tange in his Great Roll. Wilde plausibly explains the new appeal of the legend as a response to the pressure brought to bear on Edward by Pope Boniface VIII's bull, *Scimus fili*. Faced with the papacy, 'an institution whose very power was founded upon its historical primacy and ancient authority', Edward needed 'a case which could claim the oldest possible precedent in the British isles ...: the crown suddenly stood in need of Brutus the Trojan'.[60]

One of the houses that responded to Edward's first call in 1291 was the priory at Bridlington.[61] This is not surprising: the north-eastern parts of England stood to lose most if the border with Scotland was not protected and perhaps also the dominance in the wider area of Bek – then still Edward's loyal adviser – was a factor in Bridlington's ready compliance. In 1296, as a result of the earlier events, tensions flared into war between England and Scotland. At some point soon after this conflict, Pierre de Langtoft in the priory of Bridlington began his chronicle, a version of Brut-history with a disproportionate focus on the reign of Edward I. He continued his narrative up until 1296, perhaps moved to do so by what must have seemed at the time a decisive English victory, and there he stopped.

Langtoft had learned the lesson well that the past – and particularly the Arthurian past – validates the present. He was fully aware of the record search in 1291, and includes as a detail in his chronicle that Edward, at Norham castle near the border with Scotland where the Great Cause was heard:

> fet venir de abbeye e priorye
> Tutes les cronicles de auncesserye.
> La gest examyne, trop ben certifie
> Ke sire Eduuard ad drait à la seygnurye.
>
> (190:6–9; 254–7)

[causes to be brought from abbey and priory all the chronicles of our forefathers. Examines the history, very clearly ascertains that Sir Edward has the right to the sovereignty.]

He immediately adds that this was Bek's idea. What then happened, if Thiolier's identification of some manuscripts as belonging to the late thirteenth century is correct, is that the chronicle began to circulate. At the same time, when it proved that 1296 was *not* the end of the story of Anglo-Scottish conflict, the chronicle was continued: perhaps by Langtoft himself, perhaps by others. Langtoft possibly also wrote around this time a translation into Anglo-Norman alexandrines of Edward I's letter, dated 17 May 1301, to Pope Boniface concerning Scotland's vassalage: 'Whether in the translation or in the authentic text, the spirit of this reply recalls Langtoft's chronicle itself, and the argument displayed is the one Edward I and Antony Bek expected from the monasteries when they consulted them about the succession of Scotland in 1291.'[62] If Langtoft were the author of the versified letter, it shows the same sense of the uses of poetry in furthering bureaucratic and diplomatic discourse. Legendary material was not of much interest in 1291 in this cause; just a few years later, it certainly was.

Hence there is a simpler explanation of the manuscript evidence than either Thiolier's or Summerfield's accounts. The genesis of the chronicle was in the original call for documentary support in 1291 – of which Langtoft was certainly aware by 1296 but possibly was involved in, in 1291. The continuing interest of events – particularly from a viewpoint in north-eastern England – was sufficient to cause the continuation of the chronicle. But how, in this view, to account for the attitudes to the king displayed in the chronicle? Did Langtoft become disillusioned as the years went by, as Legge suggested? Was his work a bid for Edward's attention by Bek, as Summerfield has it? Or are the different positions the work of different continuators, as in Thiolier's view?

There is clearly nothing so simple in the chronicle as praise for Edward as an ideal king and a general appeal to his ego. Both Langtoft and Edward were interested in consolidating the sense of a border and of the people beyond it as alien. But Langtoft's chronicle was not really a form of letter to the king. There *is* a sense in which Langtoft was giving to King Edward the sort of history he wanted. But in doing so Langtoft asks in return for the kind of king he, and the church to which he belonged, wanted. So for example, to his largely favourable portrait of Edward the Arthurian militarist, Langtoft adds such dramatic moments as Edward's speech to the Lincoln parliament of 1301. Seeking to raise a tax of a fifteenth, Edward instead faced a raft of demands in a bill put forward by a knight of the shire, beginning with a requirement 'for the observance of Magna Carta and the Forest Charter'. As Prestwich records the demands:

Statutes contrary to the Charters should be annulled, and the magnates ought to define the powers of justices appointed to maintain the Charters. The per-ambulation of the Forest should be completed, and its finding put into effect. Offences against the regulations in the *Articuli* of 1300, about prise, should be properly dealt with. Sheriffs ought to be charged with the income from their shires, the annual farm, as in the time of Henry III, and increments recently added should be cancelled.[63]

Langtoft depicts Edward (plausibly enough) as angered at these obstacles placed in the way of the tax. He has Edward say:

> 'La chartre de fraunchises et du puraler
> Defrount ma corune, si jeo les day graunter;
> Laquel ovoke moi vus devez supporter,
> K'el ne sait blemye par prise ne par prier.

Pur quai je vus graunt le drait examiner
Par xxvj. descrez, que voisent juger,
A vos peticiouns si purray encliner,
Et salver la corune en taunt desmembrer.
De altre part vus dye, jeo suy saunz dener,
Dunt ayde de ma tere me covent aver,
Si la gwere d'Escoz day recomencer.'

(330:14–24; 1947–57)

['The charter of liberties and of the perambulation will undo my crown, if I were to grant them, which you ought to join with me in supporting, that it be not damaged by taking by force or by legal entreaty. Because of which I grant you the right to examine, through twenty-six discreet men who will give judgement, on whether I can yield to your petitions and save the crown from such dismembering. In another matter, I say to you that I am without money, because of which I must have aid from my land, if I am to recommence the war with Scotland.']

Langtoft goes on to tell how the twenty-six 'descrez' make their inquiries and conclude that Edward must pay what he owes. 'Sir', they tell him, 'n'est paas maner / A rey ne à prince covenaunt tregeter' ['Sir, it is not the manner for a king or a prince to overturn his covenant'] (332:4–5; 1964–5). The king answers the twenty-six 'covertement … Cum cil ke n'ad talent ses genz du soen eser' ['covertly, as one who has no desire to ease his people with that which is his'] (332:13–14; 1973–4). They, in their turn, do not want to give him 'doun' or 'tayler' – gift or tax. The situation is so tense that 'De pees ou de la gwere le pople fu en wer' ['the people were in doubt between peace and war'] (332:19; 1979). Fortunately, God intervenes, and as a result of his grace everyone is agreed; the king confirms the charters, while the people consent to the fifteenth. A situation which was in actuality very tense is, in the chronicle, conveniently defused by godly intervention.

Such passages make it quite clear that the author is not writing *for* the king. In fact the knight of the shire who put forward the bill at Lincoln was eventually imprisoned by an angry monarch.[64] In those circumstances, repeating the events in verse with a marked sympathy for the position of the twenty-six 'descrez' was hardly calculated to be flattering to the king. The answer to the apparent conundrum of Langtoft's varying attitudes is that while he is keen to praise Edward, he wants to do so within the terms of a specific and limiting political discourse. In order to get what he wants at Lincoln, Edward must conform to the charters and the perambulation. This is familiar: it is the kind of political theory, aiming to circumscribe kingship, which was in evidence in *The*

Song of Lewes in the 1260s. In aligning himself with the bill presented at
Lincoln, Langtoft is in these passages far more like a follower of Simon de
Montfort than an uncomplicated admirer of the king.

If, as Summerfield argues, Bek was the patron behind the chronicle, it
would seem a strange and risky strategy on his part to show that God was
on the side of the charters. One alternative would be to argue that chronicler and patron were already looking ahead to the reign of Edward II and
were not too concerned about Edward I's reception of the work. But I
suggest that this chronicle was never meant to find its way into the hands
of a king, whether the first or the second Edward. Rather than a bid
for patronage, this was a work which sent out signals of the kind which
announce to others that the chronicler had some point of contact with
the great and powerful. It did so with considerable success; others wanted
to espouse, and wanted to be seen to espouse, Langtoft's position. The
chronicle was copied, recopied, adapted, continued and became, numerically at least, the most popular Anglo-Norman chronicle after that of
Wace. This fact, evident from the state of the manuscripts, suggests, first
that the work left the control of Langtoft at an early stage, and second
that other monastic houses wished to be able to demonstrate – perhaps
only for their own internal purposes – their identification with the position of pro-English, anti-Scottish sentiment and the praise for king and a
limited monarchy so neatly expressed by Langtoft's chronicle. Making a
copy of Langtoft's chronicle could have been a statement of solidarity for
a given monastic house, but as it is also firmly in support of the charters
it is more an advertisement of solidarity with fellow houses than of adher-
ence to the king. It is possible to advertise one's love for the king without
ever really believing that a direct link to the king will be established – just
as a man who puts a bumper sticker on his car in support of the president
does not imagine the president will see it (though his neighbours will).

It is a necessary corollary of this argument that Langtoft was not actively
responsible for the dissemination of his text. Both Summerfield's and
Thiolier's explanations are wedded to the notion of the chronicle as essentially the work of a single, named, sovereign author. In order to adhere to
this idea, they are each forced into improbabilities. Summerfield's argument requires a fast-working Langtoft, producing the essentials of his
8,000–line text very quickly, and ignores the manuscript evidence that
the first version of the text was produced soon after 1296 – about four
years before Bek's quarrel with Edward and hence nothing to do with it.
Thiolier's ingenious theory of a lengthy period of composition, by contrast, seems concerned to explain how such a varied set of manuscripts

can still be pinned to the authorship of a single man, while at the same time conceding that the bulk of the manuscripts, fourteen out of twenty, display a version which was *not* principally that of Langtoft.

What I see is more like the 'intrinsic variance' to which medieval writing, in the view of Bernard Cerquiglini, is subject and which in this case arose in a text which soon escaped its author's control.[65] Far from being new, this conclusion with its scepticism about authorial control of this particular text was anticipated by Thomas Wright in 1868, who wrote that it was impossible to reconcile the variants of the manuscripts of the chronicle. Wright found *E*, for example, 'not to be a copy of Pierre de Langtoft's text, but Pierre de Langtoft very much altered by another hand'. This improver of Langtoft's text, Wright thought, produced a work so different that it could only be edited as a separate text.[66] The evidence is, in short, that after initial composition in 1296, Langtoft's chronicle was treated not as the work of a sovereign author, but as a resource to be mined for various situations. As Wilde suggests, '"Langtoft" will be best thought of … as the name of a text rather than as an individual of whose responses we can speak with confidence'.[67]

The record search for the Great Cause must have been a salutary moment for many monastic houses, in which they realised that the historiography of which they were the principal custodians was actively valued by the king. That, finally, is what Langtoft's chronicle consists of: a speculative endeavour to produce *precisely* what Edward wanted – but did not get – from the monasteries in 1291. 'Langtoft's *Chronicle* is an alternative "appeal to history"', as Summerfield puts it, 'a vernacular text offering evidence on the same subject as the official records'.[68] I would go further than this; its total overview of British history from Brutus to Edward was designed to answer to the needs the king articulated as he contemplated overlordship of Scotland in 1291. The validating chronicle was not found, and so had to be invented. In turn, its presentation of Brut-history, which Edward had ignored in 1291, was so successful that the Brut-story then entered English strategy in 1300. But the chronicle was not composed *for* Edward. Instead, it was directed to those who sympathised with him and (perhaps more importantly) wished to be seen to sympathise with him. The ideological variation from manuscript to manuscript of Langtoft's chronicle is then easily explained if the authorship of the chronicle is regarded as multiple and variable. There is no *Chronicle* of Langtoft, only chronicles. It was not an attempt at forgery but rather a historiographical masquerade, and its uses lay not in asserting its own truth value before the king, but before other custodians of that historiography.

Within this larger context, the political songs were presented. It is not finally possible to say in what degree they retain popular origins and to what extent they are purely literary inventions. What is notable, however, is that in the chronicle's manuscripts, which I have characterised as marked by 'intrinsic variation', they *act* like songs – always mutating, losing and gaining words and lines, changing their emphases, never the same in any two manuscripts. They are supplements with no original, *poèmes trouvés* which Langtoft was not able to fix in his chronicle, never original, never new, simply the products of *mouvance*. Through their poetics of abuse, they perform a shift in perception, shoring up what had previously been a permeable border.

It is intriguing that Balliol, although captured by Edward, was eventually allowed to go free. Was this mimic man protected by the fact that he was a king – or because he was, at base, an English nobleman? He escaped the fate of Montfort, who had earlier defied Edward, a fate which Edward would ritualise in subsequent years for others who defied him and withdrew their homage from him. As the last of the poems in the Langtoft chronicle happily records, the head of William Wallace is in London, while his body, quartered, hangs in four towns. 'It falles in his eghe', the poet says with satisfaction, 'That hackes ovre heghe, / Wit at Walays' (364:10–12; 2372–4; *NIMEV* 313). Balliol, too, 'hacke[d] ovre heghe'. He over-reached. The tail-rhyme devoted to him noted that he had 'overhipped'. The justice that he receives focuses on his insignia and clothing: 'His tipet is tipped, / His tabard is torn.' But his body is left intact. Edward's practice would later shift from the insignia to the body of the man such devices denoted; the next chapter begins by looking more closely at the abjected bodies of those who were less fortunate than John Balliol.

CHAPTER 3

Regime Change

THE KING IS DEAD

According to Jean Froissart, Edward I's dying instruction to his son was
that his body should be boiled, the flesh buried and the bones preserved,
'and that every time the Scots should rebel against him, he would summon his people, and carry with him the bones of his father: for he believed
most firmly, that as long as his bones should be carried against the Scots,
those Scots would never be victorious'.[1] With hindsight provided by Ernst
Kantorowicz, Edward would seem to be guilty of confusing the durability
of the king's body mystical with the perishable body natural, or hubristi-
cally imagining that his own body natural could partake of the undying
character of the mystical body.[2] Froissart, with the hindsight of a few decades, told this probably apocryphal story to underline his broad themes of
good and bad rule. Edward II's twenty-year reign, already legendarily bad
when Froissart wrote, was the necessary launching point for one of the
chronicler's main tasks, the praise of the reign of his successor, Edward
III. Edward II's failure to carry out his father's wish, breaking his oath,
was in Froissart's scheme a neat aetiology for the many unfortunate things
that were to befall him.

As we saw in chapter 1, Edward I's succession was surprisingly smooth.
But transition from one reign to the next was often traumatic in late
medieval England, even when the departure of a given king was regarded
as desirable. Few chroniclers lamented the deposition of Edward II in
1327, but the fact of deposition itself created enormous anxiety. Edward's
removal from power was succeeded by a three-year hiatus in which those
who replaced him quickly came to be regarded as even worse than their
predecessor. Roger Mortimer's crackdown on suspected dissension and
the way in which he and Isabella effectively replicated the abuses of the
Despensers whom they had replaced made this a copybook example of
failed revolution. The problems attendant on deposition were of course still

81

troubling in 1399, when Richard II was replaced by Henry Bolingbroke, who then spent several years trying to shore up his own legitimacy.

Political theology made every provision for smooth succession, with its distinction between the monarch and the Crown, the man and the office. In practice – and hardly surprisingly – the man himself became the focus of intense scrutiny. The king's body natural should have been politically less important than his mystical presence. But the story about Edward I, whether true or not, focuses attention on the body natural and the powerful nostalgia created around it. At the same time, in a way already explored in chapter 1, the bodies of the king's rebellious adversaries often led lives shadowing that of the king himself. As we have seen, because of his potency as an opponent, it was necessary not just to *defeat* Simon de Montfort, but to annihilate him. Chroniclers were clear not only that Montfort's limbs were hacked off, but his genitals also, as if to reduce him to a gender-undifferentiated mere body, symbolically denied further generation. Robert of Gloucester gives the odd detail that Montfort's head was sent to the Mortimer stronghold at Wigmore, 'To dam Maud þe mortimer þat wel foule it ssende [destroyed]'. The implication that the head was a kind of trophy is bolstered by the recently discovered document on Montfort's death that specifies Maud's husband Roger Mortimer (an earlier one) as Montfort's killer.[3] Every aspect of the death of Montfort seems designed to erase all trace of the rebel.

And yet rebel bodies have a way of living on. Recent commentators on Kantorowicz have noted how the condemned man and the outlaw are subject, like the king's body, to a form of duplication, a continuance in a non-corporeal form. Michel Foucault proposed that at the other end of the spectrum from the king, 'one might imagine placing the body of the condemned man; he, too, has his legal status; he gives rise to his own ceremonial and he calls forth a whole theoretical discourse, not in order to ground the "surplus power" possessed by the person of the sovereign, but in order to code the "lack of power" with which those subjected to punishment are marked'. Similarly provoked by Kantorowicz, Giorgio Agamben notes an equivalence between the king and the figure of 'bare life' he refers to as *homo sacer*.[4] It was in the moment of his dismembering that the process of Montfort's elevation to unofficial sainthood began, when he was revealed in his true piety, through his hair shirt and his miraculously unbleeding limbs.

Clearly, then, in this instance the attempt to make the body of the rebel abject – literally to throw it away – carried risks for those in power. This chapter explores further examples, in political poems and related texts, of the relationship between the kingly and rebel bodies, particularly as it emerged in the difficult period of transition from one reign to the next in the first half of the fourteenth century.

THE TRAITOR'S ABJECT BODY

Towards its conclusion, Langtoft's chronicle becomes increasingly obsessed with executions, dismemberments, and bodily disintegrity. In part this simply reflects the historical reality of Scotland's resistance in the years after 1296, as Edward brutally pursued his enemies, inscribing 'on the scaffold his feudal fury', as Katherine Royer puts it, 'rather than a strategy to bring Scotland and Wales to heel with displays of ceremonialized violence'.[5] One after the other William Wallace, his brother John, Robert Bruce's brothers Thomas and Alexander, a knight named Christopher Seaton, and John of Strathbogie, earl of Atholl, all suffered the executioner's attentions, until even Langtoft was moved to write, 'Allas! le gentyl saunk ensint espaundu!' ['Alas for the noble blood thus spilt'].[6]

It is difficult not to suspect, however, that there is more to this effusion of blood in Langtoft's chronicle than simple fidelity to the historical record. The torturings and dismemberments demonstrate Edward I's vengeance and his judicial power, as well as issuing a warning to other potential traitors, in a medieval version of Foucault's well-known formulation about eighteenth-century torture: 'in monarchical law punishment is a ceremonial of sovereignty; it uses the ritual marks of the vengeance that it applies to the body of the condemned man; and it deploys before the eyes of the spectators an effect of terror'.[7] Langtoft says 'Alas', but he does not stint in the telling. His regret is as much for the fact that such actions are *necessary* as for the deaths themselves – which Langtoft sometimes relates with relish. In the chronicle's narrative of the year 1305, for example, five manuscripts contain the ninth of the so-called political songs, a poem on Wallace's execution. First, in the *laisse* form, Langtoft tells us how Wallace is taken by Sir John Menteith and brought to London, where he is judged, then hanged, drawn, beheaded, and quartered. The *laisse* concludes: 'Chescun pende par say, en memor de ses nouns, / En lu de sa banere cels sunt ces gunfanouns' ['Each one hangs by itself, in memory of his name; in place of his banner these are his gonfalons'] (362:22–3; 2361–2).

It is at this point that Poem 9 appears:

> Pur finir sa geste,
> A Loundres est sa teste,

Du cors est fet partye
En iiij. bones viles,
Dount honurer les ylles
    Ke sunt en Albanye.
And tus may you here
A ladde to lere
    To bigken in pais;
It falles in his eghe
That hackes ovre heghe,
    Wit at Walays.

(364:1–12; 2364–74)

[To finish his history: his head is in London; the body is divided up, in four good towns, with which to honour the isles of Albany. And thus you may hear, how to teach a lad to build in peace; he who aims over-high has it fall in his eye – take example from Wallace.]

The poem does not really act to 'finir sa geste'; we already knew that Wallace's body was hanging in four separate parts. In fact the poem restates what we have already been told, adding little to the story that had not already been said in the *laisse* apart from some proverbial force in English. Narratively, the poem is awkwardly placed and unlike Langtoft's earlier macaronic poems, it makes no attempt to coincide with the *laisse* rhyme in *-ouns*. This looks plausibly like a *poème trouvé*, included simply because whoever first gave it a place in the chronicle, whether Langtoft or a continuator, had a fragment of morality in English verse to hand, to which some self-satisfied words about Wallace's destruction, perhaps of the writer's own composition, could be prefixed.

Wallace's body parts stand as a memory of him. Gonfalons, with their armorial devices, synecdochically remind us of the man they belong to. We are invited to understand the body parts both as metaphor (for the vanity of overweening political aspiration) and as metonym (of a complete, living body). But heads on bridges and suspended body parts – like real gonfalons made of cloth – must eventually decay into nothing. The implication is that Langtoft's record will last longer; long after the traitor's body has decayed into dust, Poem 9 will stand as a warning against political treachery.

As I suggested in the last chapter, an interest in the abjection of the rebel's body shifts in emphasis in the late thirteenth-century poems, in which bodily abjection – as for example of the 'Skaterd' Scots 'tumbed in Twede' in Langtoft's Poem 2 – is used to propose racial and national Otherness. Here, something similar occurs with Wallace, whose abjection is designed to dispose of him at the same time as preserving him: his absence is required but his continuing presence is needed as a disincentive to others. By this time, it is clear that since the *ad hoc* military assassination of Montfort, certain forms for judicial execution of nobles had been established: the bringing of the victim to London, rather than the more rapid execution at or near the place of capture; once in London, the ritual mockery of the victim's pretensions with a crown of ivy or flowers; the transport of the victim on a poor horse, or dragged behind such a horse, to the place of execution; the torture on the scaffold, followed by dismemberment, dispersal and display of the body.[8] This treatment might have been pioneered with such rebel Scots as Wallace, Simon Fraser, and Strathbogie, but once the precedent was set, it was soon available to be meted out to Englishmen: Lancaster in 1322, Andrew Harclay, earl of Carlisle, in 1323, Hugh Despenser the younger and Edmund Fitzalan, earl of Arundel, in 1326, Roger Mortimer in 1330.

In March 1306, a few months after the death of Wallace, Robert Bruce defiantly had himself crowned king of Scots. In June, Bruce was defeated at Methven and went into hiding. Langtoft now characteristically refers to him, presumably in mockery, as 'le rey Robyn' (e.g., 370:1). But this nickname rebounds intertextually on the English, as Robin proves to be as elusive as his Sherwood-dwelling namesake. Meanwhile, as the English fail to find him, the list of those dismembered continues to grow:

> Fresel, ne say coment, eschapait des estours
> Pris est, menez à Loundres, traynez, penduz à fourz,
> Sa teste fu copé, et saunz chapel de flours
> Enhaucé sur le pount, le cors fust ars de jours.
> En luy par sa fausine perirent grauntz valours.
> (370:25–6, 372:1–3; 2455–9)

[Fraser, I do not know how, escaped completely from the battle {of Methven}; he is taken, led to London, drawn, and hanged on the gallows, his head was cut off and without chaplet of flowers, raised up on the {London} bridge, the body was burnt by day. In him, through his falseness, perished a great reputation {or, great valour}.]

Next follow the executions of Seaton, Strathbogie (whose drawing Edward graciously waives), and Bruce's brothers, as Edward pursued a vengeance that has been described as 'peculiarly maniacal'.[9] All the while 'Ly reis Robin uncore en mores et marais / Court [wanders] en sa riote' (376:26–7; 2535–6). 'Riote', with the senses of revel, lawlessness, discord and riot, suggests the counterposing of the increasingly tricksterish Robin in the liminal marshlands with the regulated and bodily disciplined order of English rule. A king in the marshlands is easy to mock because he cannot fully inhabit his kingly body; elusive, almost ghostly, he is not quite real. But the body that cannot properly rule cannot be properly disciplined, either, and constantly threatens a return to potency. In 1306 this must be set against increasing concerns over the body of the ailing Edward I himself. From the English point of view, a substantial poem in London, British Library, Harley MS 2253 condenses much of what is going on here.

Soon after the battle of Methven, English forces took captive, as Langtoft notes, the Scottish knight Simon Fraser. Like many other Scottish nobles, Fraser had previously sworn fealty to Edward but had gone back on his oath – according to the poem he was four times forsworn. He certainly gave his homage to Edward I in the year of the Great Cause and was present when Balliol gave homage in 1292, but later vacillated.[10] Captured, Fraser was taken in chains back to London to be tried as a traitor like Wallace before him. Duly condemned, he was led from the Tower through Cheapside wearing a sack-cloth kirtle and a garland. At the gallows, perhaps in Smithfield, 'furst he wes an-honge', according to the poet (who speaks as if he were an eyewitness): 'Al quic by-heveded, thah him thohte longe, / Seththe he wes y-opened, is boweles y-brend'. Finally, Fraser's head was mounted alongside that of Wallace on what must by then have been a rather crowded London Bridge.[11]

The poem consists of twenty-nine quatrains, each accompanied by a four-line bob and wheel. It can be dated reasonably securely to a few months in late 1306 or early 1307 as it clearly implies that Edward I is still living.[12] It begins not with Fraser's capture and execution but with that of Wallace, along with the capture of others among Bruce's supporters, and decries Scots who 'wenden han buen kynges', but whose heads are now on London Bridge (212; 11). The poet first recalls how William Wallace was drawn, hanged, and quartered as a warning to other Scots; he then details how Fraser was served in the same way, suggesting that the Scots should have taken notice of their disastrous defeat at Dunbar in 1296. Instead, despite having sworn oaths of fealty to Edward I, the Scottish leaders have gone back on their allegiance and are thus forsworn. As a consequence, continues the poet, the English have taken captive some of these leaders, such as the bishops of Glasgow and St Andrews, through whose counsel Robert Bruce was chosen king. But Bruce, the poet notes, is now skulking in moorlands and Edward of Caernarfon and Aymer de Valence will soon take care of him.

It is only about halfway through, in stanza 12, that the poet turns to Fraser, telling of his capture after the battle of Methven.[13] The poem is very detailed about Fraser's treatment, describing how he was delivered to two English knights, Sir Thomas de Multon and Sir John Jose, to be taken from Scotland in irons. Fraser was brought into London at Newgate, with a garland of green leaves on his head (later said to be a garland of periwin-kle – note Langtoft's detail, above, specifying the removal of this 'crown' when the head was displayed), so that 'he shulde ben y-knowe / Both of heȝe ant of lowe / for treytour, y wene' (218; 118–20). Fraser was taken to the Tower of London, then tried and condemned as a traitor to the king. A very detailed description of Fraser's removal to the scaffold and execu-tion follows. Concluding, the poet comments that if Robert Bruce and the earl of Atholl were brought to England, then at last people could go safely, and he closes with a warning to Scotland to fear England, while Edward I is alive.

The wealth of circumstantial detail and the poet's apparent knowledge of exactly what was to be seen suggest that he could have been, as his work implicitly claims, an eyewitness to Fraser's execution and perhaps that of Wallace as well. Hence it may be that, having seen one or both executions, the poet was struck by the parallels between Wallace's treat-ment and that of Fraser and was moved to versify. Wallace was captured, tried, and executed; so too was Fraser. Wallace was humiliated in a public procession wearing a garland of green leaves to indicate he was a traitor; so too was Fraser. Their heads end up side by side on London Bridge. And, the poet continues, exactly the same will happen to Robert Bruce when he is caught. In this respect the poem is about the historical inevit-ability of English triumph.

Yet this sense of inevitability is undermined somewhat by differences between the two captured Scots. William Wallace never swore fealty to Edward I and consequently refused to plead guilty to treason, because he was not a traitor. Fraser, as someone who *had* broken an oath of fealty, was guilty, at least in English eyes, of treason. Wallace, a former Guardian of Scotland and renowned leader, was given a crown of leaves in apparent mockery of his pretensions (no doubt entirely invented) to a true crown of his own.[14] When Fraser appears at his own trial a year later, the gar-land of green leaves now seems to have become part of the paraphernalia, though Fraser had never been the Scots' Guardian. Rather than being a dangerous rebel, in fact, Fraser was arguably no more than someone who was in the wrong place at the wrong time. Although the author of *Flores Historiarum* states that the Scots placed great faith in him after Wallace's death, this is exaggerated, probably to magnify Edward's achievement in having captured and executed him.[15] Not of great importance himself, his body substitutes, in both the ceremonial execution and the poem, for Robert Bruce. It is *Bruce* – 'Kyng Hobbe', as this poem disrespectfully names him – who is the traitor; Bruce who should be wearing the pretender's crown, in fulfilment of the mocking appellation given to him of 'kyng of somere' (216, 215; 73, 66) – a transient, summer king, to match 'toom tabard', his empty-tunicked predecessor. Hence, although the poem gloats over Fraser's grisly death, it still regrets that the body of Bruce, with its fuller possibilities for the enactment of spectacular justice, remains elusive.

The executions, as John Scattergood notes, 'are designed to demonstrate English power and to arouse fear in the Scots'.[16] In general, the poem is strikingly explicit in the way it discusses and uses torture as a technology of power in the Foucauldian sense. At the end of the description of the treatment of Wallace, the poet adds:

> Sire Edward oure kyng, that ful ys of pieté,
> The Waleis quarters sende to is oune contré,
> On four half to honge, huere myrour to be,
> Theropon to thenche, that monie myhten se ant drede.
>
> (213; 25–9)

This is one of the earliest recorded uses of 'mirror' in English in any sense.[17] It might be argued, in conjunction with the poet's understanding of the traitor's abject body as a 'myrour', that the poem fulfils the same function. If the poet *was* present at the execution, then one possibility might be that he held an official position, making the poem part of the machinery of propaganda which we know existed in the fourteenth century, in the dissemination of news through the usual channels – sheriffs, county courts, marketplaces, pulpits.[18] The poem was perhaps intended as a 'mirror' for traitors.

In fact this argument is difficult to support. There are not really any markers, internal or external, to clinch the idea that the poem had any official status and the fact that it is in Middle English probably militates against the idea. The author was, more likely, an enthusiastic clerk, possibly in a knight's following. He mentions several knights by name, at one point listing three and then saying, 'Mo y mihte telle by tale, / Bothe of grete ant of smale, / ʒe knowen suythe wel' (219; 150–2). This address implies an audience familiar with such knightly figures, but perhaps looking up to them. The poet seems particularly keen to memorialise the knight Thomas de Multon, who is mentioned twice, each time as the first in a short list of English knights. The first time he is called 'gentil baroun ant fre' (217; 107), the second, 'an hendy knyht ant wys' (219; 147). He may also be described by the words 'that gentil is ant fre', used to describe one of the three justices before whom Fraser appears (220; 153). These are purely conventional tags, perhaps, but possibly also signalling a particular desire to please, and hence closeness, on the poet's part.[19]

The poet was therefore probably someone from the retinue of Multon, or a knight like him, perhaps employed in a capacity that required the use of French.[20] It seems that English was the language in which this poet naturally expressed himself, but at the same time he was sophisticated enough to use 'myrour' in what was then a novel sense in his own vernacular.[21] The choice of English is one indicator of a form of nation-building and the imagining of a community from below rather than anything official or programmatic. The poet feels part of a national community, and he involves his readers in that community by placing them in relation to the torture. Like so many of the political verses, this one employs forceful apostrophe, as the speaker explicitly warns the Scots away from further treasons. He also addresses, in a more intimate way, an audience. In stanza 12, he does not just turn to his main subject but announces it in a way that implies a contract with an audience: 'Now ichulle fonge ther ich er let, / Ant tellen ou of Frisel, ase ich ou byhet' (216; 89–90). In the loving recreation of the scene of torture that follows there is not (as we might expect today) a mutual horror at the spectacle on the part of poet and audience; rather, the audience is enlisted to the poet's point of view by approval of what is witnessed. Fraser was hanged, beheaded, drawn, his bowels burnt, the body quartered. We are told that the beheading took place while the knight was still alive and that to Fraser it seemed long. Two positions are invited here: one is Fraser's own, imagined as wanting the torture to end as quickly as possible. The other is that of the poet and his audience, for whom the execution is to be prolonged. That is where its pleasure lies, in the contemplation of the fate of traitors. Contrary to the Foucauldian formulation about the eighteenth century, this medieval torture (like all the executions I have been discussing from Langtoft's chronicle) is clearly supposed to *delight* spectators, not to terrify them, and the poem aims to recall the pleasure of the spectacle, binding readers and hearers into an implied community, one already anticipated by the poet's own forms of address.[22] The very spectacle of the dismemberment of Fraser implies the wholeness of the viewing community. It also separates that community from the out-group, the Scots, as it is for them that the dismembered body serves as a 'myrour'.[23]

Yet for all its self-satisfied triumphalism, the poem is also marked by anxiety. Both executions, peculiarly, can be read entirely against their apparent purpose: with their crowns and humiliating processions, Wallace and Fraser are made into obvious examples of *imitatio christi*.[24] Scattergood suggests that the poet is writing in awareness of Edward I's ill-health and that the executions may be meant as a mirror for the *English* as well as the Scots, as the reign of a strong king draws to its inevitable close.[25] Perhaps it is the case, as Elaine Scarry would have it, that '[it] is … precisely because the reality of that power is so highly contestable, the regime so unstable, that torture is being used'.[26] There is anxiety around borders and those who come from beyond them and Fraser, a little like Balliol before him, is a mimic man. Many of the Scots, in a way that was once quite acceptable, had shifted allegiances from kings of Scots to Edward I. Most famously, of course, Robert Bruce was one of them. Strathbogie, earl of Atholl, was another.[27] So too was Fraser: like Strathbogie, John Balliol, and even Robert Bruce, he was once *one of us*; his crime, then, is to go back on the oaths that secure his sameness. When he abjures the oath he becomes the Scot again, the Other, and the possibility for the mimic's grotesquerie is realised. Not only does Fraser substitute for Bruce, but there is also a bad memory here of Balliol, the king who refuses to stay a client.

There are other fears of which the poet seems barely aware. Like many of these poets, this one begins with a tone of indignation as he points to the effrontery of the Scots who dared break their oaths to Edward. In this respect the poet is, again like most of the rest of the political versifiers, deeply conservative and what matters to him are the traditional bonds of homage which Fraser did not observe. Hence what seems to underlie the poem is a critique of the loosening of such ties; this, too, is a context for the critique of Fraser, who is forsworn, breaks those bonds, and with them, the possibility for safe *national* identification.[28]

To this extent, the poem is invested in a thirteenth-century world of imagined feudal harmony and the poet, like most such versifiers, is politically backward-looking and prone to conjure up imagined stable polities in the past, looking to feudalism, not nationalism. Yet the poem slips increasingly towards vilification on the basis of nationality, in a mode that will characterise later fourteenth-century political verse. Eventually it simply abuses the Scots for being Scots. The closing bob and wheel of the poem addresses a generic Scot, using the abusive term, 'Tprot': 'Tprot, Scot, for thi strif! / Hang up thyn hachet ant thi knyf, / Whil him lasteth the lyf / with the longe shonkes' (223; 230–3).[29]

In the course of the poem an anxiety about feudalism is exchanged for an anxiety about nation. We can read in this poem the early fourteenth-century shift towards an idea of Englishness which would ultimately transcend the weakening bonds of feudalism, replacing the form of community constructed by feudalism with one imagined through nation. At such an early stage of thinking about nation, however, it is much easier for a poet to construct the idea of a national community by reference to what it is not than by appeal to its positive attributes. To argue today for fourteenth-century nationhood is not to ignore the linguistic and cultural divisions which still characterised England in the fourteenth century. It is to see the firming up of a previously uncertain border and the construction of a foreign Other out of the nation lying on the other side of that border, as part of the process of imagining a community. In the poem on the execution of Sir Simon Fraser, we see a small example of this nation-building from below at the vernacular level. In later eras, of course, a 'pamphlet culture' grew up around executions; the Fraser poem might not be official propaganda, but it can be regarded as an embryonic medieval version of the pamphlet.[30] Almost certainly composed quickly enough to awaken actual eyewitness memories of the execution, the poem dwells on the pleasures of abjection for the group unified by the dismembering of the traitor.

LONG LIVE THE KING

Whether the composer of the poem on Fraser was aware of the king's ill-health or not, the last lines of the poem certainly require Edward's bodily presence as a guarantor of success against the absent body of Robert Bruce; the poet is confident of ultimate victory so long as life remains to him 'with the long shanks'. The bodily wholeness of Edward I is contrasted with Fraser who, dismembered, is scattered to all parts of the kingdom. When the poet dwells in admiring detail on the dismembering of Fraser, he is at the same time thinking not only about the integrity of the king's body, but the integrity of a body politic, that of an English nation.

Nevertheless the poet was right, of course, to be fearful of Robert Bruce. His last lines were unintentionally prophetic, the triumphalist mood unfortunately timed. Edward I had only a few months to live at the time of Fraser's execution and died en route to Scotland and yet another campaign against Robert Bruce. In another political poem found in Harley 2253, a Middle English lament for the dead king, an unknown poet expresses his hopes for the successor:

> Nou is Edward of Carnaruan
>   king of engelond al aplyht,*   *pledged, sworn*

> god lete him ner be worse man
> þen is fader, ne lasse of myht
> to holden is pore men to ryht,
>   ant vnderstonde good consail,
> al engeland forte wisse ant diht;
>   of gode knyhtes darh him nout fail.[31]

This Middle English elegy appears to be a translation of the very similar Anglo-Norman 'Elegy on the Death of Edward I'. The lines in the Anglo-Norman about Edward of Caernarfon are similar:

> Le jeofne Edward d'Engletere
> Rey est enoint e corouné
> Dieu li doing tele conseil trere
> Ki le païs seit gouverné,
> E la coroune si garder
> Qe la tere seit entere,
> E lui crestre en bounté;
> Car prodhome i fust son pere.[32]

[Young Edward of England is anointed and crowned king. May God grant him to take such counsel that the land may be governed aright and thus the crown be preserved, that the kingdom may be intact and he himself grow in grace, for his father was a worthy man.]

Commentators on the two poems are generally convinced that the English is a translation of the Anglo-Norman rather than the other way around.[33] To Isabel Aspin, the Middle English version, 'addressed to a more popular audience' is the more assured poem. She points to alterations in the sequence of events in the poem which make the English version the more logical of the two.[34]

My interest here is the way in which the Middle English is more concerned than the Anglo-Norman to place the glorification of Edward I in a specifically national context. The Anglo-Norman version is more international in its focus, putting Edward I in a larger context that is not specifically English but which focuses on the king's crusading ambitions: 'Jerusalem tu as perdu / La flour de ta chivalerie', the poet comments, in a work which barely mentions England. The word itself tends to appear in functional usages: 'De Engletere il fu sire'; 'Le jeofne Edward d'Engletere' (11, 67). The Middle English poem certainly retains this larger context, in which Edward is regarded as an important knight within Christendom as a whole. But it also displays a consistent contrast between that role and a more local view of Edward. The opening stanza of the Anglo-Norman poem focuses on Edward's qualities as 'un rei vaillaunt', a man of 'grant bounté' and 'leauté' (3–5). Readers are enjoined, 'Priom Dieu en devocioun / Qe de ses pecchez le face pardoun' ['Let us pray God devoutly to grant him forgiveness of his sins'] (9–10). The English poem, by contrast, is more active in constructing a sense of a reading (or listening) community through a clear address by an 'I', a grieving subject of Edward's, to an explicit 'us':

> Alle þat beoþ of huerte trewe,
>   a stounde herkneþ to my song,
> of duel þat deþ haþ diht vs newe
>   þat makeþ me syke ant sorewe among;
>   of a knyht þat wes so strong,
>   of wham god haþ don ys wille;
>   me þuncheþ þat deþ haþ don vs wrong,
>   þat he so sone shal ligge stille.
>
> (1–8)

As Thorlac Turville-Petre notes, the Anglo-Norman poem places itself in a literate context, while the Middle English by contrast makes an address to notional listeners and hints (in however formulaic and illusory a way) at orality and immediacy.[35] In the second stanza, the English poem sharpens its preoccupation with Englishness. The functional Anglo-Norman line, 'De Engletere il fu sire' (11) is replaced with the more pointedly imperative 'al englond ahte forte knowe' (9). When, at the end of the stanza, the English poet writes: 'for him we ahte oure honden wrynge, / of cristendome he ber þe pris' (15–16) it is true that the 'we' of the first line looks as if it is qualified by 'cristendome' to become 'us' only in the largest possible sense, the community of western Christendom. But in the context it is clearly more narrowly directed, as the poet immediately proceeds to show the king addressing the 'Clerkes, knyhtes, [and] barouns'. Edward enjoins them: 'y charge ou by oure sware, / þat ȝe to engelonde be trewe' (19–21). In the Anglo-Norman this is paralleled by Edward's request to the 'barnage' and 'ch[i]valers' only, to make his son king after him (36–7).

In both versions of the poem, the pope, on being told of the king's death, thinks of Edward in terms of the loss to the expansionary plans of Christendom: 'of cristendome he ber þe flour!' the pope exclaims (48); 'De seint' eglise il fu la flour' (50). Both poems refer to the 'sin' of the French king, who prevented Edward from going on crusade (33, 19). But while in the French version Edward's venture was to sustain 'Seint' eglise', the Middle English describes the crusade as a national venture:

> oure kyng hede take on honde
>   al engelond to ȝeme & wysse,

> to wenden in-to þe holy londe,
> to wynnen vs heuenriche blisse.

(37–40)

The Francophone poet thinks of Edward in a supranational context, without great emphasis on local boundaries. He does say that Edward's valour is demonstrated by the fact that he had lost none of his land by the time of his death and he wishes that 'la tere seit entere' under the new king (8, 72). But that land is specified consistently as England only in the Middle English poem, by an English writer speaking to a community of English men and women.

Geert de Wilde is another who has noted the more national strain of the English poem, which he regards as 'a royalist glorification'. He points to the English poem's lengthier account of Edward's command that his heart be sent to the Holy Land, which he sees as part of a 'tendency towards legend-building around the dead king'.[36] But de Wilde and others miss the fact that this is not a picture of a mighty king raised far above his subjects. The English poem in particular is strongly concerned with the law, and a *rex* who is beneath *lex*. Edward I's deathbed words in the English poem might look like standard pious wishes. They are in fact very legalistic: Magna Carta and its various reconfirmations are ultimately behind this presentation of kingship and there is a strong sense of contract as the king charges his barons by oath. The Anglo-Norman poem sees Edward II 'enoint e corouné' as he succeeds his father; in the English, Edward is 'king of engelond al *aplyht*' – the emphasis is on oaths and hence duties, rather than holy oil and divine anointment, as the poet makes clear when he enjoins Edward to maintain poor men and to keep his vows. Ventriloquising one king on his deathbed, dispensing advice to the next, the poet has little concern with what Edward I might actually have said (in a language he was in any case unlikely to have used *in extremis*) and a great interest in what a poor man might have wanted him to say. And of course the poet's words apparently addressed to God and Edward II are in truth addressed to the English-speaking audience of his poem – the kinds of readers or hearers who were less interested in the chivalric or crusading ideals of Christendom than in the community of the realm of England.

Around the same time, a man who identifies himself as Adam Davy, the Marshal at Stratford, east of London, but about whom we otherwise know nothing, was also moved to versify about the new king. In limping Middle English verse, he recounts a series of dreams about Edward II. In the first of these the king stands armed before the shrine of St Edward while two knights attack him. But their swords have no effect; the king's body is inviolate. Then four coloured streams of light issue from the king's ears, and cover the land. In the second dream, Edward is seen riding to Rome on an ass, his feet bare, wearing a grey mantle and cap. In the third, Davy dreams he is in Rome, where he sees Edward crowned by the pope, which he takes to mean that 'he shal be / Emperour in cristianete'.[37] Davy next dreams that he is in a Lady chapel, in which Christ comes down from the cross, asking his mother leave to go to protect Edward. 'In pilerinage he wil gon', Christ says, 'To ben awreke of oure fon' (230:21–2).

At this point, the poet names himself as 'Adam þe marchal of Stretford-atte-Bowe, / Wel swiþe wide his name is yknowe' (230:31–2) and recounts how a voice told him that he should tell his dreams to King Edward. Adam responds to the voice by saying that he cannot go, because of the dark night, and receives the reply that there will be light enough for him. Finally, Adam dreams he sees Edward before the high altar of Canterbury Cathedral. Once again, an angel comes to Adam, enjoining him to tell his dreams. Concluding, Adam names himself again:

> Whoso wil speke myd me, Adam þe marchal,
> In Stretforþe-Bowe he is yknowe and overe al;
> Ich ne shewe noȝht þis for to have mede,
> Bot for God Almiȝtties drede
>
> (232:14–17)

Like the English elegist, Davy is to some extent concerned with locating the new king in a national role and linking his inviolate body to the health of the nation. In the first dream, the two knights who cannot harm Edward perhaps represent Scotland and France and the peculiar image of the coloured streams of light issuing from Edward's ears and covering England suggests the king's thoroughgoing unity with the land he rules. The attacking knights/countries cannot draw blood from the king's body but instead evoke an image of his union with England, at once bodily and mystical. There is a parallel image of a mystical kingly union with the land in the romance of *Havelok* (a text deeply concerned with kingship and right rule) in which the future king of England and Denmark first dreams that he embraces all Denmark in his arms, then that he encloses England in his hand and gives it to his wife, Goldeboru.[38]

However, Davy's later dreams move Edward out of the national context – and the union of his body with the nation – in order to situate him in relation to a papally sanctioned crusade, which is what the 'pilerinage' clearly represents. Davy is not ultimately interested in the French or Scots, except in so far as they might prevent the king from crusading.

In this role, Edward's divine connections are represented as impeccable, not just in that the dream locales are in holy places, but in that he appears Christly himself as he approaches Rome on a humble ass, and is discussed by Jesus and Mary as a knight who has done much for them. This leads to the last of the poem's unusual images, as Christ comes down from the torture of the cross so that he may protect Edward himself from bodily pain on crusade. Davy is in this regard more like the Anglo-Norman elegist in wanting to see Edward in the larger framework of Western Christendom.

Evidently, this obscure poem is highly flattering towards Edward II, leading its editor O. F. Emerson to assume that Davy was seeking 'the favour of the king' and the 'mede' that Adam claims he is *not* seeking.[39] Scattergood argues for an early date in 1307–8 and sees the work as specifically exhorting Edward II to go on crusade as his father had done. He links the poems to prophecy of the Six Kings type, noting in addition similarities to the 'Prophecies of Thomas à Becket', which refer to the reign of Edward III. Political prophecy was a broad influence on Davy, Scattergood suggests, proposing that Davy's composition was 'a loose and individualistic treatment of a well known and popular political prophecy'.[40]

Davy's is a peculiar performance, mixing topoi of humility with a certain confidence. He is very clear about who he is and where he is to be found, suggesting the poem is indeed a bid for favour and that the explicit denial that his poem is written to gain 'mede' is meant to raise the subject of reward rather than suppress it. He also gives very precise days and times for each of his dream visions, as if to underline their veracity. At the same time, his poem embodies the topos of difficult transmission represented by the story of the Knight of the Letter discussed in the introduction. Davy fearfully says to an angel, for example, that it will be hard for him to bring his dreams to the king's attention because of the dark which prevents him from making the journey (presumably from Stratford) to Westminster. The angels who speak to him make this performance before the king the highest priority. Attributing his performance to divine intervention in this way, Adam seems to be carefully mitigating any perception of impudence on his part in aiming so high with his address.

But can Davy's rather shapeless Middle English verse truly be imagined to have found an audience *coram rege*? By the end of his poem he still seems not to have made the journey across London to deliver the dreams in the way that the poem itself has made so imperative. It is as if the poem itself were the performance of the transmission, the reading of it reactivating the intended praise at the same time as it invites reward. Despite the framework of performance before the king, there are no examples of specific address to Edward in the poem. More often, Davy appears in fact to be addressing God himself, as the poem's opening lines propose: 'To oure Lorde Jesu Crist in hevene / Ich today shewe myne swevene' (227:10–11). The motif recurs in relation to the second dream: 'To oure Lorde of heven ich telle þis, / þat my swevene tourne to mychel blis' (229:4–5) and, more disputably perhaps, the third: 'Ich shewe þis, God of hevene, / To mychel joye he tourne my swevene' (229:22–3). The final lines enclose the poem in this structure of address to heaven.

Hence, Davy's account of his dreams is not in any realistic sense a letter to the king. The vision is rather attempting to perform that sense of address; it is in fact truly destined for an audience of likeminded Englishmen and women. It is certainly a bid for favour, but not truly an attempt to get the king's attention. Instead it demonstrates its author's favoured status as the privileged witness of the new king's divine sanction and protection. It makes that demonstration not to the king but to such fellow subjects of Adam's who might appreciate his rough and ready English verse. Much the same can be said of the elegies – the poem in Middle English, in particular, is unlikely to have had any official status. Each of these poets performs proximity to the king's inviolate body, offering their good wishes for the king's bodily health, linking that health to the integrity of the nation – at the same time as they associate themselves with the king's mystical presence through poetry, the only means available to them.

A 'RYBAUDE' AND A REBEL, 1318

The elegies clearly date from the beginning of Edward II's reign; Davy's poem was also surely an early production, given Edward's failure to fulfil any of the hopes it expresses. Froissart, as we saw above, wrote Edward's failure back into the very beginning of the reign, with his story of Edward's failure in the first task he was set. Edward's reign would be characterised by rebellion of various kinds. Although he had inherited from his father what was by then a well-defined ceremonial mechanism of justice for dealing with foreign rebel bodies – a mechanism which he turned on his own English subjects – in his hands it was rarely effective.

One well-distributed chronicle story about Edward II in many ways inverts the model of Adam Davy's attempted praise and claimed proximity to the king, in order to challenge Edward's legitimacy. It describes events which took place a year after the challenge of the Knight of the

Letter. The story concerns the appearance of an impostor at Oxford; in the English Prose *Brut* it is related as follows:

And in þe same tyme hit bifelle þat þere was in Engeland a rybaude þat men callede Iohn Tanner; and he went and saide þat he was þe goode Kyng Edwardus sone, and lete him calle 'Edward of Carnaruan'; and þerfore he was take at Oxenford, and þere chalangede þe frere Carmes chirche þat Kyng Edward hade ȝeue ham, þe whiche cherch some tyme was þe Kyngus Halle. And afterwarde was þis Iohn ladde to Northampton, and draw, and þere hongede for his falsenesse. and er þat he was dede, he confessede, and saide bifore al þe folc, þat 'þe deuel bihighte him þat he shulde be Kyng of Engeland'; and þat 'he hade seruede þe deuel iij ȝere'.[41]

The *Brut* – a late source for the story – mistakenly places it in 1314. In fact the events occurred, as all other chronicles agree, in the summer of 1318. This was a tense time for Edward II, when his rebellious cousin Thomas, earl of Lancaster, estranged from him and well armed, threatened the stability of the kingdom. At the same time the Scots, taking advantage of the lack of opposition since their success in the Battle of Bannockburn, ravaged the north of England. All of Edward I's gains in Scotland had been lost by this time, and the border stronghold of Berwick had fallen in April. Edward II was under severe pressure to do something about the north and the appearance of the impostor was no doubt a very unwelcome distraction.

The impostor's arrival in Oxford was most likely on or around 24 June.[42] The *Annales Paulini*, probably closest in time to the events, does not name him but records that 'a certain person came to the Oxford house of the Carmelite brothers, saying himself to be the heir and true king of England'.[43] The *Chronicle of Lanercost* names him as John of Powderham (a village near Exeter). He chose the Carmelite house, as several accounts make clear, because the building had until recently been in the possession of the king. John was quickly taken by the chancellor and bailiffs of Oxford and then led before the king in Northampton. There, according to *Lanercost*, Edward II greeted him derisively, saying, 'Welcome, my brother'. But John of Powderham turned this to advantage: 'Thou art no brother of mine, but falsely thou claimest the kingdom for thyself. Thou hast not a drop of blood from the illustrious Edward'.[44] John 'continued to persist with his error', the Pauline annalist states, 'that he was the heir and king of England'. He was condemned to death and finally confessed 'that he had done this at the instigation of the devil, and that he had believed in the magical arts for seven years'.[45]

Writing not many years after the Pauline annalist, the author of the *Vita Edwardi Secundi* recounts the story in a similar way, noting that it soon spread throughout the kingdom and that the queen was annoyed 'beyond all words' by it.[46] John is said to have been a *scriptor* or *literatus*, possibly professionally employed at Oxford, though not a member of the University. Other accounts, elaborating on the story, say that John based his claim on the fact that a switch had occurred at Edward's birth; *Lanercost* elaborates on the common idea that the king's predilection for non-noble pursuits was a sign that he was not the true son of Edward I.

Like the Knight of the Letter, then, John is a hostile challenger and it is intriguing that despite the likelihood of the 24 June date (St John's Day), two other chronicles place the event on 11 June – Pentecost – as if out of a latent sense that that is when such challenges ought to occur. Of course John is a rather different figure from the knightly challenger who appears in court and delivers an extraordinary message because he is compelled to do so. But the same political import is evident in what might otherwise appear to be only a curious sidelight on the real events. As Roy Haines notes, '[t]here seems little point in the chroniclers' reiteration of this tale, in several cases at inordinate length, unless it were considered to serve some useful purpose'. That purpose could have been political; the story 'reflects the unsatisfactory nature of Edward's kingship … and could perhaps indicate a focus of opposition'.[47] W. R. Childs is another who has considered the possibility that John of Powderham was manipulated by elements hostile to the king.[48]

Obviously the disruption threatened by the possibility that the king who is on the throne is not the true king must be dealt with. In relation to the Lancastrian usurpation of 1399, Paul Strohm has discussed at length the symbolic importance of putting Richard II to rest, beyond any rumours of his possible reappearance.[49] In this case from 1318, however, it is not easy to see how John could have been manipulated by enemies of the crown. The most obvious candidate for such manipulation at this time was Thomas of Lancaster himself, and it is difficult to see what could have been gained by the sending of this particular hostile challenger to court, other than its value as irritation. For all Edward II's incompetence on the throne, there was no real question over the legitimacy of his claim to it as there was later to be over the Lancastrian claim. In addition, if John had been sent by Lancaster it is not clear why he would have persisted as he did in his story of demonic inspiration on the point of death, rather than pointing to the true motivator.

Nevertheless, the occurrence does have inescapable political resonances in its context. John of Powderham does not simply seek proximity to the king; he seeks to *be* the king. His claim that *he* is the true son of Edward I threatens the convergence of the kingly and rebel bodies. The threat was perhaps never a realistic one; John was in the end no more than a *ribald*. Yet there *was* a real enough threat at the time. Exactly as John was being tried in Northampton, Edward was engaged in talks with Thomas of Lancaster which would lead to their rapprochement, sealed with the Treaty of Leake on 9 August 1318.[50] Inescapably, John of Powderham's story shadows this larger story of Edward's relations with Lancaster. Lancaster, too, threatened Edward II with the idea that he was not the true king: first, as a leader of the Ordainers in 1310–11 and later when he became in effect the ruler of the country after the disaster of Bannockburn.[51] Hence, although no contemporary accounts propose a political motivation for John of Powderham's claims – most of them choosing instead to see the story as being about the power and untrustworthiness of the devil – it is inescapably political, the story of the *ribald* mirroring the larger story of the rebel. John of Powderham was executed in the now familiar manner and his body left suspended in chains as a warning; meanwhile, Lancaster agreed to a peace treaty. That peace did not last. Lancaster finally and fully rebelled in 1322. This rebellion was quickly crushed, however, when his Marcher allies deserted him and the king's forces defeated Lancaster at Boroughbridge. The rebel earl was taken to his own castle of Pontefract and summarily beheaded.

This took place at Pontefract rather than in London perhaps to underline the element of humiliation, in that the execution was carried out in front of Lancaster's own people. But Edward might also have feared that delay would increase the chances of a rising in Lancaster's favour. The events that ensued certainly suggested that that fear would have been justified, as Lancaster entered an afterlife in a way analogous to events after Montfort's death. Perhaps an even less likely candidate than Montfort for sainthood, Lancaster was nevertheless soon associated with miracles of healing.[52] A verse 'Office for St. Thomas of Lancaster', as Wright called it, exists in London, British Library, Royal MS C.12. It contains some familiar motifs, in which Lancaster is acclaimed in terms reminiscent of those accorded Montfort: 'O flos militum regalis'. He is regarded as dying for the cause of the commons [*plebem*] and fighting for English liberty:

> Copiosae caritatis
> Thoma pugil strenue,
> Qui pro lege libertatis
> decertasti Angliae …

[O Thomas, strenuous champion of plentiful charity, who didst combat for the law of England's liberty …][53]

Miracles at Lancaster's tomb in Pontefract priory were reported within weeks of his execution; Edward sent 'an armed guard' to close the church and the following year 'there were riots as crowds of people tried to gain access to the place of his execution to pray and make offerings'.[54]

Hence the judicial spectacle of execution – as so often before – failed to have the finality that Edward would have wanted; the rebel/ribald bodies, once again, overcame their abjection to pose problems for the king.

THE COUP THAT WASN'T, 1330

The kind of crisis threatened in 1318 finally overwhelmed Edward II late in 1326, when his errant wife Isabella returned to England from France with their son Edward, heir to the throne, and her consort Mortimer. London's often unruly citizens welcomed Isabella and Edward II fled to Bristol, where his favourites, the Despensers, were caught and executed. The king himself was captured, imprisoned, deposed; his son was put in his place in January 1327 and then, as a revisionary afterthought, Edward II was made to abdicate in his son's favour. He perhaps escaped for a short time, was recaptured, and finally murdered.[55]

There was a three-month delay before a funeral at which, for the first time as Kantorowicz notes, the king's body was not on display but instead was represented by a lifelike effigy. What resulted is complicated: the king's 'normally invisible body politic was on this occasion visibly displayed by the effigy in its pompous regalia: a *persona ficta* – the effigy – impersonating a *persona ficta* – the *Dignitas*'.[56] Among other things the innovation might have been designed to convince viewers – in the absence of spectacular justice – that Edward was indeed dead. But like most kings killed in such circumstances, Edward II continued to lead a busy *post mortem* life. *Le roi ne meurt jamais*: while his actual body came to rest in the abbey of St Peter in Gloucester, Edward was 'sighted' in various locations and even, in one elaborate story in a source known as the Fieschi Letter, wandered around Europe in the guise of a monk.[57] Around this time also, a poem now known as the 'Lament of Edward II' appeared under his notional authorship, supposedly issuing from his place of imprisonment. This Anglo-Norman work is found in two manuscripts. It names no names directly but quite clearly refers to the period of Edward's deposition and confinement and the regime that succeeded in which Isabella and Mortimer ruled through the young Edward III.

When it was first edited and discussed in the 1920s, the king's authorship of this work was accepted.[58] More recent scholars have rejected this idea: there are impracticalities involved (how was such a poem disseminated from Edward's place of confinement?); there is the fact that Edward was not known for cultural ambition; and there are aspects of the poem that are unlikely, such as the wholehearted acceptance by 'Edward' that he has done wrong (the historical record, by contrast, suggests that he resisted up until the end). Edward's continuing expressions of love for Isabella (whom he perhaps never loved at all) are also unlikely. Alternative explanations for the poem's existence include the suggestion that it could have been composed by sympathisers as part of a push for Edward's canonisation; that it was a monastic forgery produced at the site of Edward's burial in Gloucester, where his tomb became a profitable shrine; and, most recently, that the poem is political propaganda composed in support of the coup of 1330 in which Edward III removed his mother Isabella and Mortimer from power.[59]

The 'Lament' has habitually been included among the political lyrics: both Wright and Aspin edited it as such. But it is evidently, in terms of its speaking position, far removed from the world of the poem on Simon Fraser or Adam Davy's dream vision. For here is the voice (albeit imagined) of that elusive king to whom so many complaints were addressed. It is all the more striking, then, that the poem does in fact have so much in common with those texts that purport to give voice to the ordinary people.

In the first place, the 'Lament of Edward II' is, without any doubt, a complaint. Although it is formally quite sophisticated, the poem shares rhetorical characteristics with the literature of complaint in English. In it, the voice of an alienated speaker rails against his oppressors, oscillating between desire for the reparation of worldly evils and the placing of faith in God, and ultimately electing for the bliss of heaven as the sole answer. The speaker is not quite in the rusticated seclusion of the 'Outlaw's Song of Trailbaston' (discussed in the next chapter), but there is nevertheless a sense of powerlessness, linked initially to nature: 'En tenps de iver me survynt damage, / Fortune trop m'ad traversé …' ['In winter time harm befell me, fortune has thwarted me too much'].[60] The speaker is held in prison and hence marginalised: 'Pener me funt cruelement, / E duint qe bien l'ai deservi. / lour faus fai en parlement / De haut en bas me descendi' ['They make me suffer cruelly, granted that I have well deserved it. Their false faith in parliament has brought me down from the heights to the depths'] (17–20).

Like the other verses examined here, this one is constructed as specifically addressed. It begins by appearing as if Edward II has written himself a letter but it ends by revealing the intention of specific transmission to the faithless wife and queen, Isabella: 'Va t'en chaunson ignelement / A la Bise du par Kenire …' ['Go swiftly hence my song to the doe beyond Kenire'] (106–7). 'Kenire' is obscure but 'la Bise' is anagrammatically 'Isabel', an encoding which adds an element to the topos of difficult transmission. It must be decoded before the addressee is known and then the problem is posed: how will the letter get to her from the king's confinement?[61] But this poem has already achieved its aim by the time it expresses how difficult it will be to achieve its aim, its message passed on to its readers even as the pretence is maintained that they are not its readers.

As Claire Valente notes, the only figure consistently rendered positively in the poem is Edward III. The speaker ridicules the regime with which he has been replaced:

> Troys roys eslu en ount.
> Le plus jofne par mestrie
> Coroune de oor porter en fount.
>
> (84–6)

[In their utter folly they have chosen three kings. By their power they compel the youngest to wear a crown of gold.]

He wishes for the safekeeping of this young king (who is obviously Edward III) –

> Jhesu luy garde, le fiz Marie,
> De treson qe Dieu confund!
>
> Deux confund ses enemys,
> E lui faceo un roy moud sage,
> Enpernant et poystifs
> De meyntenir pris e barnage;
> E qe toutz ceaux soyent jus mys
> Q'ennoy luy querount ou en damage.
> E si moy serroit acomplis
> Le greingnur desir de mon corage.
>
> (87–96)

[Jesus, son of Mary, preserve him from the treason which God confound! May God confound his enemies and make of him a king renowned for wisdom, enterprise and might in upholding fame and chivalry. And may all those be put down who seek to molest or hurt him. And in this wise the dearest part of my heart's desire would be accomplished.]

The poem is extremely vague about who the frequently mentioned enemies are. But they are clearly aligned with parliament: it is 'lour faus fai en parlement' which has led them to bring Edward II down. Apart from the fact that this is purportedly the royal voice of Edward, the voice behind that voice would seem to be writing from a royalist rather than parliamentary perspective. Later in the poem, it is not clear who elected the 'three kings'. It appears to be 'ceaux qe felons sunt', ['those who are evildoers'] (82), but in the same stanza it is apparently Isabella and Mortimer who, 'par mestrie', force the young Edward to wear a crown.

The poem is at its most specific in a final warning to Isabella:

> quant le serf se saut de ire
> et ove ses perches bestes purfent,
> Garde soy q'ele n'eyt mester de mire
> Tant se porte sagement.
>
> (109–12)

[when the stag leaps in wrath and rends beasts with his antlers, let her take care she need no physician, so circumspect be her behaviour.]

Valente convincingly argues that just as the doe is Isabella, the stag here is Edward III. The young king spent more than three years under the tutelage of his mother and Mortimer as king only in name. In that period, the only way Mortimer could sanction his own power was in effect to make himself into a royal favourite, accepting honours supposedly conferred on him by a grateful monarch. In 1328 he took the title of earl of March, in a manner reminiscent of the elevation of Gaveston as earl of Cornwall and the elder Despenser as earl of Winchester. Such moves were intended to confer legitimacy on Mortimer but unsurprisingly, they ended by ensuring he was as resented as any previous royal favourite.[62] Like all bad favourites, he left himself open to the charge that he wished to be regarded as a king, while having none of the divine sanction of a true king. As we have seen, Robert of Gloucester complained that if anyone objected to the depredations of Henry III's half-brothers, they responded 'we beþ kinges' (10998). A similar point is made by the composer of 'The Execution of Sir Simon Fraser', when he scornfully mentions Scots who 'wenden han buen kynges'.[63] '*Troys* roys eslu en ount', says 'Edward', mockingly, of the triumvirate led by Mortimer. Simply to put 'king' in the plural makes the point: such a thing is impossible, there can only be one.

Mortimer had to be a 'favourite', of course; he had no legitimacy, only power. The situation was inherently unstable; Mortimer and Isabella had to have Edward, and Edward had to grow up.[64] It is impossible to say what the young Edward might have been thinking in 1326–7, when his father was deposed and then murdered as a condition of his own coming to the throne, or when his uncle, Edmund, earl of Kent, was executed, or what his true sentiments were when he conferred the earldom on Mortimer. Or what he felt about the fact that his mother was Mortimer's lover. There are only his actions to interpret, and when he did act, he acted decisively.

In October 1330 a parliament was held in Nottingham. Mortimer, by then deeply suspicious of rebellion, shut himself up in Nottingham castle with Isabella and took the keys into his own keeping. But Edward III, possibly with the backing of Henry of Lancaster, brother and heir of Edward II's old adversary Thomas, had clearly been making plans with his nearest confidants. Their ringleader was William Montagu, who is said to have counselled in reference to Mortimer that 'it were better to eat the dog than that the dog [should eat] them'.[65] In politics, beast imagery was never far away. They entered Nottingham castle by night through a tunnel in the rock beneath it. In the castle, two knights defending Mortimer were killed; Mortimer is variously described as having been in the queen's bedroom, or in conversation with Henry Burghersh, bishop of Lincoln, and Oliver Ingham, the seneschal of Gascony. Isabella implored her son, 'Beal fitz, beal fitz, eiez pitie de gentil Mortimer', and as the words are given in French in a Latin chronicle, they are perhaps an authentic memory of what was said on the dramatic night.[66]

But there was no pity for Mortimer. He was sent to the Tower, condemned, then dragged to Tyburn, beheaded, drawn, and impaled on a wooden fork. Isabella was retired on a generous income. In the 'Lament of Edward II' the allusion to the stag leaping in wrath no doubt refers to these events. The most likely case is that the poem is a 'prophecy' about that which has already happened. Such posthumous approval of the coup in the imagined voice of Edward II lends weight to Valente's argument that the 'poem might very well have been written by someone in Edward III's circle who wanted to capitalize on the sentiment and devotion that had grown up around Edward II between 1327 and 1330 to champion his son's independent establishment on the throne'.[67] Unlike the relatively hamfisted efforts of Adam Davy at the beginning of the previous reign, this author has hit on an almost unassailably safe position from which to praise: the king's own father, here transformed into everything he was not: penitent, uxorious, reflective. Using animal imagery and anagrams instead of names, the poem codes itself, but in a code that is meant to be penetrated, concealing only in order to reveal. By this means the poem creates the sense for the reader of sharing in a clandestine knowledge, though it was in fact the notable political event of the day.

But why such elaborate mechanisms? Is there, as Valente suggests, a parallel with the Lancastrian justifications of the coup of 1399, meaning that the poem should be seen as part of a nervous justificatory reaction? The problem with this idea is that in 1330 the 'coup' did not *need* such rhetorical justification. The situation was quite different from that of 1399: Edward III was the legitimate and unchallenged heir of the dead king, he was already on the throne, and by moving against Mortimer and Isabella he was only removing two deeply unpopular leaders who had no legitimacy of their own.[68] In so far as there had been a usurpation, the man who was responsible for it was not the new king but Mortimer, who was now safely dead, the brutality of his traitor's execution perhaps in part explicable as a violent exorcism focused on his body, intended to bring a public and unmistakable end to the disorders and discontents of the previous three years.

None of this, however, rules out the possibility that someone, in or near Edward III's circle, *imagined* that the regime change (to use the currently fashionable term) needed the kind of cultural bolstering that we more readily associate with 1399 and its aftermath. As was the case with Richard II there had been considerable nervousness about the removal of Edward II in 1327, though for slightly different reasons from those which applied in 1399. Deposition in 1327 was new; it was not known how, legally, to achieve it. In justifying it, Michael Prestwich writes, '[w]hat was necessary was to ensure that every conceivable means of removing the king was adopted, and the procedures combined all possible precedents'.[69] Mortimer needed Edward II dead; the effigy used at the funeral may have been part of a demonstration that he was indeed dead. But Edward III or someone close to him needed him alive. So Edward II, somewhat paradoxically, was reanimated in this poem, in which the persistence of his kingly body and voice was invoked in support of the new regime. Everything in this poem aligns itself with the new monarch: the praise topos, the rehabilitation of Edward III's father, the delicate stepping around Isabella who, however disliked, was after all the king's mother.[70] Whoever wrote the 'Lament' demonstrated his political sagacity by accurately predicting what had just happened, using the image of the stag leaping in wrath to allude to a fresh deployment of spectacular justice: the public execution of Mortimer, on whom all the ceremonials developed in the previous thirty years were brought to bear in an exorcism of the troubles of Edward II's reign.

What such a poet really wants, as he writes to the king and expresses his hope for the new reign, is an end to writing to the king. If all goes well, this kind of poem will not be necessary any longer. '[З]if him miзt & grace', writes another author, of Edward III, around the same time as these events, 'Him to venge in eueriche place / Oзaines his enemis wiche þat it be / God it him graunt par charite'. The poem is preserved in the *Anonymous Short English Metrical Chronicle*.[71] There must have been a certain weariness as the chroniclers and poets reached for the topos of 'hope for the new reign' as these authors do. Behind the elaborate fiction of authorship in the 'Lament', the terms used are much the same as those last used twenty-three years earlier about Edward II himself.

The grisly death of 'gentil Mortimer' could be seen as a repetition of the tactics of the two preceding kings, both in its destruction of the rebel body and provision, thereby, of a mirror for rebels. And on this occasion the tactic was at last effective. There was to be no cult of Mortimer as there had been of Montfort and Lancaster. It was Edward II who was unquiet in the grave, as the 'Lament' and the Fieschi Letter suggest. But the new king's legitimacy was unquestioned and these rumours seem have posed no threat to him: 'It would be quite wrong … to suggest that Edward was much troubled by the ghost of his father.'[72] Nevertheless, Edward III did not bring his father's body back to Westminster, inter-rupting the sequence of royal burials there. Instead, a lavish tomb was built at the abbey in Gloucester, where the dead king did in a sense live on, the site becoming a lucrative pilgrimage destination, and where his alabaster effigy is both visible, and entirely contained between the tomb's cage-like bars. The bodies of earlier monarchs and rebels thus safely put in their places, the personal rule of Edward III could at last commence.

CHAPTER 4

The Destruction of England: Crisis and Complaint, c.1300–41

THE RISING THAT WASN'T

'O domine mi rex', wrote a priest near Windsor, addressing a letter to Edward III some time not long after the fall of Mortimer in 1330. He left no doubt about the work's addressee, repetitively beginning paragraphs with the formula, occasionally varying it with such phrases as 'ego dico tibi'. The work that he produced is known by the general title of *Speculum Regis Edwardi III* and exists in two versions, A and B, probably written in 1331 and 1332 on either side of a treaty agreed at Amiens between Edward III and Philip VI of France.[1] In both versions, the priest presents an image of a divided, unhappy England, the poor people oppressed and, but for the lack of a leader, prepared to revolt.[2] Underlining this, he retells a story from 1 Kings 21.2–19, in which King Ahab forcibly possesses the vineyard of a man named Naboth, having first ensured Naboth's death. God sends Elijah to Ahab to announce to him: 'In the place where dogs licked up the blood of Naboth shall dogs lick your own blood.' The priest continues: 'Therefore, I say to you, Lord King, that on account of the many kinds of injuries that your ministers did to paupers, the paupers were compelled to sell their lands, and they died in misery. And therefore, you should look out for yourself lest a similar thing happen to you.'[3] It is a clear threat. At one level the warning is in a mitigating biblical code, the permissible allegorical language of the pulpit. The raw fact of threatened revolt and deposition is legitimised by the comparison to biblical precedent and divine sanction. As such, though, this is a code that operates only in its revealing. It is designed to be penetrated by its presumed addressee, Edward III, and places the parish priest who relates the parable in the prophetic role of Elijah, the messenger of the Lord, while Edward himself (despite a rather thin use of evil counsel in the mention of the ministers) is threatened as an Ahab, one of the worst examples of kingship in the Old Testament.

Both versions of the *Speculum* are concerned with a specific abuse: their complaint is directed at purveyance, the practice whereby the king's agents took foodstuffs and other goods from their producers for a price well below the norm in order to provision his armies. Not much employed before 1300, purveyance was used by Edward I during the crisis years of 1294–7, by Edward II in 1314–16, and was then widely employed under Edward III in the early phases of the Hundred Years War from 1333 onwards. It became enormously unpopular. In some regions of England the burden of purveyance fell heavily on the peasants, who might not be paid at all for the goods taken; they certainly did not, in the majority of cases, receive full value. A common complaint was that seed corn was taken and plough teams broken up, destroying productivity for the future. The practice is raised, J. R. Maddicott notes, in all the major documents of the times which sought to restrict royal prerogative: *confirmatio cartarum* (1297), *articuli super cartas* (1300), the Statute of Stamford (1309), the Ordinances (1311), and other statutes in the 1320s and 1330s. None was effective and purveyance 'probably did as much as any other single factor to diminish the popular reputation of the crown'.[4]

While purveyance was particularly iniquitous, in the period 1294–1341 direct taxation also increased in its frequency. 'English government was becoming harsher', Maddicott notes, 'more comprehensive and more far-reaching in its impact' and 'neither the economic situation nor the crown's military policies offered much compensation to those on whom the weight of taxation fell most heavily'.[5] Alongside purveyance, two kinds of tax particularly affected the peasantry: the levy on movables and the costs of military service. But purveyance was perhaps the most visible and open to abuse. The state of the countryside '[b]y the late 1330s', Maddicott suggests, 'was such that many thought that a revolt was imminent'.[6] Preparations for Edward's 1338 campaign, according to the chronicler Knighton, provoked 'a great outcry from the people'.[7]

The revolt did not come; instead, Edward III went ahead with major military initiatives, in 1340 proclaiming himself king of France by right of his descent from Isabella, daughter of King Philip IV. After a long absence in Flanders, pursuing this claim at the head of an anti-French military alliance, Edward had achieved little when, late in the year, he had to return to England to face a challenge to his authority which had arisen because of the critical financial state of the country. Chief among the king's critics was the chancellor, the archbishop of Canterbury John Stratford. This was a serious crisis for Edward's authority. Yet it quickly melted away. Stratford, formerly very close to the king, now bore the brunt of Edward's anger; before their ultimate reconciliation, Edward carried out a purge of the administration, made various concessions and weathered the storm.

It was by such actions that Edward revealed himself as more like his grandfather than his father. Among the aspects of the crisis which distinguish it from those of his father's career perhaps the most important is that Edward did not go on to repeat his mistake. For a generation afterwards Edward III kept his magnates happy: 'An able and vigorous ruler who had the good sense to go through the motions of consulting his councils and parliaments on matters of high policy', May McKisack notes, 'to choose reasonably efficient and personally inoffensive ministers and to keep his favours to them within the limits of discretion, usually found the lords ready enough to leave him to his own business.'[8] After the crisis of 1340–1, Edward III's armies became more self-funding and purveyance was less in evidence.[9]

The magnates were placated; the commons, however, by this date a fixed feature of parliament, were a different matter. Their part in 1340–1, McKisack writes, 'stands out in sharp contrast to their passive role in 1310–11'.[10] Ordinary people in the 1330s were bearing more of the burden of tax. 'Between 1336 and 1341', Maddicott states, 'taxation thus imposed a cripplingly heavy burden on many men. In 1338, when royal demands were at their peak, the peasant in the worst affected parts of eastern England might find himself facing two successive wool levies, the lay subsidy, prises and a contribution towards his community's expenses for foot-soldiers or hobelars.'[11]

It was in this context that the two versions of the *Speculum Regis Edwardi III* issued their warning. The coup that removed Mortimer in 1330, like the one that removed Edward II in 1326, like the Despenser War and the execution of Lancaster in 1322, had changed nothing from the point of view of the poor and those clerics who spoke for them. Just a few months after the end of Mortimer's regime, the author of the *Speculum* was boldly prepared to remind Edward of his father's fall, Mortimer's execution, and the possibility of further revolt unless things changed.

Both versions of the text focus specifically on purveyance. The A version is highly learned, having frequent recourse to biblical quotation; the B version is an extensive revision and has a much lighter touch reflecting, Cary Nederman suggests, 'the style of the pulpit'.[12] It was once assumed that the author must be one or another archbishop of Canterbury, fearlessly complaining on behalf of a peasantry oppressed by such practices and telling the still-young king exactly how he saw things. In fact, as

Leonard Boyle demonstrates, the author was a much humbler man, a priest named William of Pagula living in the parish of Winkfield a few miles away from Windsor, Edward III's birthplace and one of his residences.[13] The origin of the text, Boyle suggests, is as a plea for protection for William and his parishioners from the destructive abuse of purveyance. Boyle proposes that this priest – who had taken up his parish when the future king was two years old – probably knew Edward, as is implied in the work itself, and was simply outlining in writing complaints he had made verbally.[14]

Even if William of Pagula did know Edward III personally there was a certain bravery involved in the act of writing these particular letters to the king. Although both versions of the *Speculum* make use of the device of poor counsel to distance the king from bad practices, they frequently imply that the king himself cannot be absolved from blame. William lays emphasis on the salvation of Edward's soul, which would be damned if he died with the sin of purveyance unabsolved. 'William mixes this customary advice', Nederman explains, 'with criticisms that reveal a more temporal orientation. He observes that the household supported by the king is more than the royal treasury can bear.'[15] In line with these temporal concerns, William reminds Edward several times of the example and ultimate fate of his father, through whose 'foolishness and negligence', he says, 'much evil happened in this land' (A, 39). He hints, more than once, that insurrection, just as in the time of Edward II, is a possibility if things do not improve:

No one desires your coming on account of purchases of this sort [i.e. through purveyance, below cost], and there is no one in your kingdom who is more needy for love than you, King. If, therefore, you wish to keep your kingdom for yourself and your son, you must make yourself loved by the people, but you will never be loved by the people as long as you wish to seize the things of others at a lower price than the seller wishes to sell them for. (A, 34)

For a parish priest – even one who possibly knew the king quite well – this is strong language. Combined with such passages as that which draws on the Ahab story, it could easily be imagined as giving offence. Edward III presumably had little Latin,[16] but it would have been a moment's work for (say) his counsellor and confidant, Richard de Bury, to decode this story's language and its allusions. Even allowing for the familiarity, to a medieval audience accustomed to the pulpit, of such extreme parallels and dire warnings as those in the Ahab story, to direct this to a king must have taken some bravery; it is difficult to imagine that this kind of independent critical thinking was ever welcome.

Regardless of its addressee and his possible reactions, there is one thing we may be sure of about the *Speculum*. It had no effect whatsoever in restraining Edward III from further purveyance. With renewed wars against the Scots commencing in 1332, the very year of the B-version's presumed writing, the rest of the 1330s saw the worst depredations resulting from purveyance.[17] The eventual crisis that confronted Edward in 1340–1 was then exactly what William of Pagula had foreseen earlier in the decade.

Is the *Speculum* therefore a failed letter to the king, a paradigm example of the little man trying his tactics against the big man's strategies, and losing? The answer depends on the degree to which it was ever truly meant as a letter to the king. If it was, it seems odd that there are so many manuscripts of the work in existence. Of course copies of letters to and from kings tended to end up in monastic scriptoria – as a copy of the A-version of the *Speculum* found its way to Glastonbury Abbey later in the fourteenth century, described as a tract directed 'ad regem et ministros suos'.[18] But it is difficult to imagine the king's circle promulgating something so obviously to his discredit, especially in circumstances in which everyone knew that the abuse of which the letter complained simply became worse. While Boyle sees the *Speculum* as specifically directed to Edward, Nederman, more circumspectly, states, 'Whether either version of the treatise ever made its way into the hands of members of Edward III's inner circle is unknown' and adds that the presence of a second, revised version may imply that two quite different audiences were intended. He concludes, '[w]e are unlikely ever to be sure'.[19]

In fact – like so many writings to the king – this one is not really a letter to the king. Its apparent address to him is in reality a rhetorical ploy which aims to enlist other readers to a point of view that is given authority by the very fact of that ostensible address. Like Adam Davy in the previous reign – but in the learned register of Latin and with far greater rhetorical effectiveness – William of Pagula transmits a sense of privilege to readers by letting them feel that they are reading something addressed to someone very important. It stages prophetic fearlessness when its author takes on the Elijah role to Edward's Ahab.

To this end William mobilises a vocabulary of insurrection where we cannot be sure there was any insurrection at all.[20] We know of course that revolt did not happen. But perhaps there were murmurings of revolt among the common people. William of Pagula's letter nurtures the idea. 'Sometimes', Nederman says of the *Speculum*, 'the intimation that rebellion provoked by the conduct of the royal curia may be justified is shrouded in vague terms.' But elsewhere, 'the threat to the unjust king is clearly explicated in terms of popular rebellion'.[21] I suggest that the *Speculum* does this not to unsettle Edward III who, if he ever knew what William said, ignored him completely. It does so to perpetuate the idea of revolt among the only people who could safely nourish the idea and wield it when it seemed useful to do so. These people were, of course, the clergy. Wendy Scase argues that William 'mobilizes the complaints of the poor against servitude as complaints with a relevance and charge for lords as well as peasants', and that his arguments are 'particularly supportive of ecclesiastical lords'.[22] William of Pagula's letter represents the voice of the Certeauian little man who has, nevertheless, his tactical ways of dealing with authority.[23]

In a poem entitled 'King Edward and the Shepherd', clearly set in the same period of rising tension over taxation in the 1330s and 1340s, the 'little man' appears in another guise. The poem is an example of the king-and-subject genre, in the typical narrative of which a king (in some texts Henry II, in others Edward IV) controls an encounter with a hermit or manual worker after engaging him in conversation without revealing his identity. The duped interlocutor usually compromises himself, either by abusing the king (as in 'The King and the Barker' and 'King Henry II and the Miller of Mansfield') or by revealing his good stocks of poached venison (as in 'The King and the Hermit').[24] When the king's identity is revealed the dupe is appalled at his indiscretion, but the king acts leniently, demonstrating his own munificence. King-and-subject poems, then, stage the same kind of confrontation imagined in the *Speculum Regis Edwardi III* between a monarch and humble subject, but they reverse the terms. William of Pagula's text mobilises the recurrent fantasy in popular medieval thought of the unmediated access to the king which circumvents the ministers who surround him and their evil counsel – the Elijah–Ahab scenario. In king-and-subject poems the king controls the encounter and the subject realises far too late the privileged access he has had, but has abused.

'King Edward and the Shepherd' makes quite clear allusions to purveyance and its effects, but in such a way that it is not usually regarded as a complaint verse at all. While Wright excerpted it in an appendix to *Political Songs of England*, another edition presents it among metrical romances.[25] In it, a king named Edward who says he was born at Windsor is out hunting on his own when he encounters a shepherd, Adam, who, not knowing whom he is addressing, complains bitterly about the purveyors who have taken his goods, driven him out of his home, and raped his daughter. The peasant's first indiscretion is abuse, albeit indirect, of the king (who ultimately is the one who sanctions purveyance). Adam invites the king (who gives his name as Robin) back to his home. The disguised king suggests to Adam that he use his sling, at which he is expert, to kill some rabbits, but Adam indignantly objects that he is no poacher. Once at home, however, he reveals a larder healthily stocked with venison. He then engages the king in a drinking game. After this entertainment, the king tells Adam to come to court, where he will ensure that he receives redress.

Once at court, Adam unwittingly makes a fool of himself through his ignorance of manners and his continuing failure to realise that he is deal-ing with the king. Several magnates – the earl of Lancaster, Earl Warenne of Surrey and Ralph Stafford – have much fun at his expense. The poem breaks off, apparently unfinished, but what appears to be in store is a typical result in this kind of narrative: once the extent of Adam's indiscre-tions is revealed, he will be mortified, but the king will pardon him and perhaps make him a knight.

The king in question is obviously Edward III and the specific com-plaint about purveyance and taxation, along with the magnates named, suggests a date around 1340. But the complaint about purveyance is, as Wright recognised when he printed only that part of the poem in *Political Songs*, entirely incidental; it is topical, but has merely been dropped into a standard narrative form which otherwise functions perfectly well without it. In the closest analogue, 'The King and the Hermit', the Hermit's indis-cretion is the gradual revelation of his plundering of the king's forests and his overfamiliar enjoining of the king in a drinking game. In 'King Edward and the Shepherd' Adam's indiscretions are the same, and are compounded by his ignorance of how to behave at court. The complaint about purveyance adds a topical motif, but is not integral.

In this poem the voice of peasant complaint is entirely contained, in a text that is both a parody of romance and a parody of the motif of access to the king. The narrative inverts romance by depicting first the wan-dering 'knight' (Edward) and then showing a hostile challenger coming to court. That 'challenger' is Adam, but his hostility results from igno-rance: he refuses attempts to remove his staff and he does not doff his hood because he has no idea of the social niceties of court. He is an ironic version of the young Sir Perceval, the ignorant but innately gentle knight who similarly does not know how to act in Arthur's court (as is seen in the Middle English *Sir Perceval of Galles* in the Thornton manuscript, also composed around this time). If, as presumably would have happened in the text's continuation, Edward knighted Adam, then the romance integration of the outsider into the chivalric order simply does away with the element of complaint. The poet makes the peasant problem go away by making the peasant go away. Whether or not this actually occurred in the missing ending of the poem (assuming it existed), in the text as it stands Adam already seems comfortable with forgetting – as he familiarises himself with the world of the court – the recent rape of his daughter by the king's officers. Adam's elevation by knighting might rescue him from the embarrassment of his social indiscretions and would pardon him his poaching, but it would be no kind of solution to the problem of corrupt royal officers.

The complaint about purveyance implies not that the iniquities of purveyance are genuine concerns but that the audience knew what peasants were complaining about that year and could be expected to laugh at a traditional story of the misdoings of a peasant, to which a patina of local realism has been given. The precise nature of that audience is difficult to specify, but it was perhaps among members of the middle ranks of fourteenth-century society, ideologically leaning more towards the magnates than the labouring classes. In a poem which superficially obscures identity by refusing to name the king, the poet is nevertheless very clear about the names of magnates around the king. The voice has something in common, then, with that of the 1306 poem, 'The Execution of Sir Simon Fraser', in which the king is a remote and mystified presence but the magnates and knights are praiseworthy mediators between the king and his anonymous, versifying admirers. The poem on Fraser, as we have seen, glories in an incipient sense of nationhood, which is itself connected to enthusiasm for the king's military endeavours.

At the same time, as William of Pagula's writing shows, military endeavour has another side to it in the burden placed on the poor. William's work in turn can be seen in a context that included a substantial tradition of vernacular verse which reacted *against* the punitive demands made on the rural poor, often specifically as a result of the costs of warfare. These versifiers are in their way interested in a construction of nationhood – but a very different one from that seen in the poem on Fraser. Theirs are poems in which nation can only emerge as an absence, as something already broken. In the thirteenth century, clerical writers wrote of *Anglia*, constructing out of Latinate and legalistic discourse a phantasm of the nation to counterpose to kingly attempts at absolutism. In the early fourteenth century, as we have seen, some surviving poems proclaim a strident (but fragile) sense of nation.

These two final chapters examine two chronologically overlapping, but distinct, traditions. In the final chapter, the work of Laurence Minot will be examined: nationalist verse that extends the concerns already seen in the Langtoft tail-rhymes and 'The Execution of Sir Simon Fraser'. First, however, in this chapter, the tradition of sceptical verse is discussed, poems of complaint in which nation becomes visible only as something deeply compromised.

'ENGLOND IS SHENT': FROM THE 'OUTLAW'S SONG OF TRAILBASTON' TO *THE SIMONIE*

The Anglo-Norman 'Outlaw's Song of Trailbaston' is another poem found in London, British Library, Harley MS 2253 which does not fit the conventional notion of 'The Harley Lyrics', as constructed by G. L. Brook's edition of poems from the manuscript.[26] It is a more than competent performance and would undoubtedly be better known, as Richard Firth Green notes, if it were in English.[27] The title, which is Wright's, is a good one: a key feature of the poem's rhetorical perform-ance is the alienation of its supposed speaker, the outlaw, and the com-plaint is directed at the commissions of trailbaston created at the end of Edward I's reign, '[w]hen there was particular alarm … at the state of the country'. Although trailbaston inquiries were occasionally used up until the 1340s, 'they were unpopular, and did not in the end become a perma-nent part of the peacekeeping machinery'.[28]

In this poem the speaker is led to rhyme and to make a *geste*, he says, because of an ordinance (*purveaunce*), which will bring about war if God does not prevent it:

> Ce sunt les articles de Trayllebastoun.
> Salve le roi meismes, de Dieu eit maleysoun
> Qe a de primes graunta tiel commissioun …[29]

[These are the articles of Trailbaston. Saving the king himself, may he have God's curse who first of all granted such a commission.]

In the familiar topos of evil counsel here, the king himself is exempted from blame. Who, then, is the speaker addressing a few lines later when he says, 'Sire, si je voderoi mon garsoun chastier / De une buffe ou de deus, pur ly amender, / Sur moi betera bille, e me frad attachier' ['Sir, if I want to punish my boy with a cuff or two, to correct him, he will take out a summons against me and have me attached?'] The speaker goes on to complain that, having been arrested, he has to pay up and then the sheriff comes for his cut to keep the speaker out of prison: 'Ore agardez seigneurs, est ce resoun?' ['Now judge, sirs, is this right?'] (9–11).

The address to these 'seigneurs' perhaps has no greater force than that to 'lordynges' in dozens of Middle English poems. It is a generalised form of address with the effect less of including a community than of marking the speaker's own exclusion from it. This sense of rhetorical exclusion is underpinned by the more serious exclusion that has led to his withdrawal to the woods, an outlaw:

> Pur ce me tendroi antre bois, suz le jolyf umbray;
> La n'y a faucceté ne nulle male lay,
> En le bois de Belregard, ou vole le jay
> E chaunte russinole touz jours santz delay.
>
> (17–20)

[Therefore I will keep within the woods, in the beautiful shade; there is no deceit there nor any bad law, in the forest of Belregard, where the jay flies and the nightingale always sings without ceasing.]

'Belregard' appears to be a fiction, '[a] fancy name, no doubt', as Isabel Aspin suggests, 'chosen to support the alleged attractions of a life under the greenwood tree'.[30] It would be a *locus amoenus* but for the enforced character of the seclusion it offers. The depths of the alienation implied by the rustic setting are not fully realised until the conclusion, where the poet reiterates that he is composing in rustic seclusion: 'Cest rym fust fet al bois … / Escrit estoit en perchemyn pur mout remenbrer / E gitté en haut chemyn qe um le dust trover' ['This rhyme was made in the wood …; it was written on a parchment to keep it the more in remembrance, and thrown on the highroad that people should find it'] (97–100). Once, the speaker tells us, he was at the grassroots of royal service, having fought for his sovereign in Flanders, Scotland, and Gascony. He is a Robin Hood figure, then: formerly a loyal servant of the crown, wrongfully outlawed, convinced that if only his king knew the truth about the abuses of the day all would be well. But he is a Robin Hood deprived of agency. Wielding a pen instead of a longbow, he puts his complaint into circulation only in the most marginal manner imaginable. It is far from being thrust under the sovereign's nose.

Abuse of the commission of trailbaston, unlike purveyance, did not necessarily fall principally on the peasantry and this, along with the fact that the poem is in French, would appear to remove it from the realms of specifically *peasant* complaint. The poem is saturated in legal discourse and arises, as Scase argues, from a context of criminal complaint, 'engag[ing] with the language and forms of contemporary practices of

bill and indictment'.[31] It might have been composed, then, in a town in a
literate, perhaps bureaucratic or legal milieu. So far as its fictional *speaker*
is concerned, however, there is less sense that he is meant to be, as Green
suggests on the basis of the use of French, 'a man of some social standing'.[32]
The speaker mentions his military service but there is no implication that
he is a knight. His has been yeoman service; if the actual poet might
have been someone working in a legal or clerical capacity, his speaker is
differentiated as a plain-speaking man with little time for the perceived
lunacies of the law: 'est ce resoun?'

Similarly, the macaronic poem which Wright entitled 'On the King's
Breaking His Confirmation of Magna Charta' clearly arises out of a
knowledge of a legal–political culture. The poem plays wittily with the
idea of documentary impermanence:

> La chartre [est] fet de cyre,
> Jeo l'enteink et bien le crey,
> It was holde to neih þe fire,
> And is molten al awey.[33]

[The charter {is} made of wax, I understand it and well believe it.]

Wright edited this poem from the only version known to him, in the
Auchinleck manuscript (National Library of Scotland, Advocates 19.2.1)
where it is used as the preamble to a widely known sermon-poem, *The
Sayings of the Four Philosophers*. He argued that its ironic commentary
on the failure of a charter was an allusion to the repudiation by Edward
II of the 1311 Ordinances. However, a second and earlier version of the
poem edited by Aspin, in Cambridge, St John's College MS 112 (*NIMEV*
2831.44), bears the rubric 'De Provisione Oxoniae', pointing to the events
of 1258. As internal evidence shows, however, it cannot date from much
earlier than 1305. Aspin suggests that this version of the poem is a retro-
spective comment on the last acts of the 'struggle for the charters' in the
1290s. Various arguments have been made about the dating of the two
versions, with the clear consensus that the later poem does, as Wright
suggested, refer to the 1311 Ordinances.[34]

Standing alone, *The Sayings of the Four Philosophers* constitutes a general and unlocalisable complaint. The first philosopher's statement, for
example – 'Ne may no king wel ben in londe, / Under God Almihte, /
But he cunne himself rede, / Hou he shal in londe lede / Everi man wid
rihte' – could have been made at any time in the Middle Ages.[35] The pref-
aced lines which link the poem to the Ordinances, however, allow a spe-
cificity which means that the four philosophers' comments can easily be

seen as directed at Edward II himself and his reign. The first philosopher's statement just cited then becomes a very apt comment on Edward. Laura Kendrick sees even more specific references, in the second and fourth wise men's statements, to Edward's well-known predilection for water sports:

> That other seide a word ful god,
> 'Whoso roweth aȝein the flod,
>   Off sorwe he shal drinke …'
>
> The ferthe seide, that he is wod
> That dwelleth to muchel in the flod …[36]

It would be entirely in character for the Auchinleck compilers either to have selected a revised version of the poem or, more likely, to have revised the earlier poem themselves for a new context.[37] The Auchinleck version is more specific than the earlier one in situating itself as a 'condition of England' poem by inserting typical laments. For the Cambridge manuscript's very general opening, for example, Auchinleck substitutes the complaint that 'Engelond is shent', introducing the sayings of the four philosophers by referring to them as wise men who will explain 'Whi Engelond is brouht adoun'.[38]

Like many poems of this kind, this one finds its resolution in conventional piety:

> Be we nu gode and stedefast,
> So that we muwen at the last
>   Haven hevene blisse.
> To God Almihti I preie
> Lat us never in sinne deie,
>   That joye for to misse.[39]

With this conclusion, the poem focuses on a tension between worldly pressures and faith in heaven that is frequently seen in political verse: the poems often retreat from the preoccupation with real worldly problems, simply failing to propose any kind of remedy. Where reforming documents fail, when writing is worth nothing, the only answers are transcendent.

There is much less sense of such retreat, however, in one of the longest and most bitter poems of the period, the poem edited by Wright as 'On the Evil Times of Edward II', but now known as *The Simonie*.[40] In its earliest version, in the Auchinleck manuscript, the text is clearly rooted in the events of the reign of Edward II.[41] In her seminal article on the poem, Elizabeth Salter argues 'that Langland had read *The Simonie*, and used it to good effect'. She further proposed that the presence of the poem in a London manuscript, and its apparent circulation prior to that appearance, 'argues, for many years before Langland's arrival in the capital, an atmosphere and a public favourable to the sort of poem he was projecting: a poem of satire and complaint, which would mingle criticism with constructive advice, and which would be more preoccupied with lively communication than with elegance or richness of language'.[42] Dan Embree and Elizabeth Urquhart also see *The Simonie* as the kind of poem 'a serious-minded cleric (like Langland a half-century later) might be expected to write'.[43] Thorlac Turville-Petre situates the poem as an important text in relation to his overall argument about the Auchinleck manuscript's contents as a national history. For him, what is notable is the poet's emphasis on the fact that he and his readers belong to a community, one which is under threat. That community is 'the nation, *þis lond* (434), England'. Like the author of the Auchinleck version of 'On the King's Breaking His Confirmation of Magna Charta', this author proposes that 'Engelond is shent', giving as the causes 'falsnesse' and 'pride' (456). '[T]he national community' as projected in the poem, Turville-Petre argues, 'exists as individuals in mutual dependency but with individual responsibility. By reversing the proper roles of individual and community, neglecting the community out of self-interest, but giving it the blame when trouble strikes, we have destroyed "our" nation.'[44] *The Simonie* appears at the very end of the Auchinleck manuscript, therefore acting, in Turville-Petre's view, 'as a coda to the history of the nation offered by the manuscript; it provides a grim portrait of the nation now'.[45]

In its Auchinleck manifestation *The Simonie* is a bitter complaint about the bad times of Edward II. But like other poems from the period this one stops short of blaming the king, instead adopting the topos of evil counsel and the related notion that if only he were aware of the extent of abuses, the king would do something about it. Concerning the misdirection of taxation, for example, the poet writes,

> Ac if the king hit wiste, I trowe he wolde be wroth,
> Hou the pore beth i-piled, and hu the silver goth …

'[W]ere the king wel avised', the poet concludes, 'and wolde worche bi skile, / Litel nede sholde he have swiche pore to pile.'[46]

The poem lacks elaborate fictions of address. It opens by appearing to suggest a community of hearers:

> Ye that wolen abide, listneth and ye mowen here
> The skile.
> I nelle liyen for no man, herkne who so wile.
>   (3–6)

This is not much more than a standard minstrel invocation and rhetorically it does not seem very confident of finding its audience in calling for 'Ye that wolen abide'. The poet is perhaps aiming here to invoke the atmosphere of mendicant preaching.

The poem consists of quatrains rhyming *aabb*, accompanied by a bob and a final line rhyming *cc*; there is also light alliteration.[47] Stanzas are usually self-contained, the closing two lines often capping off the sense, with the last line in particular heavily endstopped. Embree and Urquhart say that 'Alliteration is haphazardly and clumsily employed in a little less than half the long lines in each version' and suggest that the poet might not even have understood the technique.[48] But the poet's metrical technique, though it might be crude, is effective. The bob frequently consists of a redundant tag (doing little more than carrying the rhyme with such formulae as 'I-wis' and 'In londe'). But in many stanzas the bob enforces a pause which draws attention to the closing line, heightening the sarcastic effect of the voice. The following stanza is about priests:

> Summe bereth croune of acolite for the crumponde crok,
> And ben ashamed of the merke the bishop hem bitok;
> At even he set upon a koife, and kembeth the croket,
> Adihteth him a gay wenche of the newe jet,
>> Sanz doute;
> And there hii klateren cumpelin whan the candel is oute.
>>> (115–20)

[Some (priests) bear a crown of acolite for the crumpled crook (?) and are ashamed of the mark the bishop gave them; at evening he (a priest) puts a cap on and combs out his curled locks, provides himself with a gay wench of the latest fashion, without doubt; and there they 'recite compline' when the candle is out.][49]

The neat ironic shot fired at bad priests is amplified by the final line's alliteration, which emphasises the euphemising of sex as the recitation of compline. The poet used alliteration when he wanted to, not according to modern views of its consistency and he did so lightly, in a way that provides a sometimes urgent rapidity. A few stanzas of complaint about the knightly orders, for example, conclude with an effective use of both alliteration and end-rhyme in the service of a galloping pace, leading up to a sententious line of great finality:

> Knihtshipe is acloied* and deolfulliche i-diht;   *hindered*
> Kunne a boy nu breke a spere, he shal be mad a kniht.
> And thus ben knihtes gadered of unkinde* blod,   *non-noble*

And envenimeth* that ordre that shold be so god   *poisons*
      And hende;
Ac o shrewe in a court many man may shende.

                                              (265–70)

The speaker of *The Simonie* constructs his argument in the assumption that there *are* likeminded hearers. He works his way through various sectors of society; after the opening invocation, the clergy at all levels is attacked (7–210) in the most sustained section of the poem. The poet then takes on 'false fisiciens', considering them as a sub-branch of the clergy (212–40). He then speaks of 'thilke that han al the wele in freth and in feld, / Bothen eorl and baroun and kniht of o sheld' (241–70), then squires (271–88), then justices, sheriffs, mayors, and bailiffs (289–94).

The poem begins, then, with what appears to be a conventional version of the theory of the three estates, as revived in the fourteenth century. As it leaves out any critique of the third estate, the labourers on the land, it is by implication the *laboratores* on whose behalf it complains and from among whom it suggests itself to have emerged. In reality it is unlikely in the extreme to have been a genuine peasant production. Janet Coleman sees the complaint verses as:

largely … a literature by and for that most fluctuating estate, the wide-ranging 'middle class', newly literate and newly vocal. The literature of complaint does not, therefore, appear to be a literature of the 'peasantry' at all, even when it deals with the poor ploughman. Rather, it appears to be the literature of that generation caught in the social shift off the land and dependent economically on urban life.[50]

Of *The Simonie*, Embree and Urquhart suggest that despite sympathy for the peasantry, the poem takes the view from town, and they conclude that it is probably clerical in origin. The opening lines suggest to them an address to 'readers who are … assumed to be more down-to-earth, more public-minded, in a sense more worldly than either the would-be *lordyngis* who read romances or the would-be perfect Christians who read moral treatises. [The poet's] audience is assumed to share his interest in the connections between spiritual and social well-being'.[51]

Unsurprisingly, this is one of the political verses which has been most closely connected by modern commentators to the sermon tradition. 'Who, indeed, from the first', asks G. R. Owst, 'were more likely to give voice to the sufferings and wrongs of the common people than the early friars, those ardent champions of the poor and down-trodden, those natural enemies of misrule and luxury, vice and injustice in all ranks and classes of the community?'[52] Such figures are also good candidates in having the requisite literacy. The use of sermon techniques, arguably, does not do much to narrow down a likely speaking position, as such techniques were presumably almost as familiar to many of the recipients of sermons as they were to those who delivered them. But the opening attack on the clergy might suggest that the composer feels anger over the failings of those like himself, making the poem, as Stephen Knight puts it, a 'good example of clericization', the appropriation by the clergy, that is, of 'a labouring voice', a 'speaking position apparently made for "the pore"'.[53]

The nature of the address in the poem leads Turville-Petre to suggest that a sense of community is constructed through its address to like-minded individuals; its assumption that these are not simply one man's grievances. This is also, ultimately, a national audience, as Embree and Urquhart conclude: 'By making frequent references to *þis lond* or *Engelond* or *al Engelond, þoþe norþ and souþ*, the author invites his reader to take a long, national view of his society.'[54] It is clear that there *is* a deep concern for 'England' in the poem. It is important to note, however, that this is only exhibited negatively, through the idea that 'England is shent'. 'England' really only exists in a complete state, the poem implies, in the past; it is best viewed when it appears to be on the point of imminent collapse.

The emphasis on England the nation seen by Turville-Petre and others in this period, then, comes when the nation is troubled as it had not been for several generations. From the negative construction – the critique of clergy, the knights, the barons – some sense of inclusiveness inevitably begins to emerge, constructed by this, the most bitter, the most marginalised and alienated voice of the whole tradition. This is why it is important to think about this poem in terms of 'imagined community' and as a performative rather than a descriptive document. What *The Simonie* adds up to is a somewhat coy letter to the king – as indirect and unlikely to reach him as any piece of parchment left in the high road. The several addresses that masquerade as non-addresses to the monarch are, finally, the measure of the poem's rage-driven incapacity to make a difference. It can only be a rhetorical performance of anger, unable to effect change *unless*, in its improbably staged scenario, the king should pick up this missive from a loyal subject, thereby gaining a true view of the state of the land.

Every stanza gives witness to the alienation and marginalisation of the speaker, which suggests that Turville-Petre's emphasis on community in the poem needs be modified. The community which he sees as constituting the nation is not actually present in the poem, which is more obviously a lament for the *absence* or failure of community. To the extent that it envisages social inclusiveness, this poem does so by exclusion. There is certainly, as Turville-Petre emphasises, great concern for something explicitly called 'England'. But 'England' is an entity that can only be defined negatively. If England is coming into view as an ideological object in the late thirteenth century and early fourteenth, then it is doing so precisely at the moment when according to contemporary writers its integrity is most threatened. The worse things become in the early fourteenth century, in fact, the more interest there is in 'England'. It is significant, in this respect, that the Auchinleck manuscript, which is securely dated to the 1330s, was therefore put together shortly after the culmination of a period of strife in which civil war frequently threatened, several times broke out, and in which 'England' correspondingly was most threatened as a functional category. *The Simonie* itself proposes that England only exists in a complete state in the past. 'We' are all guilty:

> Alle wite we wel it is oure gilt, the wo that we beth inne;
> But no man knoweth that hit is for his owen sinne.
> Uch man put on other the wreche of the wouh;
> But wolde uch man renczake* himself, thanne were al wel i-nouh   *scrutinise*
>   I-wrouht.
> But nu can uch man demen other, and himselve nouht.

(463–8)

The verb *renczake* here means 'scrutinise'; other primary senses at the time include the searching of a wound, or the scrutiny of the conscience or soul, each representing appropriate lexical equivalents to what, in the poet's view, needs to be done for a nation that has already been 'ransacked' in what was then the slightly less common sense, 'plundered', 'robbed'.[55]

Of these poems from the first half of the fourteenth century, none conclusively speaks for the peasant. The 'Outlaw's Song of Trailbaston' is perhaps furthest from that voice. At the same time, neither 'Trailbaston' nor the other poems discussed here share the self-satisfied view of the nation's political integrity found in the 'The Execution of Simon Fraser'. Emerging from a similar milieu, 'On the King's Breaking His Confirmation of Magna Charta' invokes an incipient nationhood only to describe it as already *shent*. 'Trailbaston' likewise has deep concerns over political integrity, while *The Simonie* takes the clearest view of a morally shattered nation.

It is difficult to see any of this as the confident self-expression of a new and growing national awareness, 'a strident and self-confident Englishness'.[56] That confident national sentiment can only be seen by focusing on a narrow section, the knightly class, its speakers, and its emergent poetry. In the same period, the desperate voices of a small group of vernacular composers in search of a basis for communal thinking also clamour for attention.

The poem of complaint entitled by Wright 'Song of the Husbandman' inverts the tale told in 'King Edward and the Shepherd'. The title is another of Wright's which has stuck, though there is nothing to suggest that the text is a song and there has even been some discussion over whether the speaker is actually a husbandman. For Knight, however, this is a 'rare text', one 'which speaks throughout in something very much like the voice of labour'.[57] The author is unlikely to have been a peasant himself, of course, and a sympathising clerk is the more likely candidate in Coleman's view.[58] George Kane, however, attacks the very idea of the representation of peasant consciousness in this and other complaint poems and regards the fictional speaker *not* as a husbandman but a man of substance.[59]

In the opening lines the speaker proposes an *identification* with the plight of the tillers of the soil which is unmistakable, even though this is accompanied by a typical statement of clerkly distance. At first, the speaker of these lines merely reports the troubles of the day:

> Ich herde men upo mold make muche mon,
> Hou he beth itened* of here tilyynge: *wearied*
> Gode yeres and corn bothe beth agon;
> Ne kepeth here no sawe ne no song synge.*[60]   **They neither preserve their
>   [old] sayings nor sing songs*

This quite clearly offers itself as the voice of an apparently disinterested observer moving through a landscape, hearing complaint. It is a persona interested in the *preservation* of complaint, as the last line suggests: the 'men upo mold' do not preserve their sayings, nor sing songs. They do not, in other words, preserve things in verse as *Ich* am now doing and there is an implicit contrast between *their* orality and *my* literacy.

Though this suggests a clerkly sympathiser and observer who is clearly not himself one of the 'men upo mold', a rapid repositioning of the speaker immediately follows. The first-person plural is adopted as if the speaker has heard these things not from a lofty position but because he is among the complainers:

> Nou *we* mote worche, nis ther non other won,
> Mai ich no lengore lyve with mi lesinge;*   *falsehood*
> Yet ther is a bitterore bid to the bon:*   **Yet is there a more bitter*
>   *command into the bargain*
> For ever the furthe peni mot to the kynge.
> Thus we carpeth for the kyng, and carieth ful colde …
>
>   (5–9; emphasis added)

Thereafter, this identification with the peasant position is central to the poem's complaint and its 'grim music'.[61] The speaking 'I', having metamorphosed into a 'we', is at the heart of the complaint and the pronouns ensure that 'the reader, too', as Richard Newhauser puts it, 'becomes involved in these actions'. Newhauser notes that although the speaker records the effect of taxes on himself, 'it is *vs* whom the green wax grieves and *vs* whom the officals accompanying moral dissolution are hunting as a hound does the hare'.[62]

'Luther is to leosen ther-ase lutel ys' (13) says the poet – it is grievous to lose things, where there is little left to lose. He goes on to express the grievances of a whole community, if not a class:

> The hayward heteth us harm to habben of his;
> The bailif bockneth us bale and weneth wel do;
> The wodeward waiteth us wo, that loketh under rys;
> Ne mai us ryse no rest, rycheis, ne ro.
> Thus me pileth the pore, that is of lute pris.
>
>   (15–19)

[The hayward promises us that we shall have harm from him; the bailiff summons up misery for us and thinks he does well; the wood-keeper that waits under the branches plans woe for us; no rest, riches, or repose may come to us. Thus they rob from the poor, who are worth little.]

'Thus', reiterates the speaker, 'wil walketh in lond, and lawe is forlore' (23). In this variation of an old complaint, going back to Robert of Gloucester and beyond, *wil* represents the unbridled desire of the powerful. The poet continues with another of the 'Thus …' clauses that punctuate this narrative:

> Thus me pileth the pore and pyketh ful clene,
> The ryche me raymeth* withouten eny ryht;   *steal*
> Ar* londes and ar leodes liggeth fol lene,   *their*
> Thorh biddyng of baylyfs such harm hem hath hiht.
>
>   (25–8)

'Will' walks in the land, the poet then repeats. 'Thus we beth honted from hale to hurne / That er werede robes, nou wereth ragges' (35–6).

Although these lines seem to cement the speaker's identification with the rural poor and to justify Wright's choice of 'Husbandman' in the title, Kane uses them as part of his argument that the speaker is not a husbandman at all. The manuscript reading of line 26 is 'The ryche me raymeth withouten eny ryht.' Dean retains the manuscript reading; Wright omitted 'me' altogether; other editors emend to 'me[n]'. Regardless of the reading, editors are generally agreed that it is the rich who steal. Wright translated, 'the rich lord it without any right; their lands and their people lay full lean'; Elisabeth Danninger glosses, 'The rich grab everything for themselves, without any right.'[63] But Kane argues that the manuscript reading should be retained and that lines 26–7 must read: 'the rich are unrightfully despoiled; their lands and households are in a wretched state'. Scase accepts and builds on Kane's reading: 'like many other complaints that mobilize peasant plaint', she suggests, 'the poem focuses on *reduction in social status*. The rich are *reduced* to the condition of the peasant, and not merely economically but also socially.' Kane goes on to suggest that Wright's appellation of 'Husbandman' is misleading as line 66 ('When I thenk o mi weole wel neh I wepe') suggests that the speaker was formerly a man of substance. Hence the poem's complaint is not that of a poor man at all, but of someone who has lost considerable wealth.[64] The peasant vanishes.

Everything else in the poem makes this a difficult reading to support, however. Line 26 seems most likely to be another example of the ethic dative used at several places in the poem. Dean suggests that the similar *me* of line 19 – 'Thus me pileth the pore, that is of lute pris' – is to be read as an ethic dative with the sense: 'Thus they rob from the poor, who are worth little.' The sense is similar in line 25 (above), which suggests that line 26 is to be read: 'the rich unrightfully despoil us, without any reason.' Furthermore, *weole* does not necessarily translate as 'wealth' in the modern sense; in Middle English it clearly can denote, quite neutrally, 'possessions' or 'goods' rather than 'riches', as it does in the poem 'Man haue hit', in Oxford, Bodleian Library, Digby MS 102, which makes a reference to 'pore mennys wele'.[65] The *weole* that the speaker laments at line 66 is clearly the little he had (and with which he was content) before he was left with nothing. The sentiment needs to be compared with that expressed in line 13, 'Luther is to leosen ther-ase lutel ys'.

None of this is to suggest that the lines in question demonstrate a true peasant author. But the complaint about poverty clearly *stages* a peasant voice, even as the opening lines actually draw attention to that staging and give it an inescapably clerical or, at least, literate context. In trying to wrest the poem away from the fictive peasant voice, Kane conflates 'politics' with 'radicalism'. His essay takes issue with a series of articles written in the 1960s and 1970s which were disposed to find expressions of protest in the political verses and argues (rightly) that almost nothing in the political songs can be regarded as revolutionary in spirit. But a poem does not need to be revolutionary to be political (to say this would be to equate the *non*-political simply with 'what *I* think'). These poems are about political situations and problems and they take political approaches to those problems. Certainly, they are short on political *answers* but the lack of such answers is precisely the tension they are dealing with.[66]

In fact the 'Song of the Husbandman' is more politically focused than most of the poems. In the central section of the poem the speaker explains how the beadle has come to him and said, 'Greythe me selver to the grene wax. / Thou art writen y my writ, that thou wel wost!' (38–9). The green wax refers to the seal attached to exchequer documents delivered to sheriffs; it acts 'as a sign of authority as he [the beadle] extracts taxes from the husbandman'.[67] 'Mo then ten sithen', the speaker continues, 'told I my tax' (40). So the speaker is advancing the beginnings of a quite sophisticated understanding of the economic damage being wrought, which lay not simply in the immediate shortages caused by the purveyancers' prises, but the problems posed for the future. The taking of seed corn and livestock could mean there was nothing to sow for the following season, nor a ploughteam to work the earth.

Unusually, in the larger context of political verses, 'Husbandman' does not turn its energies towards assertions of faith in God as the only sure hope. The speaker remains within the persona of the husbandman, whose positioning is all too earthly and material, as the closing lines affirm:

Ruls* ys oure ruye* and roted in the stre*,	*spoiled; rye; straw*
For wickede wederes by broke and by brynke.	
Thus wakeneth in the world wondred* and wee*	*dismay; woe*
Ase god is swynden* anon as so forte swynke.	*perish*
	(70–3)

For Steven Justice these lines are evidence of the poem's 'empirical cast of thought' and they consequently expose its limitations. If bad weather, 'like the appropriations by royal officials, cut[s] into the margin of subsistence', it also 'negate[s] the possibility of critique' by implying 'that the human phenomena are no more open to change than the others'.[68] But an alternative way of looking at the complaint about the weather is to see it as a refusal of the gaze on the transcendent, a shift of attention from heaven to the heavens, but not because the poem has any alternative, material answers to its final, gloomy antithesis, death/labour. The practices described, says the speaker, simply create beggars, marginal people who drop out of the feudal world altogether. 'What happened to such unfortunates and to their holdings is not always clear', as Maddicott writes; 'Some, at least, were reduced to begging.'[69] The speaker of this poem makes a rather more convincing potential social marginal than the outlaw listening to the birds in the forest in the 'Song of Trailbaston'.

The 'Song of the Husbandman' is very difficult to date, with estimates ranging from 1294 to 1340. Newhauser, summarising the various positions, is careful to avoid making a specific recommendation, noting that the poem 'complains about conditions which are applicable in a general way' and that its 'lack of topicality contributes to the point the poet wishes to make'.[70] Nevertheless, its presence in a manuscript compiled in the late 1330s or early 1340s obviously suggests its relevance to at least one small group of readers in the context of the taxation of those times even if, as is quite possible, it was originally written in reference to a slightly earlier time. Harley 2253 provides other evidence of its interest in the issue in the poem named by Wright 'Song Against the King's Taxes'. This text makes an initial reference to the king's departure overseas and then complains about the resultant taxes raised to fund the campaign. It seems fairly clearly, then, to have been composed in the context of Edward's 1337–8 campaign in Flanders and the exactions which funded it.

In many respects, nevertheless, 'Against the King's Taxes' is a poem full of puzzles and contradictions. Its principal target is the wool collection, the ambitious and ultimately failed plan for a royal monopoly on wool that was to have financed the Flanders campaign; it also rails against the fifteenth levied at the same time. The poem makes many expressions of sympathy for the rural poor (who had most to lose from the wool plan) and delivers the opinion that it is the rich who ought to be funding the king's campaign. Quite obviously, however, the poem does not emanate from the rural poor themselves and does not, unlike 'Husbandman', make any attempt to appear to do so. In fact, as an overtly learned display, written in French and Latin with the Latin, as Aspin notes, always completing rather than translating the French, it clearly implies a literate, well-read audience. The ordinary English-speaking people on whose behalf the poem complains, then, could not have read its expressions of concern and as a poetic performance it is conducted – a little like some of the productions of the 1260s – as if their participation in its textual world were of no importance.[71]

The poem opens with one of the typical tropes of complaint verse, using evil counsel to distance the king from the bad state of affairs:

> Dieu, roy de magesté, ob personas trinas,
> Nostre roy e sa meyné ne perire sinas.
> Grantz mals ly fist aver gravesque ruinas
> Celi qe ly fist passer partes transmarinas.
> Rex ut salvetur falsis maledictio detur.[72]

[God, King of majesty, for the sake of the threefold Persons, let not our king and his household be undone. Whoever caused him to cross the seas brought great ills and grievous ruin on him. May deceivers be accursed, so that the king may prosper.]

The next stanza, however, verges on censure of the king, proposing the justness of parliamentary restraint on him, albeit in a way that could be taken as a piece of general political advice: 'Roy ne doit a feore de gere extra regnum ire / For si la commune de sa terre velint consentire' ['A king ought not to go forth from his kingdom in manner of war unless the community of his realm consent to it'] (6–7). The third stanza attacks the fifteenth and the way in which it forces the *commune gent* to sell their cows, dishes, and clothing (11–15). Then, the poem once again avoids censuring the king by saying that the problem is not just the tax, but the fact that 'la meyté ne vient al roy' ['not half the tribute … reaches the king'] (17). What is due to the king is being siphoned off by the collectors, in another familiar trope whereby the king is shown to be innocent of the abuses of his officers.

The idea, however, that 'Non est lex sana quod regi sit mea lana' ['The law that makes my wool the king's is no just law'] (25) could be read as censure of the king, though it is not exactly the king who is blamed. Just as the poem maintains a shuttling movement between French and Latin, it swings between blame and absolution for the king. In stanza 7, it is stated that the king would be better taxing the rich and this is rounded out with a moral injunction reminiscent of William of Pagula: 'Qui capit argentum sine causa peccat egentum' ['He who takes money from the needy without good cause commits sin'] (35). But, on the other hand, the poet continues, one must not blame the king, who is a 'jeovene bachiler', so much as his 'maveis consiler' (36, 37). The poor pay and the rich do not; the rich should have been taxed instead (stanzas 9 and 10). The poem then takes on an increasingly religious tone, reminding the great that the day of judgement is at hand and it concludes with a standard appeal:

Dieu pur soun seintime noun confundat errores,
E ceux que pensent fere tresoun et pacis turbatores;
E vengaunce en facez ad tales vexatores,
E confermez e grantez inter reges amores.
    Perdat solamen qui pacem destruit. Amen.

(81–5)

[May God for the sake of His most holy name confound errors, and bring low those who meditate treason and disturbers of the peace. May He take vengeance on such oppressors, and confirm and grant brotherly love between princes. May he who destroys the peace lose consolation. Amen.]

The harsh last line once again, if only by implication, censures King Edward. But as Scase notes, the poet's complaints are addressed, 'not to the king, fount of common law justice, but to God ... In the absence of the king, and during the reign of corrupt royal agents, the poet must plead in the divine court on behalf of his plaintiffs.'[73]

Amongst the poem's puzzles, then, is the position of the author. The writer purports to speak from the position of *la commune*. But in the 1340s this is difficult a term to define. Aspin remarks:

It can scarcely be equivalent to 'the commons in parliament', i.e. the knights and burgesses, because the king was under no obligation to obtain their consent to go abroad. It may imply the community of the realm, i.e. the earls and barons, or the commonality as opposed to those in authority, or the whole nation. There is possibly a hint of the increasing influence of parliament over external policy ...[74]

She finds the composition of a popular complaint in a learned form something of a puzzle, and speculates that it might have come from a political pressure group opposed to Archbishop Stratford, who was perhaps the 'maveis consiler' (107). The familiar idea of evil counsel was nothing new; many readers and writers in the late 1330s would have had strong memories of its mobilisation in the days of Edward II. But in 1338–40 there is no one who fits the description of 'maveis consiler' very well. Stratford, the principal councillor, was in fact at the core of *opposition* to the continental campaign.[75] Anyone wanting – as this poet does – to object to the king's military plans and the taxes they entailed would have had common cause with Stratford.

As reflections on the *Song of Lewes* in the first chapter have shown, the composition of popular complaint in learned form is not an insurmountable paradox. Certainly, the author expresses sympathy for the rural poor in an idiom the rural poor could not have read. But that simply means that the complaint is directed outwards; rather than aiming to foster a sense of solidarity among a caste or venting class-rage (as in 'Song of the Husbandman'), this author looks to present the plight of the poor to another audience. The precise nature of this audience is a little unclear. But this poem makes most sense as a version of the 'letter to the king' in a code that is not a code. The macaronic discourse here reserves the poem for a few readers. Anyone restricted to French can get partial access to what the poem is about. As all the sentences are completed in Latin, however, another level of learnedness is necessary to complete the poem. It is coded at this level, and further coded in its shifts from specific invocation of contemporary conditions to more general and vague Christian admonishments of the rich, along with basic political advice to kings. It embodies the paradoxes of political critique of this period: to say anything, you have to put yourself in some danger and so you encode the message. But then you effectively hand over the key to the code as well, because without it the message is pointless. It displays the mechanisms of concealment but in a mode that is concealment as revealing.

So the poem veils itself in what was, at the time, the commonplace idea of the 'maveis consiler'. Yet there is no truly convincing candidate for the role. This poem gives every appearance of having been written in 1338–9, *before* the crisis of 1340–1, the rift between Stratford and the king, and the subsequent purge of the administration. The poem then dates from before a time when it was expedient to characterise Stratford as a bad adviser. The bad counsel that sent the king abroad, lamented in the first stanza, is a chimera, whether the poet knew it or not. The continental campaign was King Edward's own idea; to suggest otherwise was disingenuous, or ignorant – or, perhaps, a standard use of the code of evil counsel as a safety device for the author.

Of course the poem is anonymous. Perhaps it circulated anonymously before it reached Harley 2253. Perhaps it was the work of a member of the commons – a knight of the shire. Its latinity would suggest rather a cleric who was involved in government, perhaps in attendance on a member of the commons, perhaps among the clerical estate, yet someone who also had some understanding of the peasant's world.[76] His poem might not have emanated from a specific faction but must have appealed to like-minded people who had the keys – the French and Latin languages, the concern about the rural poor and Edward III's warmongering – with which to unlock the poem's code. One person who is well described by these criteria is Stratford himself, the counsellor who eventually aligned himself against the war and who was as likely as anyone to view the king as poorly advised, inasmuch as the king was not taking *his*, Stratford's advice. The evidence is lacking, and there is nothing to say that the poem was not some maverick production. But it could well have come from *within* Stratford's circle. It is most likely taking the view from town and its sympathy for the poor is analogous to that of 'King Edward and the Shepherd'. It is concerned, finally, with the relations between the king and his magnates, and only enlists peasant politics in the service of that struggle.

In the end the peasants in the 1330s remain stubbornly silent, and do not rebel, despite tactical efforts apparently made on their behalf. Despite all the hints, rebellion, which we might regard as strategic rather than simply tactical, did not happen. In 1340, Edward III's return from the continent and able handling of the crisis seem to have settled the fears. That was perhaps not very difficult where the countryside was concerned. William of Pagula, to be sure, wrote with a memory of very recent revolts in mind. But what he and everyone else had witnessed was *baronial* revolt, not the popular rebellion of which he and the poets hint. That would have been something new and, taking on Elijah's mantle, William is in fact not so much urging an early occurrence of what would come to pass in 1381 as nostalgically drawing on the memory of 1258 and perhaps his own living memory of the struggle for the charters in the 1290s.[77]

The series of military successes from the battle of Halidon Hill in 1333 onwards by which Edward III asserted himself perhaps came just in time. Certainly after the Crécy–Calais campaign of 1346–7 Edward's armies became more self-funding in a way that meant purveyance was less necessary. Such protest writings as the 'Song of the Husbandman', understandably, show little interest in the international context. To such authors, the opening manoeuvres of the Hundred Years War appear as barely explicable, unnecessary matters. Indeed the Husbandman-speaker shows no consciousness of what it is the taxes are being raised for, while the author of 'Against the King's Taxes' exhibits a slightly grumpy attitude towards an unnecessary breaking of the peace.

This means that *nation,* in so far as it exists in these poems, operates very differently from the way in which it is seen working in Langtoft's verse or the poem on Simon Fraser. There is no concern with borders in these poems, and hence no racial Other. The only colonising activity visible here is that produced by manorialism in keeping the peasants in their place (and it is arguably not useful to think of this through colonial discourse at all). As they lack any interest in the incursions of aliens, or the trouble that happens at borders, what is central to the vision of these poems is *internal* community. For the Husbandman, that is the immediate community of the third estate, but seen in relation to the barons and clergy who should exist symbiotically with the tillers of the soil. It is the ruptures in that tripartite community that he laments (and in that respect the poem is backward looking rather than revolutionary, certainly, though hardly the less 'political' for that). The author of 'Against the King's Taxes', without invoking a sense of Englishness or even using the native vernacular, has a vision of a king who remains in his realm and governs it in peace, working in harmony with *la commune*. He has no interest in Edward's expansionist policies. Neither poet is interested in that transnational ideology, chivalry, which fascinates the chronicler Jean Froissart, his readers, and his patrons. Chivalry, in Froissart's hands, is pan-European. It replaces the waning image of the crusade as something that can unite the knighthood of western Christendom. 'Husbandman' and 'Against the King's Taxes' are not interested in anything beyond the borders of their own land. But they are not essentially nationalist, either; each is more concerned with the discourse of kingship and kingship's impact on a local community or class fraction.

Before long Edward's success in the renewed hostilities from the mid-1340s allowed new possibilities. After the crisis of 1341 had passed there was, Maddicott argues, some respite for the common people in England. '[T]he compromises then forced upon Edward III's government gave some relief from the intolerable taxation of the previous six years.'[78] Additionally, when war resumed in the mid-1340s it showed a profit, while post-plague conditions benefited survivors amongst the common people.[79] A combination became possible, a fusion of the kind of sentiment expressed in the poem on Simon Fraser (nationalism focused in the person of the king, related to chivalry through the war effort), with the already existing sense of an internal community (as explored, albeit imagined as *shent*, in *The Simonie* and 'Song of the Husbandman'). One result of this combination was an aggressive new nationally based sentiment.

CHAPTER 5

Love Letters to Edward III

NOVISSIMI

In 1337, as part of a reorganisation in preparation for war, Edward III created a new noble rank in England by making his son duke of Cornwall. At the same time he created several new earls, prominent among them his allies in the overthrow of Mortimer in 1330 now, it would seem, receiving their reward. The chronicler Thomas Gray was unimpressed by these elevations, believing that it must entail the diminution of the king's estates, leaving him 'obliged to subsist upon levies and subsidies'.[1] Perhaps Gray was instinctively appalled by what he saw as favouritism on a large scale. But for most, as the silence of the chroniclers on the subject suggests, the elevations passed without special note. The new earls of Salisbury, Suffolk, Huntingdon, Northampton, Gloucester and Derby were not, like Gaveston or the Lusignans, rapacious foreigners.[2] They were not, like Gaveston when he was made earl of Cornwall, suspected of improper access to the king; nor were they old and past making war, like the elder Despenser when he became earl of Winchester, nor believed to be running the country themselves, like Mortimer when he became earl of March in 1328. They were all about the king's age or a little older; they were, like him, able-bodied enthusiasts for the tournament and for war.

At times, no doubt, the line between despised favourites and the worthy elect (regardless of national affiliation) might still have been a fine one. Yet Thomas Gray's objections to the creations of 1337 seem to belong to an earlier age. Gray, an old soldier accustomed to border warfare, was perhaps the last of those who felt they had endured the burden and heat of the day with a king who nevertheless rewarded the *novissimi*. Gray's specific objection was in any case not entirely justified, given that Edward endowed the earls not with his own estates but with lands forfeited by, among others, Mortimer himself. As Chris Given-Wilson and Michael Prestwich remark, the new earls do not look like favourites.

135

Nevertheless, given the controversies over earlier promotions of such men as Gaveston and Mortimer, 'it remains surprising how few objections there seem to have been' in 1337 and Gray's opinions 'are a useful reminder that, although it is easy to look back at Edward III's comital creations of 1337 and depict them as a master-stroke of royal policy, it is similarly easy to imagine how things might have turned out rather differently'. The lack of controversy, Given-Wilson and Prestwich conclude, 'suggests that Edward's "patronage policy" had indeed been an effective one'.[3] 'Edward III', Michael Prestwich bluntly states, 'was the king who got it right', showing 'that it was possible to create new earls without at the same time generating jealousies '.[4]

W. M. Ormrod takes a somewhat different view, however, remarking that there has not been sufficient recognition of 'Edward's tendency to create political factions among the nobility by promoting a small group of personal friends' and saying that 'the royal clique of the 1330s was almost as exclusive as those which had dominated the court of Edward II'.[5] Edward III was able to concentrate his patronage in this way – without leaving himself open to the same accusations levelled at his father – by turning attention elsewhere. Ormrod notes that when Edward began his personal rule after the fall of Mortimer, he 'had to re-establish some respect for himself and some sense of order in the society over which he theoretically ruled. In the long term, he achieved these ends by diverting the latent hostilities within his realm towards a common external enemy.'[6]

It is now a commonplace to see the Hundred Years War as having contributed to a stronger sense of Englishness in the fourteenth century.[7] But even before the war began, as the creations of 1337 strongly suggest, a new sense of a specifically *English* magnate class seems to have developed, with English birth and descent as the main criteria (even if, as they no doubt did, these magnates continued to speak and read French for much of their day-to-day discourse). Edward III himself seems to have made a distinction between English magnates, and those foreigners who were established at the English court. To the latter – such men as Henry Beaumont, Robert of Artois, and Godfrey Harcourt – he certainly extended his patronage. But they could not expect the same kind of treatment as the young Englishmen and would not become English earls. Henry Beaumont, through his marriage to a Scottish heiress, could aspire to the earldom of Buchan – but that, as a foreign title, was evidently different. The creations of 1337, then, seem designed to avoid the ambiguities raised by the hybridity of the earlier nobility.

Both the foreigners at court and the new earls were, nevertheless, all instrumental in Edward's war plans; the time of the *novissimi* had come, and their appearance allowed a quite different telling of the years on either side of the crisis of 1340–1 from that we see in such poems as the 'Song of the Husbandman'. To writers far better known today than William of Pagula, the incipiently rebellious peasants and kingdom groaning under taxation discussed in the previous chapter are simply invisible.

FROISSART AND MINOT, CHIVALRY AND NATION

Jean Froissart, perhaps writing for Queen Philippa, chronicles Edward III's largely fruitless campaigns in the Lowlands in 1338–40 as a pageant of tourneying and courtly amusement, the glittering prelude to the glorious first phase of the Hundred Years War. Narrating a great war between *nations*, Froissart, a Hainaulter writing in French at the English court, effortlessly transcends nation, grounding his writing instead on the transnational ideology of chivalry. In Froissart's narrative knights on opposite sides are courteous to one another in their encounters on and outside the field of combat, their chivalric duty to one another frequently transcending their national interests. So, as Caen burns in 1346 and the English soldiers who have torched it rampage through the streets murdering the inhabitants, English knights rescue their French counterparts, the count of Eu and the lord of Tancarville, constable of France and chamberlain respectively, thereby acknowledging bonds of caste which cut across nationality (if also enriching themselves with ransoms at the same time).[8]

Writing about the same events, the patriotic poet Laurence Minot shared with Froissart the obsession with Edward III's martial achievements. But Minot's perspective was probably far from court and magnates. He may well, in fact, have lived in rural Lincolnshire or Yorkshire, not far from those whose grievances were expressed in poems of complaint. Nevertheless, he was as oblivious as Froissart to the concerns of a William of Pagula. His literary remains consist of about 1,000 lines of English verse celebrating England's wars with Scotland and France between 1333 and 1352; they suggest a positioning very different from that of Froissart, both socially and linguistically. Minot wrote in a northern dialect of English, adopting and adapting both alliterative long lines and end-rhyming tetrameter. He shows little sign of any true affinity with the world of the magnates and is more likely to have been a member of the county gentry.[9] Hence he has been regarded by Rossell Hope Robbins as the poor man's Froissart, duplicating '[t]he myth which Froissart constructed for

the rich and highborn ... for the humble'.[10] David Wallace similarly sees
an inversion of Froissart by Minot, suggesting of his gleeful retelling of
the siege of Calais in Poem 8 that it 'reads like an appalling antiromantic
riposte to Froissart'.[11]

While Minot's poems everywhere exhibit enthusiastic glorification of
Edward's ambitions and wars, there are few traces of chivalry in them.
It is the destruction of the Scots and French that is important, not the
military ethos surrounding the achievement. Froissartian respect for a
defeated but chivalrous enemy is in Minot replaced by exultant invective:

> Whare er ye, Skottes of Saint Johnes toune?
> The boste of yowre baner es betin all doune;
> when ye bosting will bede, sir Edward es boune
> for to kindel yow care and crak yowre crowne:
>   he has crakked yowre croune, wele worth the while;
>   schame bityde the Skottes, for thai er full of gile.[12]

In this apostrophe (Minot's favourite rhetorical technique), ordinary Scots
are apparently addressed. Minot's tone of lofty scorn does not change even
when he singles out specific nobles, whether Scottish or French; for him,
nation clearly comes before caste. *English* nobles are routinely praised: in
one poem the earl of Northampton is called a 'wise man of wordes and
worthli in wede' (5.38; *NIMEV* 2189) and the earl of Huntingdon and
duke of Lancaster are also singled out for praise (47, 41). Minot does not
name many English nobles but when he does, they are always members
of the group promoted in 1337. In the same poem, however, Philip VI is
simply labelled 'unkind coward' (11).

This distinctly patriotic, frequently xenophobic, tone has helped ensure
a critical fate for Minot very different from that of Froissart. At the end of
the nineteenth century, when his work was edited by English and German
scholars several times, Minot was clearly regarded as an important writer
in the canon of Middle English.[13] Critical opinion turned firmly against
him, however, after the First World War, when the poet's glorying in war
evidently became deeply unfashionable. In the twentieth century, Minot
was routinely represented by just two or three examples in anthologies
and so declined into minor exemplary status: it was sufficient to point to a
couple of Minot's poems to indicate that his was one way of writing about
politics during the Hundred Years War, with crude energy but no style.
Kenneth Sisam's judgement that Minot 'was a better patriot than a poet'
is quite typical and historians, in particular, are entirely dismissive.[14]

A more complex recent reaction comes from Thorlac Turville-Petre,
who begins by noting that there is hardly any 'critical assessment' of

Minot and ends by saying in effect that such assessment would be wasted. Turville-Petre regards Minot as having a voice that is not 'interesting or complex', characterised by 'a single tone and a single, crude message repeated time and again'.[15] At times he seems to find some merit in Minot's poems, but a rapid turnaround always follows. 'There is no lack of a personal voice and emotion in Minot', he states. But 'it is the voice of hatred, reinforced by the hammer of the verse form'. Of Minot's Poem 8, on the siege of Calais, Turville-Petre comments that the episode of the burghers of Calais 'is material out of which really moving lyric poetry might have been fashioned'. But once again Minot fails the test:

It is, though, not to Minot's purpose, whose only concern throughout is to glorify the warlike deeds of the English and to deride the weakness and wickedness of the French. That war causes appalling suffering which all must regret, and that there are Frenchmen noble enough to sacrifice themselves in order to relieve that suffering is a complication that Minot is not prepared to explore.

'Boys (of whatever age)', Turville-Petre concludes, 'love war, and it is for them that Minot writes.'[16]

Here, the Middle Ages are seen in familiar guise as the childhood of modernity, with Minot as the laureate of masculine arrested development. The charge is a particularly harsh one in the case of the burghers of Calais, a story Minot might have left untold because there was nothing to tell. It seems likely that Minot was composing five years at most after the conclusion of the siege in August 1347; the episode of the burghers was told by the chronicler Jean le Bel about a decade later, when it may well have been embellished to show Edward's kingly forbearance.[17] It is certainly true that pathos is not Minot's mode (though he *is* capable of it). But what Turville-Petre criticises here is Minot's failure to have written poetry which envisages an anti-war sensibility. That, from 1917 to the present day, has been Minot's crime.

Minot also poses a problem which seems to arise from the approach to ideology developed by modern critical theory. We have become accustomed to the idea of a textual or political unconscious and the idea that, in Pierre Macherey's classic formulation, 'What is important in the work is what it does not say.'[18] Similarly, though in a more psychoanalytic guise, Paul Strohm argues in his essay 'What Can We Know About Chaucer That He Didn't Know About Himself?' 'that the *fullest* understanding of a text must include attention to what it represses, to the gaps, traces, and other derivatives of a textual unconscious'. It is those 'matters' on which a text 'remain[s] silent' and which 'cannot be pursued in a text's own terms' which Strohm regards as most important.[19]

But Minot's verse, far from 'circl[ing] about the absence of that which it cannot say, haunted by the absence of certain repressed words which make their return', makes all too *present* an aggressive ideological content.[20] What can we know about Minot that he didn't know himself? On the face of it, there is not much hidden behind the poet's strident patriotism and 'the hammer of the verse form'. He is all too appallingly self-aware, making it impossible to read his work without becoming aware of, even complicit in, its overt ideological projections, and aware of Minot himself as 'the first true national propagandist, violent, abusive, narrowly prejudiced, with a repellent glee, very appropriate to the genre, in gloating over the downfall of the enemy'.[21] But why is this so much more of a problem to us than (to take a notorious example) anti-semitism in the *Prioress's Tale*? Although many critics are prepared to concede that that tale's ideological positioning might well have been Chaucer's own, there is no question of casting Chaucer from the canon as Minot has been ejected.[22] The difference is that Chaucer's tale is told by a Prioress who is being narrated by 'Chaucer the pilgrim' who is being written by Chaucer: in the gaps between those positions there is plenty of room for a textual unconscious. By contrast what we see very actively in Minot's poetry is the lyric ego (in Minot's case, it might be called the lyric id) which allows and even promotes the absorption of the reader into the poems' speaking positions. To read out loud some of Minot's lines is automatically to abuse the Scots:

> Rughfute riveling*, now kindels thi care,   *Rough-footed one in your
>   rawhide boots*
> berebag with thi boste,* thi biging es bare;   *boasting bag-carrier*
> fals wretche and forsworn, whider wiltou fare?
> Busk the unto Brig* and abide thare …   *Bruges*
>
>   (2.19–22)

The words do not simply perform Minot's abuse of the Scots, they entail the performance of it by others; this nationalist abuse remains a latency to be activated by succeeding readers. '[T]he poem remains an invitation to each hearer to displace himself, as particular ego', writes Judson Boyce Allen of medieval lyric, 'into the ideal monologue (or dialogue) of the poem.' The first- and second-person pronouns in such works 'exist as ideal or universal to each member of the audience's own particularity and invite him to perfect or universalize himself by occupying that language as his own'.[23] Gregory Stone, likewise, remarks of the troubadour lyric that it 'expresses … the will or desire of *everyone and no one*, and it thus always appears as an anonymous or universal language, as essentially identical to the language of others'.[24] Minot's poems – despite his own self-naming in them – similarly work to produce a universal language.

Douglas Gray writes of Minot's verse that 'it is rare, for poems such as these, however topical in their own time, to live on to engage the interest of later readers'.[25] In fact it was *precisely* their engagement with later readers that ensured the poems' survival. The sole copy of the poems is found in London, British Library, Cotton MS Galba E.ix, generally considered to be of the first quarter of the fifteenth century, and hence certainly made long after Minot's death. Thomas Beaumont James and John Simons suggest that the poems might have been copied as anti-peace propaganda in either the reign of Henry IV or the infancy of Henry VI – a suggestion which relies on Minot's creation of a 'universal language' through which a new war can be thought about in terms set up by the old.[26]

There is nothing in the manuscript, however, to suggest any capacity for or circulation as propaganda. Cotton Galba E.ix consists of 114 folios; it is partly decorated, but not lavishly, and is the kind of book a moderately wealthy household in town or country might own. It has the appearance of a digest of a library: it opens with a chivalric romance (*Ywain and Gawain*) and concludes with a very popular religious text (*Prick of Conscience*), which occupies the final third of the manuscript and, more lavishly ornamented than the rest, clearly has a privileged position. It also contains a collection of generically varied tales in *The Seven Sages*, *The Gospel of Nicodemus*, the Merlin prophecy *Of the Six Kings*, and religious verses on penance and the seven deadly sins which are elsewhere found as part of the *Cursor Mundi*. Neatly written in two columns on folios 52r–57v are Minot's poems, offering – from the viewpoint of the early fifteenth century – a nostalgic paean to martial England.

This suggests that Minot is not *exactly* the inverse of Froissart. His readers were unlikely to have been 'humble', but rather in the middle ranks of society, perhaps the county gentry to which Minot himself possibly belonged, as well as town-dwellers below knightly rank. This is not to revive the suggestion of any form of official status as propaganda for Minot's work, however. James and Simons describe Minot as a kind of court poet, 'one amongst the increasingly large retinue of minor functionaries who thronged the later medieval courts and who decided to seek preferment through the production of laudatory poetry in a style which may have appealed to the king himself'. Douglas Gray implicitly endorses this, suggesting Queen Isabella, Philippa of Hainault or Edward himself as possible patrons.[27] But this view of Minot (as almost a proto-Chaucerian poet) does not address the question of why any writer would have tried to attract the attention of Edward III (still less of Isabella or Philippa) with alliterative verse in English.[28]

Minot's verses can be viewed, by way of alternative, as having their origins in a vernacular language of abuse as it had been developing since the 1290s (at the latest). They have some affinity with the abusive rhymes in Langtoft's chronicle, but they are several steps further on in formal sophistication. Minot either knew the tradition of complaint verse directly or was steeped in the same language used in some of them: Osberg points out that his phraseology has strong affinities with the York Plays; there are links with such poems as the 'Song of the Husbandman' and, as suggested by Minot's use of stanza forms and alliteration, with the alliterative poems of Harley 2253 more generally.[29] Whatever he absorbed from such works as the 'Song of the Husbandman', however, ideologically Minot was in a very different position. He was much closer to the work being done by the crude tail-rhymes in Langtoft's chronicle and 'The Execution of Sir Simon Fraser' (also in Harley 2253): he saw, not a realm riven by discontent and internal disquiet, but borders that needed to be made firm.

In the context of Ormrod's suggestion that Edward 'divert[ed] the latent hostilities within his realm towards a common external enemy',[30] I argue that although Minot is unlikely to have been an *official* representative of this foreign policy, his verse nevertheless reads as if written for it. Minot's lovingly crafted missives were not really written *to* Edward III, but they were certainly, in one sense, *for* him. Edward can be seen, Ormrod suggests, as 'in certain cultural respects the first "English" king of post-conquest England'.[31] Minot's poems do not necessarily show that an official policy of nation-building had filtered down to the level of the county gentry. But they do suggest that a spirit of nationalism was filtering *up* from a social level at which it had become very easy for members to think of themselves in national terms as English.

LAURENCE MINOT'S WAR

Minot begins his poem sequence in a fashion very familiar from earlier political verse, opening in the voice of a speaker languishing in isolation because of the state of the country:

> Trew king that sittes in trone
> unto The I tell my tale
> and unto The I bid a bone
> for Thou ert bute of all my bale*.   *remedy for all my pain*

Als Thou made midelerd and the mone
and bestes and fowles grete and smale
unto me send Thi socore sone
and dresce my dedes in this dale.
In this dale I droupe and dare*   *cower*
for dern dedes that done me dere*;   *harm*
of Ingland had my hert grete care
when Edward founded first to were.

                                (1.1–12; *NIMEV* 3801)

The lines are marked by the same suggestion of complaint and alienation, coupled with a disempowered rural or natural confinement made
necessary by a corrupt social world, that is a feature of such verses as the
'Outlaw's Song of Trailbaston' and the 'Song of the Husbandman'. Like
the alienated speakers of those verses Minot is concerned with questions
of address and the political effectiveness of address. He has only God to
speak to – but in making a verse at all he testifies to the possibility that
there might be someone else to listen.

Yet this mood changes almost immediately; the 'socore' of God is
forthcoming, and the sequence of lyrics begins. On the basis of the rubri-
cated divisions in the manuscript, it is conventional to consider what
Laurence Minot wrote as consisting of eleven separate poems, most critics
maintaining that Minot wrote occasional lyrics in response to events and
soon after the occurrence of each.[32] In fact the manuscript presentation is
capable of an entirely different explanation, which I want to explore here.
Minot's oeuvre is actually written out as if it were one continuous work,
like those that surround it in the manuscript.[33] James and Simons see it as
a reading experience which 'would have been analogous to the experience
of reading a short romance, divided into fitts, with appropriate features
and generic markers and satisfying the expectations which romances
generally fulfilled'.[34] In this view, the rubrics would be seen as staging
posts in a narrative rather than decisive breaks between lyrics. Instead of
writing short lyrics at intervals of several years and later collecting them,
Minot could well have begun trying to write exactly what is in the manuscript, in or soon after 1352: a single coherent narrative about events in the
Hundred Years War. Whatever he actually did, the poems can certainly
be reconsidered as a political *narrative*.[35]

After the opening lines, quoted above, Minot finds his mood very rapidly ameliorated, despite the French threat he fears:

The Franche men war frek to fare
ogaines him [Edward III] with scheld and spere;

> thai turned ogayn with sides sare
> and al thaire pomp noght worth a pere.
>
> (1.13–16)

A rapid generic shift is signalled here. The lamenting narrator has disap-
peared from view altogether as military success dispels the gloom and
the rusticated speaker fearing for England's future gives way to a speaker
rapidly realigning himself with magnate and royal interests. In the 'Song
of the Husbandman', the beadle, bearing the sheriff's writ, 'us hontethe
ase hound hare doth on hulle', where the 'us' refers to the rural poor with
whom the speaker identifies. When Minot uses the same image it is to
tell the people of Calais what Edward III will do to them: 'He sall yow
hunt als hund dose hare, / that in no hole sall ye yow hide.'[36] The change
in pronouns reflects different kinds of use of the lyric ego: in the 'Song
of the Husbandman', 'we' fear the official; in Minot's poem, 'we' admon-
ish the French. Minot can picture an England that is threatened, but the
threats come exclusively from outside England, not from internal disorder
as imagined in 'Husbandman' or by William of Pagula.

In positioning himself as a poet expressing the topos of hopes for
the new reign, Minot must be selective. The early years of Edward III's
reign give his panegyrists difficulties, with the ignominious time under
Mortimer followed by another three years before there is any significant
achievement from the military point of view.[37] For Minot, Edward's reign
effectively commences in 1333 with the shattering of the Scots at Halidon
Hill. Minot's first two poems position Edward by seeing Halidon Hill
as revenge for Bannockburn, thus erasing the whole sorry history of the
English monarchy between 1314 and 1330.

After the relatively restrained tetrameter and regular stanzas rhyming
abababab of Poem 1, the second poem unleashes a more expansive form
in stanzas of four monorhymed alliterative long lines, accompanied by a
couplet refrain:[38]

> Skottes out of Berwik and of Abirdene
> at the Bannok burn war ye to kene!
> Thare slogh ye many sakles, als it was sene
> and now has king Edward wroken it I wene:
> it es wrokin I wene, wele wurth the while;
> war yit with the Skottes, for thai er ful of gile.
>
> (2.1–6)

The refrain's chief rhyme-word, *gile*, appears at the end of each stanza;
the repetitive effects carry the hearer briskly through abusive formulae which represent the Scots as a miserable, scattered race in a manner

reminiscent of some of the Langtoft poems. The accompanying rubric says the poet will speak of Bannockburn; in fact he merely mentions it and the poem's true subject is the aftermath of Halidon Hill, regarded as revenge for Bannockburn and the 'many sakles [innocent]' the Scots slew there (2.3). A notable feature of the poem is the implied physical and martial effectiveness of Edward contrasted with the *verbal* inadequacies of the Scots. 'The boste of yowre [the Scots'] baner es betin all doune' the poet says, for which Edward will 'crak yowre crowne' (2.8, 10). The Scotsman is pictured as exiled to Flanders: 'The Skotte gase in Burghes and betes the stretes, / all thise Inglis men harmes he hetes [promises harm to]; / fast makes he his mone to men that he metes' (25–7). But he has become an empty vessel of words: 'he uses all threting with gaudes [pretence] and gile' (30). In the final stanza the poet continues on his theme of the emptiness of words when confronted with a powerful adversary:

> many man thretes and spekes ful ill
> that sum tyme war better to be stane still.
> The Skot in his wordes has wind for to spill
> for at the last Edward sall have al his will …
>
> (2.31–4)

The fact that it is their 'crowns' that Edward will crack is a word choice dictated both by rhyme and alliteration. Nevertheless, it presupposes some familiar ideas; foreign enemies must not simply be defeated, but made abject. They are miserably exiled from the homeland that, by implication, is not really theirs and it is important to cut off or in this case crack their heads to end any threat they may pose.

After the announcement that, in this way, 'Edward sall have al his will', the sequence shifts to Edward's campaign in the Lowlands – the fruitless manoeuvres of the late 1330s which achieved no military results of any consequence, did not trouble Philip VI, and brought England to the brink of revolt. Minot effortlessly avoids all mention of such matter. Instead, Poem 3 begins by describing, now in rhyming couplets, Edward's alliance formed in Brabant and the angry reaction of Philip VI. Once again, the rubric to this poem ('How Edward the king come in Braband / and toke homage of all the land') does *not* act like a poem title so much as a narrative marker. The poem shifts quickly away from Brabant to describe Philip's response to Edward's action: the assembly of a fleet to attack Southampton in October 1338. The bulk of the poem is about the French attack and the English response. The damage inflicted by the French is minimised and Minot prefers to dwell on the ensuing battle for the defence of the town, and later on the sea, where the French defeated the outnumbered English.[39] The French remain at sea, acting as pirates and robbing 'pouer men thaire gude'. Minot closes by warning that the French actions 'mun be ful dere boght' (3.122, 119; *NIMEV* 987). The poem's closing couplet may be conventional, but it cements the sense of a nation encircled by enemies: 'Now Jhesus save all Ingland / and blis it with his haly hand. Amen' (3.125–6).

The use of couplets, and the description of battle, make this section more romance-like than most other parts of Minot's work. Despite the lack of a rubric following, most editors follow the hint provided by the preceding 'Amen' and see a division here, marking the next section as Poem 4. The narrative thread returns to Edward in Brabant, where the king, again in romance fashion, 'has his woning / with mani cumly knight' (4.2–3; *NIMEV* 709). Philip VI is now seen in the character Minot typically imputes to him as Edward advances into France. Philip is a coward: despite an army outnumbering Edward's seven to one, 'durst he noght cum nere' (4.42). 'Than the riche floure de lice / wan thare ful litill prise,' Minot says: 'fast he fled for ferde' (4.25–7). The Battle of Flamengerie (23 October 1339) is an anticlimax. Philip and his allies the kings of Bohemia and Navarre are cowardly and ultimately flee: 'Sir Philip of Fraunce fled for dout / and hied him hame with all his rout –/ coward! God giff him care' (4.88–90). The two poems that follow detail first the sea-battle of Sluys (24 June 1340) and the siege of Tournai in the same year, the first returning to the energetic alliterating monorhymed quatrain, the second to the octet rhyming *ababababab*. It is in this second poem that Minot first uses what will become a dominant image in the remainder of the sequence. 'A bore with brenis [byrnies] bright / es broght opon yowre [Tournai's] grene' (6.3–4; *NIMEV* 3796). The boar is Edward III, in a guise deriving from the prophecies of Merlin which – in their form in the poem *Of the Six Kings* – appear two leaves before Minot's poems in the manuscript. Minot's remarkable poem on Tournai consists principally of an extended, elegiac apostrophe to the city and its inhabitants, describing what will happen when Edward has his way and warning them to have no faith in Philip VI. At the end Minot hints at treachery on the part of John, duke of Brabant, Edward's nominal ally whose actions at the siege may well have led to its abandonment.

To this point then, Minot has been able to enthuse over the victories at Halidon Hill and Sluys. But behind his rhetoric it is quite clear that there is in truth not a great deal to celebrate: Southampton is near destroyed; the French are superior at sea (until Sluys); the Tournai siege has failed;

Philip VI has not been decisively brought to battle. This all changes with the long sequence that now commences.

Minot opens Poem 7 by referring explicitly, for the first time, to Merlin and his prophecies: 'Men may rede in romance right / of a grete clerk that Merlin hight' (7.1–2; *NIMEV* 2149). The reference to a boar in the previous poem is now clearly linked to Merlin's prophecies:

> Merlin said thus with his mowth:
> Out of the north into the sowth
> suld cum a bare over the se
> that suld mak many man to fle.
> And in the se, he said ful right
> suld he schew ful mekill might
> and in France he suld bigin
> to mak tham wrath that er tharein.
>
> (7.7–14)

It is at this point also that Minot makes the second and clearer of his two self-nominations, giving the sense that he is indeed composing for Edward III:

> Untill the se his [the boar's] taile reche sale
> all folk of France to mekill bale*.   *woe*
> Thus have I mater for to make
> for a nobill prince sake.
> Help me, God, my wit es thin;
> now Laurence Minot will bigin.
>
> (7.15–20)

There is then a metrical shift back to what seems to be Minot's favoured form for the more narrative sections of his poetry: octets rhyming either *abababab* or *ababbcbc*, with stanza linking.[40] He continues in this mode for the remaining 153 lines of Poem 7 and the 96 of Poem 8 (*NIMEV* 585). Even when the meter changes for Poem 9 with a return to alliterative long lines (with a clearly marked caesura) Minot continues a narrative. This is the most congenial material for him, taking in the English sack of Caen and the victory at Crécy (1346); the siege of Calais (1347) and, back in England, the defeat of the Scots at Neville's Cross (1346).

After the description of the fall of Calais to Edward, Poem 9 deals with the Scots king David and his defeat at Neville's Cross, which involves a necessary flashback to the previous year. David Bruce states that he will 'ride thurgh all Ingland' and his horses will stand at Westminster Hall (9.10; *NIMEV* 3117). The second stanza repeats this phrase exactly and states that the *chevauchée* in England is the idea of the Scots' ally, Philip

VI, as there is no one in England 'to let hym the way' (9.18). The third
stanza hammers home the message that David aims 'all Ingland to win .
fro Twede unto Trent' (9.22). That 'Ingland' itself is at stake is repeatedly
made clear: the archbishop of York and his forces will not hesitate to win
with their weapons 'the wirschip of Ingland' (9.32); David Bruce says that
'of all Ingland' he has 'no drede' (9.36). The poem goes on to tell how
David and his forces are defeated outside Durham, David himself captured and taken to the Tower of London, fulfilling his own prophecy that
he will ride the length of England and come to London, but only in an
ironic manner. As ever, Philip VI – even when he is nowhere near – is the
real culprit: 'Philip the Valais, thou made me be here', David says:

> 'this es noght the forward . we made are to yere.
> Fals es thi forward, . and evyll mot thou fare
> for thou and sir John thi son . haves kast me in care.'
>
> (9.57–60)

The final stanza gloats over the failed Scottish intention 'for to win
Ingland . whils Edward was out' (9.62).

Two poems remain. They are relatively short and focus respectively on
the battle of Les Espagnols-sur-mer (30 August 1350) and the capture of
the castle of Guines near Calais in 1352 (a minor event which, as all commentators have noted, brings the poems to a relatively downbeat end). The
closing lines, with their conventional commendation of Edward to God's
care and expression of the hope 'that he may at his ending . have hevin till
his mede', seem to make it clear that this was intended as the sequence's
close (11.40). After this, for unknown reasons, Minot fell silent.

MINOT'S ENGLAND

Laurence Minot begins his poem sequence by showing the identification
of the national and sovereign bodies. '[O]f *Ingland* had my hert grete care',
he says, 'when *Edward* founded first to were' (1.11–12). As the French 'war
frek to fare / ogaines him with scheld and spere' (13–14), there is an implicit
admission of the vulnerability of the young, untried king. The poetry that
follows is about the removal from harm of that kingly body and, conversely, the abjecting of the foreign bodies threatening it. Hence, nation
and king are equated and – as in the song on Fraser and Froissart's story
about Edward I's bones – the health of one is the health of the other.

Minot quickly recovers from the early state of fear. '[A]nd yit es Ingland
als it was', he writes in Poem 7 (132), despite everything the French can

do. The very act of perceiving and depicting an *external* threat is crucial to the way in which Minot constructs England. While he adopts some of the political complaint traditions, he reverses their impact by aligning himself with royal interests. Minot does not have chivalry, but instead deploys an incipient ideology that will ultimately fill the gap left when chivalry has evolved into a purely ceremonial function. That ideology is nationalism.

One of the major objections raised by Benedict Anderson to the existence of medieval nationalism is the idea that nationalism cannot co-exist with strong monarchy. Monarchic dynasties, he proposes, are among three factors which must lose 'their axiomatic grip on men's minds' before 'the very possibility of imagining the nation' can arise. Anderson links the rise of nationalism to the era of print-capitalism with its capacities 'for rapidly growing numbers of people to think about themselves, and to relate themselves to others, in profoundly new ways'.[41] While print indisputably had the effect of allowing greater and more effective dissemination of ideas, the notion that the kind of thinking it allowed was 'profoundly new' is more open to dispute. I have earlier suggested that the equivalent of a pamphlet culture is represented in some of the poetry examined here and have pointed to evidence of public posting of poetic works. The reach of such poetry within a manuscript culture could not, of course, have been anything like that made possible by print. Indeed, Minot's poetry – existing as it does in a single late copy, having left no other traces of itself – appears, like many of the poems examined here, to prove the fragility of the transmission of such works rather than otherwise. Nevertheless, as the poems in Langtoft's chronicle suggest, with their afterlife in Robert Mannyng's translation, the Prose *Brut*, and beyond, circulation certainly did occur. Print *furthered* something which already existed, but it should not be credited with a revolutionary effect in this regard.

I am suggesting that the same kinds of imagined comradeship and community which become evident after print were promoted by the kinds of poems discussed here. In Minot's poem sequence the figure of the monarch, Edward, far from precluding the possibility of a nationalism, actually forms a focus for it. It might not be possible to impose, via print, a widespread sense of what the nation is; but we can, Minot might be suggesting, all look to this one figure as a guarantee of national integrity: 'and yit es Ingland als it was'.

One peculiar aspect of Minot's poems as praise-biography of Edward III helps confirm this: the simple fact that the hero-king remains strangely inscrutable throughout the poems. Minot makes considerable use of

techniques of literary fiction, and represents the interiority of the characters, their emotions, and depictions of them engaged in dialogue. A consistent picture of King Philip as vacillating and cowardly, for example, is
built up through the speaker's supposed knowledge of his emotions – just
as if Minot's speaker were an omniscient narrator.[42] In the Neville's Cross
poem this fictional creation of characters' sentiments is elevated into an
effect of pathos, when Minot skilfully depicts David Bruce's changing
states of emotion after his wounding and capture at the battle (see 9.15–18,
55–60). The exchanges between David and Philip – quoted above – can
hardly have happened while Philip was in France and David in the Tower
of London: this is Minot's literary fiction.

Yet despite the success with which Minot creates such characters,
Edward III himself never says a word in Minot's verse. Nor do we learn of
his thoughts, as we do with the rival kings. Hence as the object of praise he
is strangely remote and unknowable within this text. Minot is in the position of all political versifiers in relation to the king: he cannot truly know
the subject of his verse and much as he addresses him adoringly, there is
no sense that his missives will reach such a remote figure. By the end of
the sequence, Minot's narrator is as distant from his hero as he was in his
dale at the outset. In fact as the sequence progresses Edward increasingly
appears to exist on a different plane from the rest of the characters. He is
not referred to as 'the boar' until the Tournai poem (6); after the discussion of the Merlin prophecy at the beginning of Poem 7, the appellation is
frequently used, underlining Edward's role as the fulfilment of prophecy.
At the same time the king is an agent of God-directed destiny:

> Haly Gaste, Thou gif him grace
> that he in gude time may bigin
> and send to him both might and space
> his heritage wele for to win.
> And sone assoyl him of his sin
> hende God that heried hell
> for France now es he entred in
> and thare he dightes him for to dwell.
>
> (7.29–36)

Between Arthurian prophecy on the one hand and Christian destiny as
conqueror of France on the other, Minot has taken the narrative very far
from its opening as a rustic lament on evil times. With this twin teleology
operating, Edward is increasingly the fulfilment of a larger design and,
while he might consequently be unavailable as a conventional character,
the sense of a larger narrative structure is strengthened.

Making use of techniques that would later be perfected by Chaucer and the *Gawain*-poet, Minot explores the interiority of his characters. But he reserves this aspect of character construction for those belonging to the enemy side: King Philip, his son John, and to a lesser extent, David Bruce. He uses interiority in the construction of the Other. Hence his regular use of apostrophe; Minot is constantly halting the narrative to address the enemy. After the scene-setting of Poem 1, he shifts into this typical mode in order to begin Poem 2: 'Skottes out of Berwik and of Abirdene, / at the Bannok burn war ye to kene!' Extensively used as the device is, it is nevertheless (like fictional interiority) reserved exclusively for addresses to the enemy. Some of the addresses are to real people: 'Say now sir John of France, . how saltou fare / that both Calays and Gynes . has kindeld thi care?' (11.25–6; *NIMEV* 3899). Some are to imagined individuals:

> Was thou noght, Franceis, with thi wapin
> bitwixen Cressy and Abuyle
> whare thi felaws lien and gapin* *gape*
> for all thaire treget* and thaire gile? *magic*
>
> (7.133–6)

Others are to personifications or imagined collective identities:

> Towrenay, yow has tight* *determined*
> to timber trey and tene*. *to build affliction and sorrow*
> A bore with brenis bright
> es broght opon yowre grene.
>
> (6.1–4)

Also in this mode there are addresses to 'Calays men' and 'Ye men of Saint Omers' (8.1; 11.31).

Like an omniscient author Minot 'knows' his characters: he knows what Philip VI and David Bruce are thinking and what they say to one another; he knows Philip VI's frame of mind at all times. He knows how the denizens of various cities feel. Minot *commends* certain Englishmen – but he does not address them, and certainly does not address Edward III.[43] The lyric ego uses pronouns which never presume to tell Englishmen what to do or feel via apostrophe. Conversely, that ego aligns the reader against those behind the second-person pronouns, the Scots and French. Rather than apostrophising Englishmen, Minot's text constitutes what the community of Englishness is *not* by fixing the opposing discursive position. To read and perhaps even to hear abusive apostrophes of this kind is automatically to be constituted as a subject who is *not* the object of the apostrophe. This imperative address has the effect, by fixing the

'Other' in this way, of securing precisely that 'deep, horizontal comrade-ship' which, in Anderson's phrase, is part of what constitutes a nation.[44] Laurence Minot's poetry is an example of mid-fourteenth-century nation-alism in full-throated cry.

English in the fourteenth century cannot be considered, as Tim William Machan warns, an 'ennobling vernacular'. There is nothing to suggest that Minot wrote with any kind of official sanction, or that he was much read or well regarded. In this respect his self-portrayal as a lone speaker 'droup[yng]' in a 'dale' – like the speaker of the outlaw in the 'Trailbaston' poem – might have had some accuracy about it. Minot's missives to Edward III are far more competent than Adam Davy's address to the previous king, but, acceptable as we might imagine them to be to the monarch, they seem to have passed as unregarded as William of Pagula's complaints about purveyance.

Edward III, as has already been suggested, could easily have had William of Pagula's letters translated for him. No doubt there were those at court who could unravel alliterative verse for him as well. But the nation-loving Minot is unlikely to have been so blinded by patriotic sentiment that it did not occur to him that the medium in which he wrote was hardly the best by which to catch the attention of the king. Minot's 'letters' do not literally address the king. Via apostrophe, they are instead addressed to the enemies on the other side of the border. But before outsiders can be resisted, insiderdom must be created and hence outsiderdom invented.[45] Minot is doing that work, contributing to the construction of the French and Scottish as members of an outgroup. We can see this in his Poem 9 which, lacking conventional stanza linking, instead has the thematic link of the idea of 'Ingland': that place that, suc-cessively invoked, David resolves to ride through (10); Philip encourages him to ride through (17); Philip encourages him to win (22); the 'wirchip' of which the archbishop of York will win (32); that David does not fear (36); that the Scots, with their falsehood, aim to win while Edward is away (62). At the end of the poem, 'Ingland' has resisted all depredations. However limited Minot's own impact, the sense of outsiderdom on which he drew has marked Anglo-French and Anglo-Scottish relations until the present day.

Fourteenth-century England and its populace shared blurred edges with Wales and Scotland; it still had internal divisions between Francophones and Anglophones, south and north. In recent history, as we have seen, determining the Scottishness of the Scots around the border and the Englishness of the English had not always been a straightforward matter.

Even distinguishing Frenchman from Englishman – as has been seen in earlier chapters – was not always simple. On this territory, Minot's poetry imagines a community. It is focused on the monarch but at the same time is resolutely committed to Englishness in the choice of language (which additionally enacts a reconciliation between south and north through its use of both the northern alliterative and southern accentual-syllabic verse traditions). Minot's community is also constituted along national lines through opposition to the foreign Others near at hand. The verses perform that nationalism through the rhetorical technique of apostrophe, which automatically places readers in the privileged subject position, defined against the foreign Others. Minot imagines this community *through* the figure of the monarch, who becomes less a character to be lauded in the poems than an expression of English national destiny. The horizontal comradeship to which Anderson refers is secured by the vertical relations between the monarch and his subjects.

Minot's verse is not the expression of a shared and demonstrable attitude of the mid-fourteenth century, a *Zeitgeist* revealing the growing perception of a national destiny. But that is not the point. Minot was performing, not describing, an attitude. I have mentioned several times that it is now common among historians to see a 'a strident and self-confident Englishness' (in R. R. Davies' words), from the late thirteenth century onwards.[46] And I have suggested that this self-confidence, a little like the bravery of the playground bully, is illusory. Minot's verse, I contend, demonstrates an *emerging* sense of English identity that is fragile rather than strident – so fragile that it had to be constantly demonstrated and reiterated. Nationhood *is* largely illusory and imagined, as Anderson has so influentially argued. By definition, its foundations are shaky and it is consequently demonstrated in defiant and overcompensating aggression against foreign Others.

This is the work, for better or worse, that Laurence Minot was doing as he wrote on the cusp of the revolution in vernacular writing that would occur at the end of Edward III's reign and in that of Richard II. As what we might call a 'high Edwardian' writer, Minot lacks those subtleties, ironies, and psychological insights which classically characterise the Ricardian writers. This means that he can be written off as a non-literary writer, whose verse is merely raw material for historians. Perhaps nobody was ever much interested in Minot's writing, as its survival in a single manuscript suggests. But what his verse does is only a logical development from one of the currents discussed in this book. To various of the political problems posed by the poems considered here, one answer that could be provided was the nation, constantly under threat from the foreigners near at hand. The nation is an embattled place: the Scots stay awake at night 'to dere [injure] all Ingland with thaire dede' and 'to wait [damage] Ingland with sorow and schame', while the French king gathers his counsellors to think of ways in which 'to stroy Ingland and bring to noght' (1.52, 64, 3.48). But it is only through that embattledness that 'we' (the subject of the lyric ego) know what 'our' nation is.

Minot's poetry, then, seems to be evidence of an important shift across the century or so of poetry surveyed in this book. Where, once, clerical voices learnedly discussed a construct called *Anglia*, now a different voice, decidedly non-clerical and, so far as can be made out, from the middle ranks of English society, lauds and upholds England for fellow Englishmen and for a king regarded as straightforwardly English. But rather than developing a teleology out of this apparent shift, we need to recall the limitations of Laurence Minot's construction of nation. As has been seen, Minot counterposes his uniformly positive English characters – such figures as William Bohun, earl of Northampton, William Clinton, earl of Huntingdon, and Edward himself – to their adversaries Philip VI, his son and successor John, and David Bruce, reserving especial scorn for Philip. The vituperative certainty of the difference between foreign and native exhibited by Minot seems to make his the most strident of nationalist voices in the late Middle Ages.

Yet even Minot is not so clear about nation. I stated above that whenever Minot mentions an English noble, it is one of Edward III's 1337 comital creations he refers to, that class of newly English 'new men'. But this is not precisely true. In his list of those on the English side at the Battle of Sluys in Poem 5, Minot includes, between his mention of William Bohun and the duke of Lancaster, 'Sir Walter the Mawnay, God gif him mede, / [he] was bold of body in batayl to bede' (5.39–40). Walter Mauny was a Hainaulter who arrived in England as a page in the retinue of Philippa in 1327. He fought loyally in Edward's campaigns for many years and married a noble Englishwoman. Foreign-born, he nevertheless was, it would seem, another in the category of honorary Englishmen. Minot certainly shows no sign of seeing in Mauny anything other than a figure to be ranked with the English earls, which underlines the capaciousness of his category of nation: it is imagined rather than constrained by the considerations of blood, descent, or birthplace which would have meant Mauny's expulsion from Englishness.

Interestingly, Edward III himself does not seem to have shared quite the same capacious vision: for all the patronage he bestowed on Mauny, there seems never to have been any question that he would be elevated to comital rank, even though he was married, for the last eighteen years of his life, to the countess of Norfolk.[47] The creations of 1337 remained Edward's most extravagant gesture in this regard, and they fit a general pattern through which Edward bolstered the English nobility's sense of its own dignity. While the creations could be seen as a nationalist gesture, the event was also consistent with the consolidation of a caste, which is how Thomas Gray saw it – worrying that these men were not in fact worthy of the highest rank – and perhaps how Edward himself saw it. Finally, the category of 'the nation', even or perhaps particularly among its greatest admirers, is never entirely coherent. Nation must be imagined; it requires endless reiteration and fresh performance in order for its notional stability to be maintained. Even the most enthusiastic supporters of its integrity seem to sense that it is an easily troubled construct, leading them to strident restatement in an endeavour to keep it stable. The cultural traces of this struggle to maintain the useful fiction of nation are what come down to us as writings to the king.

Envoy

How 'writing to the king' might be understood in the late fourteenth century is given a clear statement by one fictional Southwark tavern-keeper. In the *Canterbury Tales,* when the Host turns to the Clerk he asks for a 'murie thyng of aventures', warning him to speak 'pleyn' so that everyone can understand. Obviously fearing the learned Clerk's capacity for rhetoric, Harry advises: 'Youre termes, youre colours, and youre figures, / Keepe hem in stoor til so be ye endite / Heigh style, as whan that men to kynges write.'[1]

Harry Bailly frequently misses the mark on the Canterbury pilgrimage and he does so again here. He forgets or is unaware that the mechanism of petitioning the king which had arisen with parliament by the early fourteenth century was still available.[2] The Clerk himself might well be called upon, in his future life, by an individual or a community to draft a letter to the king: his tale shows that he is already deeply interested in the issue of mediation between ruler and people. But the Clerk would know that 'heigh style' was not a necessary feature of petitionary writing.

As a *literary* strategy, writing to the king could be described as just coming into its own in the Ricardian period, when it was explored by Chaucer, Gower, and various anonymous writers, later succeeded by Hoccleve and Lydgate. At some point around 1400, for example, an unknown author, referring to the return of Henry of Derby to England in 1399, tells how his mind was 'troblid' for fear of strife between Henry and Richard II. Unsure, says the speaker of *Richard the Redeless*, what will happen, he resolves to write to Richard II to instruct him:

> For to written him a writte, to wissen him better,
> And to meuve him of mysserewle, his mynde to reffresshe
> For to preie the prynce that paradise made
> To fullfill him with feith and fortune above,
> And not to grucchen a grott ageine Godis sonde,
> But mekely to suffre what-so him sente were.

And yif him list to loke a leef other tweyne,
That made is to mende him of his myssededis,
And to kepe him in confforte in Crist and nought ellis,
I wolde be gladde that his gost myghte glade be my wordis,
And grame if it greved him, be God that me boughte.
Ther nys no governour on the grounde ne sholde gye him the better … [3]

And so, the writer continues, 'I fondyd with all my fyve wyttis / To traveile on this tretis, to teche men therafter / To be war of wylffulnesse, lest wondris arise' (50–2). At this point the third-person address vanishes from the poem and the speaker begins addressing the king directly, suggesting that if the work should 'happe to youre honde', he should look quickly at it, scanning a hundred lines, 'And if ye savere sumdell [relish some of it], se it forth overe [look over all of it], / For reson is no repreff … (53, 55–6). And furthermore, the speaker recommends that if the king should find fault with it, he should correct it, both through his own wisdom and with the help of the learned (59). Yet as soon as it is offered, this address to the king is withdrawn; for now, the speaker continues, the 'tretis' shall remain private, till 'wyser wittis' (62) have looked at it, as he wants it to be pleasing.

Despite these various evasions and disculpatory strategies, as a piece of 'writing to the king' *Richard the Redeless* goes on to take an aggressively critical approach to the monarch. The poem was, of course, probably addressed primarily to readers other than the king – who might well have been dead or in custody at the time of writing, in which case there was never any risk.[4] The writer could have been masquerading as a fearless critic.[5] Whether or not Richard II was alive to receive it – and whether or not it was ever likely that he would read it – *Richard the Redeless* makes a very full exploration of the possibilities of writing to the king, in which the document itself is offered in a way that proposes an interactive process: the king will read a little to see if he likes it, then he might read more; he will suggest corrections, and meanwhile the author will be letting others have their say on possible improvements.

Such a self-conscious exploration of the motif in this text might suggest that *Writing to the King*, far from ending at 1350, should have begun there, taking Laurence Minot's paean to Edward III as the beginning of a literary phenomenon that saw a fuller realisation in such texts as *Richard the Redeless*, Chaucer's *Complaint to his Empty Purse*, and the more complicated relationships between king and writer established by such a figure as John Lydgate.

By way of response to that imagined possibility, I want to point first to one of the remarkable – and in many ways very welcome – facets of late medieval literary study in recent times: the construction of a coherent period out of the years 1350–1550 and the concomitant erasure of 1485–1500 as a necessary, limiting, boundary. This is visible in a range of major works, including the key literary histories of recent times, one of which justifies its inception date of 1350 by pointing to 'a newly articulate vernacularity' visible in the second half of the fourteenth century.[6] To the extent that it breaks down long-held prejudices about the beginning of the so-called 'Renaissance' – ideas long since abandoned by many historians – this seems a valuable critical move. But, as Nicholas Watson has warned, there is 'an unintended consequence of our current interest in the moment of transition between the medieval and the early modern', in the 'downgrading of work on the 300 years of vernacular writing, Middle English and Anglo-Norman, *before* Chaucer, and its reinscription of the false and multiply exploded view that Chaucer is the place where discussion of English literature can legitimately begin'.

In sympathy with Watson's view, this book has attempted to avoid the diminution of pre-1350 literature by showing that however important a hinge the mid-fourteenth century was, it is nevertheless appropriate to reattach the period *preceding* it to the Ricardian explosion of vernacularity. I agree with Watson when he writes, 'For Middle English scholars … Chaucer and the late fourteenth-century are our inevitable centre of attention, but must be considered the *fulcrum* of our period, not the moment when it gets interesting enough to talk about.'[7]

There is much to work against when venturing back before 1350. Studies of fifteenth-century poetry were for decades if not centuries hampered by a Whiggish notion of literary history which could not fathom the apparent falling-away of poetic technique after Chaucer; it is only recently that criticism has dealt with the apparent abjection of the fifteenth-century writers before Father Chaucer, and the result has been a remarkable revival in the study of Thomas Hoccleve, John Lydgate, and other less well-known fifteenth-century figures.[8] After the rehabilitation of fifteenth-century writing, however, literature before 1350 is perhaps in an even worse position than before: that of being abject without the excuse of a master whose example it can fail to come up to. In the fierce glare of retrospection, the flaws of Robert Mannyng's framed story-collection, *Handlyng Synne*, are thrown into sharp relief by the *Canterbury Tales*; *The Simonie* can seem only an incoherent burst of rage when placed next to Langland's lifelong project, *Piers Plowman*; Robert of Gloucester's Arthurian story, desperately tedious next to the *Alliterative Morte Arthure*; the early English romances, crude when compared with *Sir Gawain and*

the Green Knight. If the early fifteenth century is a time of awkward filiation of childish poets learning to live without their fatherly master, as
Seth Lerer has it, then the early fourteenth century is the even more
embarrassing primal scene of Ricardian writing, from which it is best to
avert the gaze.

It has not been part of my argument to make claims for previously
unconsidered poetic gems in the material I have examined in the period
before 1350. Nevertheless, it seems to me clear that much of the writing
of that period has been downgraded only for failing to live up to the
Ricardian example, while, correspondingly, Ricardian writing is where
it is because it can be taken as the first inklings of modernity – the more
so since the Ricardians have been reconnected, via Thomas Wyatt, to
the Tudor period. At the very least, it is abundantly clear that some of
the anonymous authors whose work I have examined here were interested in English verse and the uses of English for poetry. This was in
many cases clearer to our antiquarian scholarly predecessors than it is
to modern scholars. The poem 'The Execution of Sir Simon Fraser', for
example – in some ways the least poetic of productions – was the object
of frequent interest in the revival of Middle English literature after the
1760s, being printed by Joseph Ritson in his *Ancient Songs* and again by
Thomas Wright. It attracted very little attention in the twentieth century,
however. Despite its place in the most celebrated manuscript of Middle
English lyrics, its bloodthirsty approach to the execution of Fraser and
Wallace was probably enough for it to be put aside as something of an
embarrassment. Yet, like many of the more conventionally lyrical poets
in the manuscript, this poet was clearly interested in verse itself. His frequently effective use of a basic bob-and-wheel feature, for example, anticipates the same device in *Sir Gawain and the Green Knight*. If the verse is
not as skilful as the work of the Gawain-poet, this author was nevertheless someone who had a notion of vernacular poetry as a craft, not simply
as a vehicle for political sentiment.

Laurence Minot is another who was quite evidently interested in verse
forms in English; he was, by early fourteenth-century standards, a poetic
innovator and effective stylist. As Richard Osberg points out, 'Minot is
the only fourteenth-century poet known to us whose poems are com-
fortably composed in both [the alliterative and accentual-syllabic] styles.'
Osberg also favourably compares Minot's use of stanza linking with similar techniques employed by Machaut.[9] This was clearly appreciated by his
numerous readers at the end of the nineteenth century and the beginning of the twentieth. But like the poem on Simon Fraser, Minot's poems

interpellate the reader too powerfully; they offer a sense of belonging in the community they imply and in a context of imperialist war in the early twentieth century, critics for the most part chose to resist the inclusion so aggressively forced on them. The critical turn away from Minot after the First World War is in fact demonstration of the power of this kind of address. Michael Prestwich's condemnation of Minot's work as 'bombastic patriotic poetry … perhaps some of the worst to be produced in that undistinguished genre' is, I think, very wide of the mark.[10] If Minot had brought the same style and verse to poems in praise of daisies we would now be hailing him as the grandfather of English poetry.

Minot and others of the period are indeed precursors of Chaucer and the other Ricardians in ways that are rarely acknowledged. James Simpson, as I have noted, sees the period after 1350 as marked by 'a newly articulate vernacularity'. Robert Meyer-Lee focuses that vernacularity still further; for him, something new happens to the first-person voice in the Ricardian period. There is a fundamental difference between the Chaucerian 'I' and that of pre-Ricardian poetry, he suggests. The 'I' of the English lyric before 1350, for example, is simply Leo Spitzer's 'poetic I' – representative rather than pointing to a historical individual: 'The "I" of most pre-Ricardian lyrics is the common property of a community of singers and listeners.'[11]

The lyric ego or poetic 'I' is certainly much in evidence in lyrics before 1350, as I have shown here. Yet the performances of Laurence Minot and Adam Davy in particular complicate the picture painted by Meyer-Lee. Davy is especially keen to pinpoint his name and his place; Minot is scarcely less so. To the extent that both poets create a space for the lyric ego, they are also each quite obviously concerned with an empirical 'I' as well. Their work, it seems to me, undermines the possibility of a boundary drawn at 1350; they may not have the articulacy of a Chaucer, but they are articulate in the vernacular, nevertheless. They stand near the end of a long and evolving tradition from the 1250s (at the latest) in the course of which verse in English explores the possibilities of both speaking position and the nature of address.

We run the risk of reintroducing the discredited narrative of the 'Triumph of English' by avoiding that phrase while also avoiding anything that does not fit that familiar narrative. What I have aimed to do in *Writing to the King* has not been to discover, yet again, how all that is modern, all that we can recognise, began around the middle of the fourteenth century; I hope instead to have contributed to a fuller sense of the conditions out of which later medieval English literature emerged.

The tail-rhyme poems of Langtoft's chronicle

Table 1: *The Poems*

Poem	Opening line	*NIMEV* No. of ME sections	Robbins's titles, *Manual*	Language	Edition*	Mannyng's translation and other appearances †
1	Dount li rays Eduuard		*Against Balliol*	AN	Wr p. 222; Th 'Rédaction II', lines 647–52	Mannyng, part II, lines 6423–8
2	Pykit him	2754	*Jeering of the Scots at Eduard's Earthworks*	ME	Wr pp. 234–7; Th lines 901–17	Mannyng, 6599–604; Rishanger, p. 373. Brie, *Brut*; Fabyan
3	De nos enemys	2686	*The Messenger's Speech to Balliol*	AN with 6 concluding lines in ME	Wr p. 244 ; Th lines 905–22	Mannyng, 6683–8
4	The fote folk‡	3352	*Diatribe at the Defeat of Scots at Dunbar*	ME	Wr p. 248; Th lines 956–67	Mannyng, 6711–16
5	For Scottes†...	841	*Against the Scots II*	ME	Wr p. 252; Th lines 999–1004	Mannyng, 6735–6; Brie, *Brut*; Fabyan
6	Calays, Yrays...	814	*Admonition to Eduard for Vengeance Against Balliol*	AN with 6 concluding lines ME§	Wr pp. 254–8; Th lines 1036–89	Mannyng, 6765–78

7	Les xii. peres…	310	*Against the Scots III*	AN with 12 concluding lines of ME	Wr pp. 260–4; Th lines 1119–60	Mannyng, 6813–26
8	Ses enemys…		*Merlin's Prophecies Fulfilled in Edward*	AN	Wr pp. 266–8; Th lines 1178–213	
8a	For thar wer thai bal brend‡	848		ME	Wright, *Political Songs*, p. 318, lines 720–8	Only in CUL Gg.I.1
9	Pur finir sa geste…‡	313	*Exultation over the Execution of Wallace*	6 lines AN, 6 ME	Wr p. 364; Th 2363–74	Mannyng, 8063–8

* Wr = Wright, *Langtoft*, vol. II; Th = Jean Claude Thiolier, *Édition Critique et Commentée de Pierre de Langtoft: Le Règne d'Édouard Ier* (Créteil: CELIMA Université de Paris, 1989).

† Mannyng = Idelle Sullens (ed.), *Robert Mannyng of Brunne: The Chronicle*, MRTS 153 (Binghamton, NY: MRTS, 1996); Rishanger = Henry Thomas Riley (ed.), *Willelmi Rishanger, quondam Monachi S. Albani … RS 28.2* (London: Longman, Green, Longman, Roberts and Green, 1865); Robert Fabyan, *Neue Cronycles of Englande and of Fraunce* (London: Pynson, 1516).

‡ These poems do not pick up rhyme of the *laisse*.

§ One manuscript, CUL Gg.I.1, has a further six lines of ME.

Table 2: *The Manuscripts*

MS	Sigla*	Wright's sigla, 1839	Contains poems	Remarks
London, British Library, Cotton Julius A.v	A	C	2, 3, 4, 5, 6, 7, 9	
London, British Library, Royal 20 A.xi	B	R2	2, 3, 4, 5, 6, 7, 9	
London, British Library, Royal 20 A.ii	C	R1	2, 5, 6, 7, 9	Colophon of first section rebukes Langtoft for reducing Wace; MS also contains the 'Lament of Edward II'
London, College of Arms, Arundel LXI	D		2, 4, 5, 6, 7, 9	
London, College of Arms, Arundel XIV	E		2, 4, 5	Contains only Reign of Edward I to April 1307; has Wace in place of *Brut* history
Oxford, Bodleian Library, Fairfax XXIV	F		2, 4, 5	'Rédaction I', closest to Langtoft himself (Thiolier, 'Pierre de Langtoft: Historiographe d'Edouard Ier', p. 383)
Cambridge, University Library, G.I.1	G	Base text	2, 3, 4, 6, 7, 8a	
London, British Library, Harley 114	H		2, 3, 4, 5, 6, 7	
Cambridge, Trinity College 883, olim R.14.7	I			
London, British Library, Harley 202	J			
London, British Library, Lansdowne 227	†			
Oxford, Bodleian Library, Laud Misc. 637	L			

Table 2 *(cont.)*

MS	Sigla*	Wright's sigla, 1839	Contains poems	Remarks
Aylsham, Blickling Hall	N			Damaged; the reign of Edward I after 1290 lost
Oxford, Bodleian Library, Douce 120	O			
Paris, Bibliothèque Nationale, fonds français 12154	P_1 & P_2	2, 3, 4, 5, 6, 7, 9		
London, Phillipps 25970	R			
Oxford, All Souls, 39	S	2, 3, 4, 5		Contains Latin text of Geoffrey instead of *Brut* section
London, British Library, Stow 1047	§			
Cambridge, Sidney Sussex College, 43	U	2, 4, 5, 6, 7		
London, British Library, Cotton Vitellius A.x	V			Contains Wace in place of *Brut* section
New York, Pierpont Morgan Library, MS 930	Y			
Dublin, Black Book of Christ Church	Z			

* MSS A–E were used by Wright in his RS edition; he gave them the sigla still in use (Wright, *Langtoft*, vol. i, pp. xxii–xxv).

† 'Il ne semble pas nécessaire d'attribuer un sigle à un manuscrit qui présente seulement une copie d'un extrait du second livre de la *Chronique*.' Thiolier, 'Pierre de Langtoft: Historiographe d'Edouard Ier', p. 97.

§ Contains extracts from Langtoft copied by Francis Thynne in the 1580s, from MS A.

Table 3: *Manuscripts containing poems, rearranged according to Thiolier's chronology (late copies omitted)*

MS	Historical terminus	Contains poems	Suggested MS date (From Thiolier, *Règne d'Édouard Ier*, pp. 35–141)
S	1295	2, 3, 4, 5	composed by 1303?; written, first third 14thC
P₁ & P₂	1296	2, 3, 4, 5, 6, 7, 9	1296–1307 & third quarter, 14thC
F	Death of Wallace, August 1305	2, 4, 5	Completed 1305–7
H	1307, with 31-line continuation on Edward II	2, 3, 4, 5, 6, 7	1312–40
C	Beginning of reign of Edward II	2, 5, 6, 7, 9	1316–27
E	April 1307	2, 4, 5	1307–20
A	End of reign of Edward I	2, 3, 4, 5, 6, 7, 9	1st quarter, 14thC
B	End of reign of Edward I	2, 3, 4, 5, 6, 7, 9	1327–77: probably first half, 14thC
G	1296	2, 3, 4, 6, 7, 8a	Reign of Edward III
U	Beginning of reign of Edward II	2, 4, 5, 6, 7	Edward III
D	End of reign of Edward I	2, 4, 5, 6, 7, 9	1350–1410?

Notes

PREFACE

1 [Joseph Ritson, (ed.)], *Poems on Interesting Events in the Reign of King Edward III … By Laurence Minot* (London, 1795).

2 Thomas Wright, *Political Songs*; reissued in facsimile, Hildesheim: George Olms Verlagsbuchhandlung, 1968 and as *Thomas Wright's Political Songs of England: From the Reign of John to that of Edward II*, with a new intro. by Peter Coss (Cambridge University Press, 1996).

3 Among major recent works revitalising the study of Lydgate and Hoccleve are Larry Scanlon, *Narrative, Authority, and Power: The Medieval Exemplum and the Chaucerian Tradition* (Cambridge University Press, 1994); Ethan Knapp, *The Bureaucratic Muse: Thomas Hoccleve and the Literature of Late Medieval England* (University Park: Pennsylvania State University Press, 2001); Nicholas Perkins, *Hoccleve's 'Regiment of Princes': Counsel and Constraint* (Cambridge University Press, 2001); Maura Nolan, *John Lydgate and the Making of Public Culture* (Cambridge University Press, 2005); Larry Scanlon and James Simpson (eds.), *John Lydgate: Poetry, Culture, and Lancastrian England* (Notre Dame, Ind.: University of Notre Dame Press, 2006). Also important is James Simpson's discussion of Lydgate in *The Oxford English Literary History, Vol. 2, 1350–1547: Reform and Cultural Revolution* (Oxford University Press, 2002).

4 Note the dates in Simpson's *Oxford English Literary History, Vol. 2, 1350–1547*; cf also Robert J. Meyer-Lee, *Poets and Power from Chaucer to Wyatt* (Cambridge University Press, 2007) and SunHee Kim Gertz, *Chaucer to Shakespeare, 1337–1580* (Basingstoke: Palgrave, 2000).

5 Emily Steiner, *Documentary Culture and the Making of Medieval English Literature* (Cambridge University Press, 2003). Wendy Scase, similarly linking literature and documentary practice, looks back to the earliest days of parliament in *Literature and Complaint in England, 1272–1553* (Oxford University Press, 2007).

INTRODUCTION: WRITING TO THE KING

1 Henry Thomas Riley (ed.), *Johannis de Trokelowe, et Henrici de Blaneforde … Chronica et Annales …* RS 28.3 (London: Longman, Green, Reader and Dyer, 1866), pp. 98–9.

2 J.R. Maddicott, *Thomas of Lancaster 1307–1322: A Study in the Reign of Edward II* (Oxford University Press, 1970), p. 197; Antonia Gransden, *Historical Writing in England, c.1307 to the Early Sixteenth Century* (London: Routledge and Kegan Paul, 1982), p. 7.

3 Tim William Machan, *English in the Middle Ages* (Oxford University Press, 2003), p. 33.

4 Michael Clanchy, *From Memory to Written Record: England 1066–1307*, 2nd edn (Oxford: Blackwell, 1993), p. 51. S. H. Rigby notes that despite the law that said only free men should use seals, even serfs used them on occasion. *English Society in the Later Middle Ages: Class, Status and Gender* (Basingstoke: Macmillan, 1995), p. 29.

5 Michael Clanchy, *England and Its Rulers, 1066–1307*, 3rd edn (Oxford: Blackwell, 2006), p. 132. Nevertheless although it is 'certain', as Patrick Geary states, '[t]hat the nature and quantity of writing changed' in the later eleventh and the twelfth centuries, the assumption of a necessary overall shift from orality to literacy needs to be avoided. Geary argues for 'the early Middle Ages as a period during which writing penetrated deeply into medieval society'. *Phantoms of Remembrance: Memory and Oblivion at the End of the First Millennium* (Princeton University Press, 1994), pp. 13, 14.

6 On the rise of the petition under Edward I, see Paul Brand, 'Petitions and Parliament in the Reign of Edward I', in Linda Clark (ed.), *Parchment and People: Parliament in the Middle Ages*, Parliamentary History special issue (Edinburgh University Press, 2004), pp. 14–38. On its more general development, see J. R. Maddicott, 'Parliament and the Constituencies, 1272–1377', in R. G. Davies and J. H. Denton (eds.), *The English Parliament in the Middle Ages* (Manchester University Press, 1981), pp. 61–87 and G. L. Harriss, 'The Formation of Parliament 1272–1377', in Davies and Denton (eds.), *The English Parliament*, pp. 29–60.

7 On the role of the Eyre's collapse see Alan Harding, 'Plaints and Bills in the History of English Law, Mainly in the Period 1250–1330', in Dafydd Jenkins (ed.), *Legal History Studies 1972: Papers Presented to the Legal History Conference Aberystwyth, 18–21 July 1972* (Cardiff: University of Wales Press, 1975), pp. 65–86, esp. p. 76; and Harriss, 'The Formation of Parliament 1272–1377', p. 34.

8 Maddicott, 'Parliament and the Constituencies', p. 62.

9 Harding, 'Plaints and Bills in the History of English Law', p. 67.

10 It has been widely thought that petitioning waned in popularity with the changing role of parliament from the middle of the fourteenth century. However, Gwilym Dodd argues that it continued, though for various reasons it became obscured from the historian's view. See 'The Hidden Presence: Parliament and the Private Petition in the Fourteenth Century', in Anthony Musson (ed.), *Expectations of the Law in the Middle Ages* (Woodbridge: Boydell, 2001), pp. 135–49, esp. pp. 137–47.

11 Maddicott, 'Parliament and the Constituencies', p. 63.

12 Steven Justice, *Writing and Rebellion: England in 1381* (Berkeley, Calif. and London: University of California Press, 1994), pp. 59, 61.

13 *NIMEV* 4165. I quote from the version in the Auchinleck Manuscript (Edinburgh, National Library of Scotland Advocates MS 19.2.1) edited by James M. Dean in *Medieval English Political Writings*, TEAMS Middle English Texts (Kalamazoo, Mich.: Medieval Institute Publications, 1996), lines 312–14. The poem was also edited by Wright, *Political Songs*, pp. 323–45.

14 W. M. Ormrod, 'Robin Hood and Public Record: The Authority of Writing in the Medieval Outlaw Tradition', in Ruth Evans, Helen Fulton, and David Matthews (eds.), *Medieval Cultural Studies: Essays in Honour of Stephen Knight* (Cardiff: University of Wales Press, 2006), pp. 57–74. See the edition of the poem in Stephen Knight and Thomas H. Ohlgren (eds.), *Robin Hood and Other Outlaw Tales*, TEAMS Middle English Texts (Kalamazoo, Mich.: Medieval Institute Publications, 1997).

15 Ormrod, 'Robin Hood and Public Record', pp. 66–7. The poem is edited in Knight and Ohlgren (eds.), *Robin Hood and Other Outlaw Tales*.

16 'Vulneratur Karitas', in Aspin, *ANPS*, pp. 149–56, lines 13, 9, 1–8. Further references appear parenthetically and give page numbers (where necessary) followed by line numbers; translations of all works in this text are Aspin's own.

17 On the former, a reforming document looking back to the demands made in 1259, see Sir Maurice Powicke, *The Thirteenth Century, 1216–1307* (Oxford: Clarendon Press, 1953), pp. 216–18; on the latter, designed to address problems of public disorder, see Michael Prestwich, *Edward I* (New Haven, Conn. and London: Yale University Press, 1997), pp. 267–82 *passim*.

18 Justice, *Writing and Rebellion*, p. 48; the point is amplified, pp. 188–92. Freedman, *Images of the Medieval Peasant* (Stanford, Calif.: Stanford University Press, 1999), pp. 265, 264. On legal conflict between peasants and landlords see further Rigby, *English Society*, pp. 105–6.

19 Aspin, *ANPS*, pp. 56–66, lines 17–20 (Auchinleck version). See also Wright, *Political Songs*, p. 253. Charters, of course, were *not* written on wax – though it is possible that they were prepared on wax tablets. I am grateful for W. M. Ormrod's explanation (made in personal correspondence) that the wax here refers to the seal on the charter, which synecdochically stands in for – is identified *as* – the charter itself.

20 Aspin, *ANPS*, p. 63, lines 21–4; trans. p. 65.

21 Aspin, *ANPS*, pp. 69–73, lines 25–6. See also Wright, *Political Songs*, pp. 231–6.

22 Emily Steiner, *Documentary Culture and the Making of Medieval English Literature* (Cambridge: Cambridge University Press, 2003), p. 3.

23 Matthew Giancarlo, *Parliament and Literature in Late Medieval England* (Cambridge and New York: Cambridge University Press, 2007), p. 9.

24 See Wendy Scase, *Literature and Complaint in England, 1272–1553* (Oxford University Press, 2007), pp. 8–10.

25 I am thinking here of the way in which the new *Oxford English Literary History* divides the Middle Ages in two either side of 1350; only volume 2, James Simpson's *Reform and Cultural Revolution, 1350–1547* (Oxford University Press, 2002) has so far appeared. But there are many other examples; for a fuller bibliography on this point, see the Envoy, note 6. By way of major contrast, one must note Thorlac Turville-Petre's *England the Nation: Language, Literature, and National Identity, 1290–1340* (Oxford: Clarendon Press, 1996) and Christopher Cannon's *The Grounds of English Literature* (Oxford University Press, 2003): even these books, however, to some extent work to consolidate the divide by closing, respectively, with 1340 and c.1300.

26 Geert de Wilde, 'The Stanza Form of the Middle English *Lament for the Death of Edward I*: A Reconstruction', *Anglia* 123.2 (2005), 230–45 (230).

27 Janet Coleman, *English Literature in History: 1350–1400, Medieval Readers and Writers* (London: Hutchinson, 1981), p. 125. Richard W. Kaeuper sees continuity from as far back as the twelfth century. See *War, Justice, and Public Order: England and France in the Later Middle Ages* (Oxford: Clarendon Press, 1988), p. 325.

28 Brie, *Brut*, p. 249, lines 31–2.

29 Very similar rhymes appear in a late fifteenth-century poem in London, British Library, Harley MS 372 which Wright entitled 'On the Corruption of Public Manners' and which begins: 'Ye prowd galonttes [gallants, men of fashion] hertlesse, / With your hyghe cappis witlesse, / And youre schort gownys thriftlesse, / Have brought this londe in gret hevynesse.' In this poem the link between extravagant fashion and thriftlessness is made explicit. *NIMEV* 4255; see Thomas Wright (ed.), *Political Poems and Songs Relating to English History*, RS 14.2 (London: Longman, Green, Longman and Roberts, 1861), vol. II, p. 251.

30 Brie, *Brut*, p. 249, lines 24–6.

31 On negotiations see E. L. G. Stones, 'The Anglo-Scottish Negotiations of 1327', *Scottish Historical Review* 30 (1951), 49–54, esp. 51. If there is anything in the chronicle's description of the English as being 'alle in cotes & hodes' (line 27), this perhaps makes more sense in February than July.

32 Michel de Certeau, *The Practice of Everyday Life*, trans. Steven Rendall (Berkeley, Calif.: University of California Press, 1984), p. xiv.

33 V. J. Scattergood, *Politics and Poetry in the Fifteenth Century* (London: Blandford, 1971), p. 29.

34 Justice, *Writing and Rebellion*, pp. 28–9.

35 May McKisack, *The Fourteenth Century, 1307–1399* (Oxford: Clarendon Press, 1959), p. 84. It should also be noted that actual graffiti was quite commonplace in the Middle Ages; see V. Pritchard, *English Medieval Graffiti* (Cambridge University Press, 1967); for written material see especially pp. 172–4, 181–3.

36 Certeau, *Practice of Everyday Life*, p. 19.

37 *Thomas Wright's Political Songs of England: From the Reign of John to that of Edward II*, with a new intro. by Peter Coss (Cambridge University Press, 1996), pp. lxv–lxvi.

38 Judith Ferster, *Fictions of Advice: The Literature and Politics of Counsel in Late Medieval England* (Philadelphia, Pa: University of Pennsylvania Press, 1996), p. 36.

39 Aspin, *ANPS*, pp. 93–104, lines 106–7.

40 Scattergood gives some examples (*Politics and Poetry*, p. 21), including that of a Lucas de la Barre, condemned to death for writing anti-royal poems in 1124. He committed suicide before the sentence could be carried out.

41 Certeau, *Practice of Everyday Life*, pp. xiv–xv. 'Discipline' here is avowedly similar to Foucault's understanding of it.

42 *Thomas Wright's Political Songs*, intro. Coss, p. lxv.

43 See G. R. Owst, *Literature and Pulpit in Medieval England: A Neglected Chapter in the History of English Letters & of the English People* (1933; 2nd edn Oxford: Basil Blackwell, 1961), p. 220.

44 J. R. Maddicott, 'Poems of Social Protest in Early Fourteenth-Century England', in W. M. Ormrod (ed.), *England in the Fourteenth Century: Proceedings of the 1985 Harlaxton Symposium* (Woodbridge: Boydell, 1986), pp. 130–44 (pp. 135–6); *Thomas Wright's Political Songs*, intro. Coss, p. lxvi.

45 Stephen Knight, 'The Voice of Labour in Fourteenth-Century English Literature', in James Bothwell, P. J. P. Goldberg and W. M. Ormrod (eds.), *The Problem of Labour in Fourteenth-Century England* (Woodbridge: York Medieval Press in association with Boydell & Brewer, 2000), pp. 101–22 (p. 102).

46 Knight, 'Voice of Labour', pp. 107, 115–16, 117.

47 Leo Spitzer, 'Note on the Poetic and Empirical "I" in Medieval Authors', *Traditio* 4 (1946), 414–22.

48 Judson Boyce Allen, 'Grammar, Poetic Form, and the Lyric Ego: A Medieval *A Priori*', in Lois Ebin (ed.), *Vernacular Poetics in the Middle Ages* (Kalamazoo, Mich.: Medieval Institute Publications, 1984), pp. 199–226 (p. 208).

49 Justice, *Writing and Rebellion*, p. 38.

50 George Kane, 'Some Fourteenth-Century "Political" Poems', in Gregory Kratzmann and James Simpson (eds.), *Medieval English Religious and Ethical Literature: Essays in Honour of G. H. Russell* (Cambridge: D.S. Brewer, 1986), pp. 82–91 (p. 91). Kane was objecting, among others, to Rossell Hope Robbins, 'Middle English Poems of Protest', *Anglia* 78 (1960), 193–203. I will deal with this objection more fully in chapter 4.

51 Aspin, *ANPS*, p. 69, line 4. On the 'inherent potential for conflict' in medieval English 'class relations', see Rigby, *English Society*, Chapter 3 (esp. p. 109).

52 Certeau, *Practice of Everyday Life*, p. xix.

53 Maddicott, 'Poems of Social Protest', p. 131.

54 Bruce Dickins and R. M. Wilson (eds.), *Early Middle English Texts* (London: Bowes & Bowes, 1951), pp. 8–9.

55 By, respectively, R.G. Latham and Joseph Ritson; see the various opinions reprinted in David Matthews, *The Invention of Middle English: An Anthology of Sources* (Turnhout: Brepols, 2000), pp. 24, 27, 106.

56 Dickins and Wilson, *Early Middle English Texts*, p. 7. Clanchy notes that there is 'No satisfactory contemporary explanation given for issuing these letters in languages other than Latin', but suggests that as the letters are specifically critical of sheriffs and other officials, it was perhaps the case that those same officials were not to be trusted to promulgate the documents – hence the added clarity given to them by production in English. *Memory to Written Record*, p. 221.

57 Clanchy, *Memory to Written Record*, p. 222.

58 Turville-Petre, *England the Nation*, p. 9.

59 See William Stubbs, *Select Charters and Other Illustrations of English Constitutional History*, 8th edn (Oxford: Clarendon Press, 1905), p. 485.

60 Machan, *English in the Middle Ages*, pp. 24, 27.

61 *Ibid.*, p. 38.

62 *Ibid.*, p. 57.

63 *Ibid.*, pp. 61–2, 63.

64 *Ibid.*, pp. 64, 63, 33.

65 *Ibid.*, p. 21.

66 W.A. Wright, *Robert of Gloucester*, vol. I, lines 7538–47. Other such reflections on the vernacular have been gathered in an essential anthology: Jocelyn Wogan-Browne, Nicholas Watson, Andrew Taylor and Ruth Evans (eds.), *The Idea of the Vernacular: An Anthology of Middle English Literary Theory, 1280–1520* (University Park: Pennsylvania State University Press, 1999).

67 Christopher Cannon remarks of this passage, 'Since Robert's own "englissh" draws copiously from Latin and Anglo-Norman, his *Chronicle* belies its own claims, but, particularly in that conflict, these lines provide important witness to the durability of a powerful *idea* about language.' *The Making of Chaucer's English: A Study of Words* (Cambridge University Press, 1998), pp. 141–2. Laura Ashe, arguing for the consolidation of Englishness in the twelfth century, when French was still culturally in the ascendant, notes that 'Englishness expressed … itself in French, and did so apparently unselfconsciously'. *Fiction and History in England, 1066–1200* (Cambridge University Press, 2007), p. 9.

68 Anthony D. Smith, *National Identity* (London: Penguin, 1991), p. 14; emphasis in original.

69 Benedict Anderson, *Imagined Communities: Reflections on the Origins and Spread of Nationalism* (1983; rev. edn, London and New York: Verso, 1991), pp. 6–7.

70 Hans Kohn, 'The Modernity of Nationalism', from *The Idea of Nationalism: A Study of its Origins and Background* (New York: Macmillan, 1944), rpt. in C. Leon Tipton (ed.), *Nationalism in the Middle Ages* (New York: Holt, Rinehart and Winston, 1972), pp. 7–13 (p. 7).

71 Kathleen Davis, 'National Writing in the Ninth Century: A Reminder for Postcolonial Thinking about the Nation', *Journal of Medieval and Early Modern Studies* 28 (1998), 611–37 (613).

72 Boyd C. Shafer, *Nationalism: Myth and Reality* (London: Victor Gollancz, 1955), p. 60.

73 Barnaby C. Keeney, 'Military Service and the Development of Nationalism in England, 1272–1327', *Speculum* 22 (1947), 534–49; excerpted in Tipton, *Nationalism in the Middle Ages*, as 'England' pp. 87–97 (pp. 88, 96).

74 Johan Huizinga, 'Patriotism and Nationalism in European History', in *Men and Ideas: History, the Middle Ages, the Renaissance*, trans. James S. Holmes and Hans van Marle (London: Eyre & Spottiswoode, 1960), pp. 97–155 (p. 117).

75 Marc Bloch, *Feudal Society*, trans. L. A. Manyon (London: Routledge and Kegan Paul, 1961), pp. 432–7; rpt. in Tipton, *Nationalism in the Middle Ages*, as 'Medieval National Consciousness', pp. 25–9.

76 Ernst H. Kantorowicz, *The King's Two Bodies: A Study in Mediaeval Political Theology* (Princeton University Press, 1957), p. 250; see also p. 268. Gaines Post, 'Two Notes on Nationalism in the Middle Ages', *Traditio* 9 (1953), 281–320. On the relation (and differences) between medieval states and nations, see further Hagen Schulze, *States, Nations and Nationalism: From the Middle Ages to the Present*, trans. William E. Yuill (Oxford: Blackwell, 1996), esp. Chapters 1, 5.

77 Adrian Hastings, *The Construction of Nationhood: Ethnicity, Religion and Nationalism* (Cambridge University Press, 1997), argues that medieval England is a special case in Europe; it 'presents the prototype of both a nation and a nation-state in the fullest sense' (p. 4). See also John Gillingham, *The English in the Twelfth Century: Imperialism, National Identity, and Political Values* (Woodbridge: Boydell, 2000).

78 Turville-Petre, *England the Nation*, p. v.

79 Susan Reynolds, *Kingdoms and Communities in Western Europe, 900–1300*, 2nd edn (Oxford: Clarendon Press, 1997), p. 253. The flexibility that makes Anderson useful for medievalists has also been remarked by Patricia Clare Ingham, *Sovereign Fantasies: Arthurian Romance and the Making of Britain* (Philadelphia, Pa: University of Pennsylvania Press, 2001), p. 8.

80 A recent cogent critique of precisely this possibility (albeit in relation to imagined nation formation in the *early* Middle Ages) is Patrick J. Geary, *The Myth of Nations: The Medieval Origins of Europe* (Princeton University Press, 2002).

81 Kathy Lavezzo (ed.), *Imagining a Medieval English Nation* (Minneapolis, Minn.: University of Minnesota Press, 2003), p. xiv. In a related statement, Patricia Ingham warns against the tracing of 'a teleological trajectory from early origins to a fully realized national present' when examining instances of medieval nationalism. *Sovereign Fantasies*, p. 9. For a similar caution, see David Wallace, *Premodern Places: Calais to Surinam, Chaucer to Aphra Behn* (Oxford University Press, 2004), p. 10.

82 Powicke, *Thirteenth Century* p. 30.

83 Prestwich and Clanchy also take national identity as a given in the period. Clanchy is careful to stress that 'like all generalized opinions about national

character', ideas about the English 'were no more than prejudice constantly repeated'. Nevertheless, he adds, 'The identity of England … became clearer in the thirteenth century in more precise ways.' *England and Its Rulers*, p. 234. See also Michael Prestwich, *Plantagenet England 1225–1360*, New Oxford History of England (Oxford University Press, 2005), p. 554.

84 R. R. Davies, *The First English Empire: Power and Identities in the British Isles 1093–1343* (Oxford University Press, 2000), pp. 20, 80.

85 It must be said that Davies does note that 'England, like most other countries, was defined in part by otherness'. *The First English Empire*, p. 196. As Clanchy suggests, 'National sentiment is often voiced under stress, when the group is threatened by a powerful neighbour or torn by civil war.' *England and Its Rulers*, p. 229.

86 Clanchy, *Memory to Written Record*, p. 221.

87 Machan, *English in the Middle Ages*, pp. 63–4.

88 *MED* folk (n) 1a(a).

89 On willing peasant involvement in the politics of the time, see D. A. Carpenter, 'English Peasants in Politics, 1258–1267', *The Reign of Henry III* (London and Rio Grande, Oh.: Hambledon, 1996), pp. 309–48. Carpenter proposes 'that ideas about the community of the realm had percolated down to the level of the village' and that 'the peasantry belonged to the community of the realm of thirteenth-century England' (pp. 309, 310).

1 DEFENDING *ANGLIA*

1 W.A. Wright, *Robert of Gloucester*, vol. ii, lines 11748–49 (*NIMEV* 727); further references by line number parenthetically in the text. The distance is more like twenty miles, but I reproduce the chronicler's own reckoning. Despite the self-naming, it is usually assumed that the chronicle had at least two authors. The person who names himself as Robert is thought to have been a monk of St Peter's at Gloucester, but could have been a secular clerk. Gransden suggests that the flattering portrait of Sir Warin Bassingbourne in the account of Henry's reign might indicate a relationship with that knight; Kennedy notes a relative lack of interest in monastic affairs. The account of Henry III's reign and the Barons' Wars in particular has some independent historical value. See Antonia Gransden, *Historical Writing in England, c.550 to c.1307* (London: Routledge & Kegan Paul, 1974), pp. 432–7; Edward Donald Kennedy, 'Gloucester, Robert of (fl. c.1260–c.1300)', *ODNB*, www.oxforddnb.com/view/article/23736, accessed 11 April 2008. When referring to the sections on Henry III's reign, I will assume the authorship of Robert, while using the term 'Gloucester Chronicle' for its other sections.

2 Thorlac Turville-Petre, *England the Nation: Language, Literature, and National Identity, 1290–1340* (Oxford: Clarendon Press, 1996), p. 15.

3 Geoffrey of Monmouth, *The History of the Kings of Britain*, trans. Lewis Thorpe (London: Penguin, 1966), p. 53. See also *The Historia Regum Britannie of Geoffrey of Monmouth I: Bern, Burgerbibliothek, MS. 568*, ed. Neil Wright

(Cambridge: D.S. Brewer, 1985), p. 2. Henry, Archdeacon of Huntingdon, *Historia Anglorum: The History of the English People*, ed. and trans. Diana Greenway (Oxford: Clarendon Press, 1996), pp. 12, 13. For a detailed account of Robert of Gloucester's sources see W.A. Wright, *Robert of Gloucester*, vol. I, pp. xiv–xxxii.

4 The story, at lines 354–469, is paraphrased from Geoffrey, who refers to Gascony as Aquitania.

5 *History of the Kings of Britain*, trans. Thorpe, p. 69; Latin supplied from *Historia Regum Britannie*, ed. Wright, p. 12.

6 *MED* comeling (n.) 1a).

7 See for example Patricia Clare Ingham, *Sovereign Fantasies: Arthurian Romance and the Making of Britain* (Philadephia, Pa.: University of Pennsylvania Press, 2001), pp. 31–50; Michelle R. Warren, *History on the Edge: Excalibur and the Borders of Britain, 1100–1300* (Minneapolis, Minn.: University of Minnesota Press, 2000), Chapter 2; Jeffrey Jerome Cohen, *Of Giants: Sex, Monsters, and the Middle Ages* (Minneapolis, Minn.: University of Minnesota Press, 1999), pp. 31–7.

8 M. T. Clanchy, *England and Its Rulers: 1066–1307*, 3rd edn (Oxford: Blackwell, 2006), p. 228.

9 Claire Valente, *The Theory and Practice of Revolt in Medieval England* (Aldershot: Ashgate, 2003), p. 66.

10 See Huw Ridgeway, 'King Henry III and the "Aliens", 1236–1272', *Thirteenth Century England* 2 (1987), 81–92. For a summary, see Michael Prestwich, *Plantagenet England 1225–1360*, New Oxford History of England (Oxford University Press, 2005), pp. 93–8.

11 See D. A. Carpenter, 'King Henry III's "statute" against Aliens: July 1263', *The Reign of Henry III* (London and Rio Grande, Oh.: Hambledon, 1996), pp. 261–80.

12 Henry Richards Luard (ed.), *Matthaei Parisiensis, Monachi Sancti Albani, Chronica Majora*, 7 vols. RS 57 (London: Longman & Co, Trübner & Co., 1872–83), vol. III (1876), p. 227. Matthew followed Roger of Wendover's work up to 1235, taking over, Gransden notes, Roger's 'hostility to king and pope' (*Historical Writing*, p. 368). On the events see further D. A. Carpenter, 'The Fall of Hubert de Burgh', *The Reign of Henry III*, pp. 45–60 and on Matthew Paris himself see also Carpenter, 'Matthew Paris and Henry III's Speech at the Exchequer in October 1256', *The Reign of Henry III*, pp. 137–50.

13 J. R. Maddicott, *Simon de Montfort* (Cambridge University Press, 1994), p. 21; N. Denholm-Young, *Richard of Cornwall* (Oxford: Basil Blackwell, 1947), pp. 35–6.

14 Luard (ed.), *Chronica Majora*, vol. III, pp. 477–8. As the vineyard image is from Psalms 79.13, it is difficult not to suspect some ventriloquism of Richard by Matthew here.

15 *Ibid.*, p. 622, see also n.22.

16 *Ibid.*, p. 630. For discussion, further examples, and Matthew's later toning down of some of his comments in the *Chronica Majora*, see Gransden, *Historical Writing*, pp. 369–70.

17 Sir Maurice Powicke, *The Thirteenth Century, 1216–1307* (Oxford: Clarendon Press, 1953), p. 163. For more detailed description of events, see Maddicott, *Simon de Montfort*, pp. 192–215.

18 See Maddicott, *Simon de Montfort*, pp. 256–8; Powicke, *Thirteenth Century*, pp. 182–3.

19 On the battle see D. A. Carpenter, *The Battles of Lewes and Evesham, 1264/65* (Keele: Mercia, 1987), pp. 22–34.

20 Maddicott, 'Poems of Social Protest in Early Fourteenth-Century England', in W. M. Ormrod (ed.), *England in the Fourteenth Century: Proceedings of the 1985 Harlaxton Symposium* (Woodbridge: Boydell, 1986), pp. 130–44 (p. 131).

21 John Scattergood, 'Authority and Resistance: The Political Verse', in Susanna Fein (ed.), *Studies in the Harley Manuscript: The Scribes, Contents, and Social Contexts of British Library MS Harley 2253* (Kalamazoo, Mich.: Medieval Institute Publications, 2000), pp. 163–201 (p. 182).

22 The principal source is the Melrose Chronicle; see Denholm-Young, *Richard of Cornwall*, p. 175.

23 Wright, *Political Songs*, pp. 63–8; Paris, Bibliothèque Nationale, MS fr. 837.

24 Wright, *Political Songs*, p. 69; *NIMEV* 3155; also edited in Bruce Dickins and R. M. Wilson (eds.), *Early Middle English Texts* (London: Bowes & Bowes, 1951), pp. 10–12. *Trichard* is a relatively rare word in Middle English. Dickins and Wilson gloss it as 'trickster', but *MED* gives 'One who engages in treachery or deceit' (*MED* trechard (*n*.)). The primary meaning at this time seems to be 'deceiver' rather than 'traitor'; the words *traitor*, *treachery*, and *treason* would converge later, in the fourteenth century. See Richard Firth Green, *A Crisis of Truth: Literature and Law in Ricardian England* (Philadelphia, Pa.: University of Pennsylvania, 1999), pp. 206–21. T. W. E. Roche, improbably and without giving a source, has the Montfortians chanting the poem's refrain at Richard in the windmill, shortly after mocking him as a *molendinarius*. *The King of Almayne* (London: John Murray, 1966), p. 184.

25 On Bigod see Maddicott, *Simon de Montfort*, pp. 216, 221, 244, 248; on Warenne see *ODNB*.

26 Wright, *Political Songs*, p. 71; cf Dickins and Wilson's edition in *Early Middle English Texts*, lines 38–46.

27 Hilmar Sperber, *Historisch-politische Gedichte im England Edwards I* (Heidelberg: Carl Winter Universitätsverlag, 1985), p. 87.

28 Denholm-Young, *Richard of Cornwall*, p. 175.

29 Carpenter notes that Montfort did not, like other foreigners, come to England landless. He states that 'Englishmen simply accepted the paradox', and that Montfort was 'an honorary Englishman'. Matthew Paris, Carpenter points out, at one point describes Simon as *naturalis*. 'King Henry III's "statute"', pp. 274–5; see Luard (ed.), *Chronica Majora*, vol. v (1880), p. 289. *Naturalis*, as Clanchy suggests, commenting on its use by Roger of Wendover, is used rather than *nativus* because of the peasant implications of the latter word; *naturalis* has the advantage of meaning both 'true-born' and

'natural'. *England and Its Rulers*, pp. 228–9. Turville-Petre, noting Robert of Gloucester's approbation for de Montfort, recalls the comparable example of the Norman Thomas à Becket and states that 'these contradictions in Robert of Gloucester's concept of the nation are never resolved'. *England the Nation*, p. 100.

30 It 'consist[s] of 968 lines of Goliardic couplets with internal rhyme. … its author … was probably a member of Simon's household'. A. G. Rigg, *A History of Anglo-Latin Literature 1066–1422* (Cambridge University Press, 1992), p. 199.

31 Valente, *Theory and Practice of Revolt*, p. 19.

32 C. L. Kingsford (ed. and trans.), *The Song of Lewes* (Oxford: Clarendon Press, 1890), line 8. Quotations and translations (in some places slightly modified) are from this edition; further references by line number parenthetically in the text. Scattergood notes the early reference to the poet's pen and sees the poem as 'highly learned' and 'literary'. 'Authority and Resistance', p. 182.

33 Kingsford thought *Policraticus* the most likely source (p. xxiv). Cary J. Nederman argues that *Lewes* 'clearly repeats ideas found in the Bractonian *De legibus et consuetudinibus Angliae* or some other legal text derived therefrom, but it turns those doctrines into the basis for justification of de Montfort's revolt against the crown'. *Political Thought in Early Fourteenth-Century England: Treatises by Walter of Milemete, William of Pagula, and William of Ockham* (Turnhout: Arizona Center for Medieval and Renaissance Studies in association with Brepols, 2002), p. 5.

34 George E. Woodbine (ed.), *De legibus et consuetudinibus Angliae*, 4 vols. (New Haven, Conn.: Yale University Press, 1915–42), vol. II, p. 33; Samuel E. Thorne (trans.), *Bracton on the Laws and Customs of England*, 3 vols. (Cambridge: Belknap Press in association with the Selden Society, 1968–77); both quoted from *Bracton Online*, http://hlsl5.law.harvard.edu/bracton/, accessed 11 April 2008. See further on Bracton and kingship Ernst H. Kantorowicz, *The King's Two Bodies: A Study in Mediaeval Political Theology* (Princeton University Press, 1957), pp. 143–92. The poet's use of Bracton is, of course, highly partial. Kantorowicz explores the paradoxes that emerge from Bracton's concept of a king both above and below the law, noting that 'The king is bound to the Law that makes him king; but the Law that made him king enhances also his royal power and bestows upon the ruler extraordinary rights which in many respects placed the king, legally, above the laws' (150). The first extant coronation oath, that of Edward II, requires the king to swear to uphold the laws and customs of the land. See Robert S. Hoyt, 'The Coronation Oath of 1308', *EHR* 71.280 (Jul., 1956), 353–83 (356).

35 Nederman, *Political Thought*, p. 10.

36 Giorgio Agamben, *Homo Sacer: Sovereign Power and Bare Life*, trans. Daniel Heller-Roazen (Stanford University Press, 1998), p. 15.

37 Valente, *Theory and Practice of Revolt*, p. 90.

38 On the development of the sense of 'community of the realm' towards 'the Commons' see Prestwich, *Plantagenet England*, pp. 183, 186–7, 205–6.

39 This property qualification exempts Montfort himself from the charge of being a foreign adventurer, as he did not arrive without land. See note 29 above.

40 Turville-Petre, *England the Nation*, p. 6.

41 The chronicle and poem are found in London, British Library, Cotton MS Claudius D.vi, fol. 101ᵛ, a-b. See James Orchard Halliwell (ed.), *The Chronicle of William de Rishanger, of the Barons' Wars; The Miracles of Simon de Montfort* (London: Camden Society, 1840), pp. 18–20. Translation (modified) from Wright, *Political Songs*, p. 121. Further references given parenthetically will be by page number to the edition of Halliwell and the translation by Wright.

42 Clanchy notes 'that the idea of "England" as a cause to fight for was familiar to thirteenth-century writers'. *England and Its Rulers*, p. 230. On the idea of fighting *pro patria* in the Middle Ages more broadly, see further Gaines Post, 'Two Notes on Nationalism in the Middle Ages', *Traditio* 9 (1953), 281–320, esp. 295.

43 Wright, *Political Songs*, p. 69.

44 Wright, *Political Songs*, p. 70. Cf. Dickins and Wilson (eds.), *Early Middle English Texts*, p. 10, lines 29, 33. They read 'top' for Wright's 'cop', with the same sense: *head*.

45 See Denholm-Young, *Richard of Cornwall*, who believes (following Rishanger) that Richard refused the offer through 'pride and his thirst for revenge' (p. 128). Sperber argues that by proposing that Richard actually *asked* for the money, the poet deliberately twists the detail to put Richard in the worst possible light. *Historisch-politische Gedichte*, p. 92.

46 Tim William Machan, *English in the Middle Ages* (Oxford University Press, 2003), p. 38.

47 Maddicott, *Simon de Montfort*, pp. 312, 329.

48 Carpenter, *Battles of Lewes and Evesham*, Chapter 7; Maddicott, *Simon de Montfort*, pp. 340–42.

49 Powicke, *Thirteenth Century*, p. 179.

50 Valente, *Theory and Practice of Revolt*, p. 12.

51 Maddicott, *Simon de Montfort*, p. 342.

52 Rigg, *History of Anglo-Latin Literature*, p. 203. The full poem is printed in Halliwell (ed.), *Chronicle of Rishanger*, pp. 139–46.

53 Valente, *Theory and Practice of Revolt*, pp. 35–6.

54 Olivier de Laborderie, J. R. Maddicott and D. A. Carpenter, 'The Last Hours of Simon de Montfort: A New Account', *EHR* 115.461 (2000), 378–412 (403 and appendix, 407–12).

55 Katherine Royer, 'The Body in Parts: Reading the Execution Ritual in Late Medieval England', *Historical Reflections* 29.2 (2003), 313–39 (323, 325). I am grateful to Catherine Batt for bringing this to my attention. Royer's general point may stand, but the dismemberment of *noble* adversaries was far from the norm at the time. The case of Montfort is quite different from those of the Scots Simon Fraser and William Wallace, discussed in chapter 2. On the basis of the recently discovered account of the battle, D. A. Carpenter notes that 'the killing of Montfort was not the result of some rush of blood to the head during the battle. Rather it was coolly conceived at a

council of war beforehand. Edward and his allies wanted Montfort dead. With no precedent in England for the execution of magnates accused of political crimes, murder on the battlefield was the only way of getting rid of him' (Laborderie, Maddicott and Carpenter, 'The Last Hours of Simon de Montfort', 403). However, the wording of the actual account does not specify this legal motive over either revenge or a more straightforward desire to end the conflict in the most decisive way.

56 Aspin, *ANPS*, p. 30, lines 91–3; translation p. 33. See also Wright, *Political Songs*, pp. 125–7. Aspin plausibly dates the poem to c.1267–8, and the period after the settlement made with the former rebels at the parliament of Marlborough late in 1267. Further references by line number parenthetically in the text.
57 Halliwell (ed.), *Chronicle of Rishanger*, p. 109.
58 The first is edited in George Walter Prothero, *The Life of Simon de Montfort* (London: Longmans, Green, 1877), pp. 388–91 (p. 391), from Cambridge, University Library MS Kk.4.20; the second by Frederic Maitland in 'A Song on the Death of Simon de Montfort', in H. A. L. Fisher (ed.), *The Collected Papers of Frederic William Maitland*, 3 vols. (Cambridge University Press, 1911), vol. III, pp. 43–9 (quotation at stanza 6).
59 Maitland, 'Death of Simon de Montfort', p. 45.
60 Powicke, *Thirteenth Century*, pp. 223, 225.
61 Michael Prestwich, *Edward I* (New Haven, Conn. and London: Yale University Press, 1997), p. 89.
62 'The Praise of the Young Edward', London, British Library, Cotton MS Vespasian B.xiii, fol. 130vº. See Wright, *Political Songs*, pp. 128–32 (p. 128).
63 Prestwich, *Plantagenet England*, p. 96.

2 ATTACKING SCOTLAND

1 G. L. Brook and R. F. Leslie (eds.), *Laȝamon: Brut*, 2 vols., EETS o.s. 250, 277 (Oxford University Press for the EETS, 1963, 1978), vol. II (1978), line 12447 (Otho text).
2 For the classic statement of Edward's personal interest, see R. S. Loomis, 'Edward I, Arthurian Enthusiast', *Speculum* 28 (1953), 114–27; by contrast Michael Prestwich argues that although '[t]he Arthurian myth was undoubt-edly of interest to Edward … it was not a dominating influence' and that Edward's self-construction in Arthurian terms 'was probably no more than a conceit he toyed with occasionally'. *Edward I* (New Haven, Conn. and London: Yale University Press, 1997), pp. 121, 122. But see also R. R. Davies, *The First English Empire: Power and Identities in the British Isles 1093–1343* (Oxford University Press, 2000), pp. 31–2, for Edward's practical uses of Arthurian symbol and the suggestion that he may not have been 'immune from such excitement' (p. 32).
3 Robert Mannyng, translating Langtoft in the 1330s, significantly altered this passage because he found it to be untrue. Wright, *Langtoft*, vol. II, p. 266,

line 3; see also Jean Claude Thiolier, *Édition Critique et Commentée de Pierre de Langtoft: Le Règne d'Édouard Ier* (Créteil: CELIMA Université de Paris, 1989), p. 372, line 1174. Further references to this chronicle will be made parenthetically to the second volume (unless otherwise indicated) of Wright's Rolls Series edition by page and line number; the second reference in each parenthesis will be by line numbers to the corresponding passage in Thiolier's edition of the so-called 'Rédaction II'. Translations are Wright's, but modified in places.

4 W.A. Wright, *Robert of Gloucester*, vol. I, lines 4038, 4040, 4041–2.

5 The exception is Langtoft, though perhaps only for reasons of compression. Arthur's speech consists in his version of just seven lines which say nothing of Julius Caesar and conclude: 'Rome dait estre nostre … / Belynus, noster auncestre, la conquist par espeye' (Wright, *Langtoft*, vol. I, p. 178, lines 24–5).

6 Peculiarly, some versions of the 'Gloucester Chronicle' – including the best known, the version in MS Cotton Caligula A.xi edited by W.A. Wright – do not actually tell the story of Belinus and Brennius and their conquest of Rome on which Arthur's words depend. Instead they pack into a single line a mention of many kings 'of wan we mote be stille' (904), so that when Arthur comes to draw on it as part of his authorisation, the Belin story is not one that the audience has actually heard. Readers might have known – and perhaps it was assumed they knew – the story from another source, such as Wace or Geoffrey himself. This in turn would mean that the authors of the chronicle assumed that readers knew more than English: though that seems strange in view of the Englishness of this chronicle and its implication that it is written for those 'lowe men' who 'holdeþ to engliss · & to hor owe speche ȝute ·' (7547). The Belinus–Brennius story *does*, however, appear at some length in what Wright identified as the chronicle's later recension, where the redactor not only makes it clear that 'þos kinges of þis lond · furst ywonne Rome / Longe er Iulius þe emperour · euere wonne þis lond' but also, as if setting up the later speech by Arthur, that 'oþere of þis lond seþþe · hadd rome on hond / Whar þoru rome auȝte bet · abowe to þis londe / Þan þis lond to Rome · wiþ riȝte ich vnderstonde' (vol. II, appendix G; p. 798, lines 252–6). Here, there seems at least to be a logic concerning who got his conquering in first.

7 For the manuscripts of Langtoft's chronicle, see the appendix. Sigla used in this chapter are those listed in table 2.

8 Idelle Sullens (ed.), *Robert Mannyng of Brunne: The Chronicle*, MRTS 153 (Binghamton, NY: MRTS, 1996); Caroline D. Eckhardt (ed.), *Castleford's Chronicle or The Boke of Brut*, 2 vols., EETS 305, 306 (Oxford University Press for the EETS, 1996); Ewald Zettl (ed.), *An Anonymous Short English Metrical Chronicle*, EETS o.s. 196 (Oxford University Press, 1935); Brie, *Brut*. See further, on these chronicles as revealing 'the existence of an "English" historical self-consciousness in the late thirteenth and early fourteenth century, a racial self-consciousness that was on [the] brink of being subsumed into a larger national identity', Douglas Moffat, 'Sin, Conquest, Servitude: English Self-Image in the Chronicles of the Early Fourteenth Century', in Allen J.

Frantzen and Douglas Moffat (eds.), *The Work of Work: Servitude, Slavery, and Labor in Medieval England* (Glasgow: Cruithne Press, 1994), pp. 148–68 (p. 160); see also Thorlac Turville-Petre, 'The "Nation" in English Writings of the Early Fourteenth Century', in N. Rogers (ed.), *England in the Fourteenth Century* (Stamford: Paul Watkins, 1993), pp. 128–39.

9 Davies, *The First English Empire*, p. 34.

10 On the Great Cause see E. L. G. Stones and Grant G. Simpson, *Edward I and the Throne of Scotland, 1290–1296*, 2 vols. (Oxford University Press, 1978).

11 Prestwich, *Edward I*, p. 366; see chapter 14 for a general account of the Great Cause.

12 See on this chapter 6, 'The Appeal to History in the Great Cause', Stones and Simpson, *Edward I and the Throne of Scotland*, vol. 1. 'For all that we know, the royal clerks may have spent some weeks working at chronicles, and searching the archives [in Westminster], before they thought of casting their net more widely, and writing to monasteries' (p. 141). See also Antonia Gransden, 'Propaganda in English Medieval Historiography', *Journal of Medieval History* 1 (1975); 363–82 (367).

13 Davies, *The First English Empire*, p. 27.

14 In one manuscript, Cambridge, University Library MS G.I.1, there is an extra verse of nine lines, as well as an extra stanza of six lines given to one poem.

15 Thea Summerfield, 'The Political Songs in the *Chronicles* of Pierre de Langtoft and Robert Mannyng', in Evelyn Mullally and John Thompson (eds.), *The Court and Cultural Diversity* (Woodbridge: D.S. Brewer, 1997), pp. 139–48 (p. 141).

16 The line referring to the 'fosse' does not appear in Wright's base text but is supplied from other manuscripts. It makes sense as the obvious referent of the opening lines of the song that follows.

17 *NIMEV* 2754. I omit six lines inserted by Wright from Mannyng's version which appear in none of the Langtoft manuscripts.

18 It is noteworthy that the Prose *Brut* – which at this point is based on Langtoft – certainly read the lines this way; words about Edward's piking and ditching are given to the Scots, and it is as a result of their mockery that Edward is driven to take the town. Brie, *Brut*, p. 189.

19 This is true in the three manuscripts used in Thiolier's edition, for example; see *Règne d'Édouard Ier*, p. 290, line 908; p. 291, line 812.

20 Does this consist of what were, in fact, originally two different poems – one actually a memory of Scottish abuse, the second half composed in England in response? The fact that Mannyng – or someone between Langtoft and Mannyng – was able effortlessly to insert six more lines suggests the adaptability of this kind of verse. Once again the treatment by the Prose *Brut* compilers is interesting; a six-line stanza, very similar to Langtoft's 'Skaterd be the Scottes' stanza, is treated as a free-standing poem in the *Brut*. Brie, *Brut*, p. 191.

21 The exact personnel vary in different manuscripts. Prestwich, *Edward I*, p. 471, gives these three names.

22 'Although it is impossible to know whether, in recitation, the continuation of the mono-rhyme was as effective as it looks on paper, there can be little doubt that an attempt at unity between the chronicle text and the insertions is being made here.' Thea Summerfield, *The Matter of King's Lives: The Design of Past and Present in the Early Fourteenth-Century Verse Chronicles by Pierre de Langtoft and Robert Mannyng* (Amsterdam and Atlanta, Ga.: Rodopi, 1998), p. 145.

23 See Thiolier, *Règne d'Édouard Ier*, p. 315, line 916; Wright, *Langtoft*, p. 244, includes the English in the speech.

24 There is considerable variation, in the last three lines, in different manuscripts.

25 The Middle English sections of Poems 6 and 7 are *NIMEV* 814 and 310. One manuscript, the highly variant Cambridge, University Library MS Gg.I.1, has a further nine-line poem in Middle English, inserted just after the mention of the Scots captured at Dunbar:

> For thar wer thai bal brend,
> He kauged ham thidre kend,
>   aut dreved to dote.
> For Scottes at Dunbar
> Have at thayre gau char
>   schame of thar note.
> Wer never dogges there
> Hurled out of herre
>   fro coylthe ne cotte.

(*NIMEV* 848; Wright, *Political Songs*, p. 318; the equivalent position in Wright's Rolls Series edition is 278:11).

26 Fergus Wilde, 'History and Legend in the Chronicle of Peter of Langtoft', unpublished PhD thesis, University of Manchester (1997), p. 14.

27 The tradition of what Maureen Barry McCann Boulton calls 'lyric insertions' was strong in *French* literature. Boulton discusses such insertions at length, though principally in relation to romance; given the close links between Brut-chronicle and romance, it is quite possible that Langtoft was familiar with the device from that genre. *The Song in the Story: Lyric Insertions in French Narrative Fiction, 1200–1400* (Philadelphia, Pa: University of Pennsylvania Press, 1993).

28 Wright, *Political Songs*, p. lxxvii; Wright, *Langtoft*, p. ix.

29 The square-bracketed line of Anglo-Norman is not in Wright's base text but is supplied from other manuscripts. Wright's translation of *karole* as 'dance' seems to fit the context, though 'song' is also possible.

30 See *Thomas Wright's Political Songs of England: From the Reign of John to that of Edward II*, with a new intro. by Peter Coss (Cambridge University Press, 1996), p. xii.

31 R. M. Wilson, *The Lost Literature of Medieval England* (London: Methuen, 1952), p. 212.

32 See M. Dominica Legge, *Anglo-Norman in the Cloister* (Edinburgh University Press, 1950), p. 74 and, at greater length, *Anglo-Norman Literature and its Background* (Oxford: Clarendon Press, 1963), pp. 352–3.

33 Lionel Stones, 'English Chroniclers and the Affairs of Scotland, 1286–1296', in R. H .C. Davis and J. M. Wallace-Hadrill (eds.) *The Writing of History in the Middle Ages: Essays Presented to Richard William Southern* (Oxford: Clarendon Press, 1981), pp. 323–48 (pp. 337–8).

34 R. H. Robbins, 'Poems Dealing with Contemporary Conditions', *Manual*, vol. v (1975), p. 1401.

35 Thiolier, *Règne d'Édouard Ier*, 16–17. Fergus Wilde is agnostic on this question, referring to Langtoft's 'preservation, or equally possibly his composition of martial and mocking songs'. 'History and Legend', p. 18.

36 Thorlac Turville-Petre, 'Politics and Poetry in the Early Fourteenth Century: The Case of Robert Mannyng's *Chronicle*', *Review of English Studies* 39 (1988), 1–28 (8–9).

37 Summerfield, *Matter of King's Lives*, pp. 144–5; see also 'The Political Songs', p. 145.

38 Of the twenty manuscripts, J. C. Thiolier observes, no two can be placed 'dans un rapport de filiation directe'. 'Pierre de Langtoft: Historiographe d'Edouard Ier Plantagenêt', in Ian Short (ed.), *Anglo-Norman Anniversary Essays,* Anglo-Norman Text Society occasional publications series, 2 (London: Anglo-Norman Text Society, 1993), pp. 379–94 (p. 379). For a detailed description of the manuscripts see Thiolier, *Règne d'Édouard Ier*, 35–141. A process of accretion of the poems over time does not seem to be supported by the manuscripts. In the appendix, table 3, I have reorganised the manuscripts according to Thiolier's dating of them. It reveals no pattern: P_1, an early text dated to 1296–1307, in Paris, Bibliothèque Nationale, fonds français 12154, contains Poems 2, 3, 4, 5, 6, 7, and 9, yet such later manuscripts of the mid-fourteenth century as *R, N*, and *J* contain no poems.

39 See Paul Zumthor, *Essai de poétique médiévale* (Paris: Seuil, 1972), p. 71.

40 Prestwich, *Edward I*, p. 470; on the even more blurred character in the tenth and eleventh centuries of this border and the affiliations of Lothian, Cumbria, and Northumberland to either side of it see Davies, *The First English Empire*, p. 55.

41 See G. P. Stell, 'John [John de Balliol] (c.1248x50–1314)', *ODNB*, online edn, Oct 2005, www.oxforddnb.com/view/article/1209, accessed 14 May 2008.

42 On the interconnections and intermarriages between Scottish and English noble families, and in many cases the descent of Scots from the Norman aristocracy, see Sir Maurice Powicke, *The Thirteenth Century, 1216–1307* (Oxford: Clarendon Press, 1953), pp. 579–82.

43 Homi K. Bhabha, 'Of Mimicry and Man: The Ambivalence of Colonial Discourse', *The Location of Culture* (London: Routledge, 1994), pp. 85–92 (pp. 87, 86, 91).

44 Robert Young, *White Mythologies: Writing History and the West* (London: Routledge, 1990), p. 148.

45 Wright, *Political Songs*, pp. 160–79, line 51. Translations are Wright's, modified in places.

46 Wright, *Political Songs*, p. 180.

47 A 'tippet' is an ornamental piece of cloth, such as a part of a hood. It is conceivable that in this context what is meant is a piece of armour protecting the lower face, neck and shoulders; either way, a piece of Balliol's clothing has been knocked awry, just as his insignia are removed from his tabard. See *MED* tippet (n.) 1a, 2.

48 'Scaffeld' has been identified as John de Sheffield, sheriff of Northumberland in 1305; see Summerfield, *Matter of King's Lives*, p. 17, who summarises the scant biographical details. But as Wilde points out, there were other royal clerks with the surname in the period, and it is not even clear from Langtoft's single reference to him that 'Scaffeld' 'was a patron as such'. 'History and Legend', p. 42.

49 Legge, *Anglo-Norman Literature and its Background*, p. 279.

50 Thiolier, *Règne d'Édouard Ier*, p. 18.

51 *Matter of King's Lives*, pp. 25–6. Summerfield first questioned Thiolier's account in 'The Context and Genesis of Pierre de Langtoft's *Chronicle*', in Donald Maddox and Sarah Sturm-Maddox (eds.), *Literary Aspects of Courtly Culture* (Cambridge: D.S. Brewer, 1994), pp. 321–32.

52 *Matter of King's Lives*, pp. 83–5; on the performance, see p. 96; for more detail see her 'The Testimony of Writing: Pierre de Langtoft and the Appeals to History, 1291–1306', in Rhiannon Purdie and Nicola Royan (eds.), *The Scots and Medieval Arthurian Legend* (Woodbridge: D.S. Brewer, 2005), pp. 25–41 (pp. 37–40).

53 'History and Legend', p. 32; he further points out that there is no known royal or even noble ownership of early manuscripts, which tend instead to be found in religious houses or in the hands of 'minor lay and clerical figures' (p. 33).

54 Summerfield suggests that the political songs would have constituted 'hilarious and raucous outbursts in English' in this performance; it seems to me unlikely, however, that material *in English* would have appealed to Bek, Edward I, or his son. *Matter of King's Lives*, p. 96.

55 *Matter of King's Lives*, p. 84. The relative compression of the sections derived from Geoffrey of Monmouth is adduced as evidence for rapidity of composition.

56 Thiolier's account of the manuscripts suggests that some copying was going on by the late thirteenth and early fourteenth century, supporting his claim of an initial phase of writing perhaps as early as (and in response to) the 1296 campaign in Scotland. See appendix, table 3. Summerfield attempts to account for the manuscript evidence of chronological development, improbably, by proposing that the markers were deliberately inserted by Langtoft as a literary device. As Wilde notes, 'the manuscript tradition presents difficulties for us if we imagine the whole to have been written at one sitting, as it were, and of a piece'. 'History and Legend', p. 31.

57 Summerfield does mention the fact that Edward I was dying, but uses this as an argument for Langtoft's haste: *Matter of King's Lives*, p. 94. A more logical deduction is that if Bek could see that Edward was dying, then there was no

need to propitiate him; rather than urging Langtoft on to completion, the better option was simply to wait.

58 Stones and Simpson, *Edward I and the Throne of Scotland*, vol. I, p. 138.
59 *Ibid.*, p. 148.
60 Wilde, 'History and Legend', p. 83.
61 The responses are preserved in Sir Francis Palgrave, *Documents and Records Illustrating the History of Scotland and the Transactions between the Crowns of Scotland and England, Preserved in the Treasury of Her Majesty's Exchequer* ([London]: Record Commission, 1837), pp. 60–7.
62 J. C. Thiolier, 'Langtoft, Peter (d. in or after 1305)', *ODNB*, www.oxforddnb.com/view/article/16037 accessed 2 April 2008. On Langtoft's translation see further Summerfield, 'The Testimony of Writing', p. 35.
63 Prestwich, *Edward I*, pp. 525–6.
64 Prestwich, *Edward I*, p. 526.
65 Bernard Cerquiglini, *In Praise of the Variant: A Critical History of Philology*, trans. Betsy Wing (Baltimore, Md and London: Johns Hopkins University Press, 1999), p. 71; see also p. 78.
66 Wright, *Langtoft*, vol. II, p. viii.
67 Wilde, 'History and Legend', p. 43
68 Summerfield, 'The Testimony of Writing', p. 27. In this revisiting of the topic, Summerfield retains her belief in the late date of composition and presentation before the king; see p. 26.

3 REGIME CHANGE

1 Sir John Froissart, *Chronicles of England, France, Spain …* trans. Thomas Johnes, 2 vols. (London: William Smith, 1842), vol. I, p. 38.
2 See for a summary Ernst H. Kantorowicz, *The King's Two Bodies: A Study in Mediaeval Political Theology* (Princeton University Press, 1957), pp. 7–23.
3 W. A. Wright, *Robert of Gloucester*, line 11733; Olivier de Laborderie, J. R. Maddicott and D. A. Carpenter, 'The Last Hours of Simon de Montfort: A New Account', *EHR* 115.461 (2000), 378–412.
4 Michel Foucault, *Discipline and Punish: The Birth of the Prison*, trans. Alan Sheridan (New York: Vintage Books, 1979), p. 29; Giorgio Agamben, *Homo Sacer: Sovereign Power and Bare Life*, trans. Daniel Heller-Roazen (Stanford University Press, 1998), p. 94; see also p. 102.
5 Katherine Royer, 'The Body in Parts: Reading the Execution Ritual in Late Medieval England', *Historical Reflections* 29.2 (2003), 313–39 (327).
6 Wright, *Langtoft*, vol. II, p. 372:19; cf. Jean Claude Thiolier, *Édition Critique et Commentée de Pierre de Langtoft: Le Règne d'Édouard Ier* (Créteil: CELIMA Université de Paris, 1989), line 2474. Further references, to Wright and the corresponding passage in Thiolier's 'Rédaction II' respectively, parenthetically in the text.
7 Foucault, *Discipline and Punish*, p. 130. This is a statement about eighteenth-century punishment; I will discuss some differences in the medieval model below.

8   Pieter Spierenburg notes the 'routinizing of public punishment' in the early modern period, when 'the carefully planned acting-out of executions …contrasts with the relative spontaneity and directness of medieval times'. As can be seen from this discussion, planned ceremonial is already evident in the executions of Wallace and Fraser – it is the reason they are brought to London rather than dealt with on the spot. Such ceremonial is invoked again in the execution of Mortimer twenty-five years later. *The Spectacle of Suffering: Executions and the Evolution of Repression: From a Preindustrial Metropolis to the European Experience* (Cambridge University Press, 1984), p. 45.

9   G. W. S. Barrow, *Robert Bruce and the Community of the Realm of Scotland*, 3rd edn (Edinburgh University Press, 1988), p. 228.

10 The poet may not have been exaggerating in his claim that Fraser went back on his allegiance four times. Fraser's *ODNB* entry (which labels him simply 'rebel', oversimplifying matters) says that he fought against the English at Dunbar in 1296 but was captured, later gaining his freedom by once again giving his loyalty to Edward and fighting for him in Flanders. Awarded office in Scotland by Edward as sheriff of Selkirk Forest, he gave concern over his loyalty by the end of the century, only to be imprisoned by the Scots. Fraser was present at the Lincoln parliament in 1301 but by 1303 was fighting in Scotland against the English; he submitted to Edward again in 1304, declined exile, was outlawed with Wallace, submitted again, then joined Robert Bruce's rebellion. Fiona Watson, 'Fraser, Sir Simon (c.1270–1306)', *ODNB*, www.oxforddnb.com/view/article/39585, accessed 18 April 2008.

11 'The Execution of Sir Simon Fraser' (*NIMEV* 1889), Wright, *Political Songs*, pp. 212–23 (p. 221); see also R. H. Robbins, *Historical Poems of the XIVth and XVth Centuries* (New York: Columbia University Press, 1959), pp. 14–21 (lines 185–7). Further references to the poem in Wright's edition by page number followed by line numbers to the corresponding passage in Robbins's edition, parenthetically in the text. Wright entitled the poem 'Song on the Execution of Sir Simon Fraser'; however, as so often there is nothing to suggest it was a song and more importantly, nearly half the poem is about Wallace and other figures. As Sperber notes, in its opening lines (with reconfirmation in the final stanza) the poem itself appears to invite a title such as 'Of the Traitors of Scotland'. Although we could label it more neutrally as 'On the Taking of the Scottish Leaders', for convenience I have used Robbins's title throughout. Hilmar Sperber, *Historisch-politische Gedichte im England Edwards I* (Heidelberg: Carl Winter Universitätsverlag, 1985), p. 245.

12 It also states quite clearly that the earl of Atholl is alive, which suggests composition between 7 September and 7 November 1306, the dates of Fraser's and Atholl's executions.

13 The poet in fact refers to the battle of Kirkencliff. There is no such place in modern Scotland, and no record of it in the Middle Ages. Wherever it took place, it was presumably a skirmish after the main battle (note Langtoft's reference, above, to Fraser's escape from the battle, 'ne say coment'). See

further Elisabeth Danninger, *Sieben Politische Gedichte der HS. B.L. Harley 2253: Textausgabe und Kommentar* (Würzburg: Konigshausen & Neumann, 1980), p. 197.

14 Evidence for a popular understanding that Wallace had such ambitions is found in the Prose *Brut*, which wrongly states that the Scots chose him 'to bene her kyng'. Brie, *Brut*, p. 192, line 37.

15 Henry Richards Luard (ed.), *Flores Historiarum*, 3 vols., RS 95 (London: HMSO, 1890), vol. III, p. 133; Danninger, *Sieben Politische Gedichte*, p. 166, accepts this judgement.

16 John Scattergood, 'Authority and Resistance: The Political Verse', in Fein (ed.), *Studies in the Harley Manuscript*, pp. 163–201 (p. 176).

17 *MED* mirour (n.) 3d. *MED* records what may be an earlier use (*c*.1300) in a similar sense in one version of the poem 'Worldes blis ne last', in Oxford, Bodleian Library, Rawlinson G.18 (*NIMEV* 4223). See Carleton Brown (ed.), *English Lyrics of the XIIIth Century* (Oxford: Clarendon Press, 1932), pp. 80–2 (line 52).

18 On the role of the marketplace in the dissemination of information in the fourteenth century, see James Masschaele, 'The Public Space of the Marketplace in Medieval England', *Speculum* 77 (2002), 383–421, esp. 392–3; on the later dissemination of news about the Hundred Years War, see H. J. Hewitt, *The Organisation of War Under Edward III* (Manchester University Press, 1966), esp. pp. 159–60.

19 It is notable that in addition to circumstantial detail about the execution itself, the poet gives many details about the original capture; compare the relatively vague account given in Langtoft, above. Multon is presumably the knight of this name active in Scottish campaigns in the late 1290s, who fought at the siege of Caerlaverock in 1300. See the biography of this figure's grandfather, C. L. Kingsford, 'Moulton, Sir Thomas of (d. 1240)', rev. Ralph V. Turner, *ODNB*, www.oxforddnb.com/view/article/19521, accessed 15 April 2008.

20 Note in addition the macaronic line on p. 216. Johanna Jahn proposes as author Richard le Harpur, whom she identifies as being in Multon's service in 1305. *Die mittelenglische spielmannsballade von Simon Fraser* (Bonn: Peter Hanstein, 1921), p. 44.

21 This use of *myrour* is reminiscent of other French terms which appeared for the first recorded time in Middle English political poems: *trichard* and *lyard* in 'Song Against the King of Almaigne' (discussed in chapter 1), and the abusive *nages* ('buttocks') in Langtoft's Poem 4 (discussed in chapter 2), a first use in Middle English which is then not followed for more than a century (see *MED* nache (n.)). This suggests bilingual, code-shifting composers, familiar with French terms not yet in widespread use in English, but who have at the same time made the decision to compose their verse in English.

22 Sperber similarly notes the immediacy of the poet's account, contrasting it with the distance of a chronicler. *Historisch-politische Gedichte*, p. 248.

23 Cf the similar attitude in the Prose *Brut* to the execution of the Welsh Prince David, whose head was sent to London, but whose four quarters were 'sende

to the iiij chief tounes of Walys, for þai shulde take ensample, & þerof be-war'. Brie, *Brut*, p. 184, lines 4–6.

24 The link between judicial execution and the image of Christ on the cross has been thoroughly explored (principally in art) in Mitchell B. Merback, *The Thief, the Cross and the Wheel: Pain and the Spectacle of Punishment in Medieval and Renaissance Europe* (London: Reaktion Books, 1999).

25 Scattergood, 'Authority and Resistance', p. 177. Similarly, Thorlac Turville-Petre finds that 'the last stanza reveals both frustration and fear'. 'Political Lyrics', in Thomas G. Duncan (ed.), *A Companion to the Middle English Lyric* (Woodbridge: D.S. Brewer, 2005), pp. 171–88 (p. 173).

26 Elaine Scarry, *The Body in Pain* (Oxford University Press, 1985), p. 27.

27 John of Strathbogie provides a classic case, similar to Fraser's own: he supported the Bruce side during the Great Cause but was present when Balliol did homage to Edward I in 1292; he was part of the 1296 invasion of England and was captured at Dunbar, receiving his freedom by serving with Edward; returning to Scotland, he may have been back on the Scottish side at Falkirk in 1298 and was prominent in Scottish affairs for the next five years. He then seems to have submitted to Edward again in 1303 and held offices under him in Scotland, yet was present in 1306 at Bruce's coronation. He was captured a few months later. To modern eyes, this might appear to be either terrible indecision or the worst politically pragmatic havering. But Strathbogie's case was not untypical; his family, like many another, had inheritances on the English side of the border and many links by marriage with English families. Because of his English noble blood, he was given the dubious distinction of a scaffold thirty feet higher than the norm. See Fiona Watson, 'Strathbogie, John of, ninth earl of Atholl (c.1260–1306)', *ODNB* www.oxforddnb.com/view/article/49383, accessed 18 April 2008.

28 Treason in this poem, Richard Firth Green notes, 'was only incidentally the hierarchical offense of a subject against the king; it was first and foremost the breach of a mutual agreement'. *A Crisis of Truth: Literature and Law in Ricardian England* (Philadelphia, Pa: University of Pennsylvania Press, 1999), p. 209.

29 This obscure abusive word is also found in a three-line scrap of verse in two manuscripts of Langtoft's chronicle (*NIMEV* 3799.3), beginning 'Tprut Scot riueling'. See Thiolier, *Règne d'Édouard Ier*, p. 300, rédaction I, lines 846–8.

30 Spierenburg, *Spectacle of Suffering*, p. 59. Spierenburg also notes, of medieval uses of execution, that 'the relation of display and exemplarity with the early phases of state formation becomes clear' (p. 55). See further pp. 77–8. I am not suggesting that the poem circulated either orally or in written form as, in effect, a pamphlet (though it might have done); we simply do not have the data to make that claim. But its function was similar, I suggest, in that it takes on the role of 'mirror' from the displayed body parts themselves. My tentative suggestion about authorship, above, would imply the further possibility that the work was offered to Thomas Multon by a member of his

retinue as a favourable comment on the way Multon had created the possibility for spectacular justice when he brought Fraser to London.

31 'The Death of Edward I', lines 73–80; Robbins, *Historical Poems*, pp. 21–4, also in Wright, *Political Songs*, pp. 246–50. The poem, *NIMEV* 205, is found in Harley 2253, fol. 73r; there are also fragments in Cambridge, University Library, Additional MS 4407, Art. 19.

32 'Elegy on the Death of Edward I', lines 67–74, in Aspin *ANPS*, pp. 79–89; translation is Aspin's. See also Wright, *Political Songs*, pp. 241–5. The poem appears at the end of an Anglo-Norman translation of the English *Short Metrical Chronicle*; see Ewald Zettl (ed.), *An Anonymous Short English Metrical Chronicle*, EETS o.s. 196 (Oxford University Press for the EETS, 1935), pp. 105–7. Further references by line number parenthetically in the text.

33 Wright, *Political Songs*, p. 245; K. Böddeker, *Altenglische Dichtungen des MS. Harley 2253* (Berlin, 1878), p. 139; Thorlac Turville-Petre, *England the Nation: Language, Literature, and National Identity, 1290–1340* (Oxford: Clarendon Press, 1996), p. 203. See also the more extensive arguments of Geert de Wilde, 'The Stanza Form of the Middle English *Lament for the Death of Edward I*: A Reconstruction', *Anglia* 123.2 (2005), 230–45.

34 Aspin, *ANPS*, p.81.

35 Turville-Petre, *England the Nation*, p. 204.

36 De Wilde, 'The Stanza Form', 231, 242.

37 'Adam Davy's Dreams of Edward II', in Oliver Farrar Emerson, *A Middle English Reader* (London: Macmillan, 1915), pp. 227–32 (p. 229, lines 32–3); *NIMEV* 3763. Further references, given in the text, are to page and then line number. The poem is found in Oxford, Bodleian Library, Laud Misc. 622, fols. 26b-27b, which is dated to 1400–25; the poem itself is usually assigned to the early years of Edward II's reign.

38 *Havelok the Dane*, lines 1295–1304, 1311, in Ronald B. Herzman, Graham Drake and Eve Salisbury (eds.), *Four Romances of England*, TEAMS Middle English Texts (Kalamazoo, Mich.: Medieval Institute Publications, 1999).

39 Emerson, *Middle English Reader*, p. 314.

40 V. J. Scattergood, 'Adam Davy's *Dreams* and Edward II', *Archiv für das Studium der Neueren Sprachen und Literaturen* 206 (1970), 253–60 (260); the Becket prophecies are in J. Rawson Lumby (ed.), *Bernardus de cura rei familiaris, with Early Scottish Prophecies*, EETS o.s. 42 (London: Trübner, 1870), pp. 23–31.

41 Brie, *Brut*, pp. 208–9.

42 The *Lanercost Chronicle* gives the Feast of the Nativity of St John (24 June), which fits best with the timing of the events immediately ensuing. Herbert Maxwell (trans.), *The Chronicle of Lanercost 1272–1346* (Glasgow, 1913), in Harry Rothwell (ed.), *English Historical Documents, 1189–1327* (London: Eyre & Spottiswoode, 1975), p. 270.

43 William Stubbs (ed.), *Chronicles of the Reigns of Edward I. and Edward II*, 2 vols., RS 76 (London: Longman, 1882–3), vol. 1, p. 282.

44 Maxwell (trans.), *Lanercost*, in Rothwell (ed.), *English Historical Documents, 1189–1327*, p. 270.

45 Stubbs (ed.), *Chronicles of ... Edward II*, vol. 1, p. 283. See also the account of the incident by W. R. Childs, "'Welcome, my Brother": Edward II, John of Powderham and the Chronicles, 1318', in Ian Wood and G.A. Loud (eds.), *Church and Chronicle in the Middle Ages: Essays Presented to John Taylor* (London: Hambledon Press, 1991), pp. 149–63.

46 Wendy Childs (ed. and trans.), *Vita Edwardi Secundi: The Life of Edward the Second* (Oxford: Clarendon Press, 2005), p. 149.

47 Roy Martin Haines, *King Edward II: Edward of Caernarfon, His Life, His Reign, and Its Aftermath, 1284–1330* (Montreal–Kingston: McGill-Queen's University Press, 2003), p. 44.

48 Childs, "'Welcome, my Brother"'.

49 See Paul Strohm, *England's Empty Throne: Usurpation and the Language of Legitimation, 1399–1422* (New Haven, Conn. and London: Yale University Press, 1998), esp. chapter 4. See also Strohm, 'Saving the Appearances: Chaucer's "Purse" and the Fabrication of the Lancastrian Claim', *Hochon's Arrow: The Social Imagination of Fourteenth-Century Texts* (Princeton University Press, 1992), pp. 75–94.

50 See Haines, *Edward II*, pp. 113–16, and J. R. Maddicott, *Thomas of Lancaster 1307–1322: A Study in the Reign of Edward II* (London: Oxford University Press, 1970), p. 226.

51 On Lancaster's rule see Maddicott, *Thomas of Lancaster*, chapter 5.

52 *Ibid.*, pp. 309–11. The comparison with Montfort is one Lancaster seems to have made himself; see pp. 321–2.

53 Wright, *Political Songs*, pp. 270, 269, 272; trans. Wright.

54 J. R. Maddicott, 'Thomas of Lancaster, second earl of Lancaster, second earl of Leicester, and earl of Lincoln (c.1278–1322)', *ODNB*, www.oxforddnb.com/view/article/27195 accessed 18 April 2008.

55 For full detail see Haines, *Edward II*, pp. 177–96.

56 Kantorowicz, *The King's Two Bodies*, p. 421.

57 For extended analysis see Haines, *Edward II*, chapter 8, with translation of the Letter, pp. 221–2.

58 As for example Paul Studer, 'An Anglo-Norman Poem', *Modern Language Review* 16 (1921), 34–46; Robbins (ed.), *Historical Poems*, p. 302; the view is repeated in William Calin, *The French Tradition and the Literature of Medieval England* (Toronto University Press, 1994), p. 7.

59 Edward's canonisation: T. F. Tout, 'The Captivity and Death of Edward of Carnarvon', *Bulletin of the John Rylands Library* 6 (1921), pp. 69–114; monastic forgery: T. M. Smallwood, 'The Lament of Edward II', *Modern Language Review* 68 (1973), 521–9, esp. 529; coup of 1330: Claire Valente, 'The "Lament of Edward II": Religious Lyric, Political Propaganda', *Speculum* 77 (2002), 422–39.

60 The poem is found in Wiltshire, Longleat House, MS 26 and London, British Library, Royal MS 20 A.ii. The latter also contains a text of

Langtoft's Chronicle with five of the political verses. Both versions are edited in parallel with translation by Aspin, *ANPS*; quotation and translation, pp. 93, 104, lines 1–2. Further references by line number parenthetically in the text.

61 On the anagram see Valente, 'Lament of Edward II', 432, who also records previous speculations about 'du par Kenire', as meaning 'around Kenilworth', or as an error for 'du parke Vire', referring to the region in Normandy. The version in Royal MS 20 A.ii has the phrase as 'la bisse du park q'enpire', or 'the Doe of the park that is deteriorating'. This makes sense historically, as referring to the regime of Mortimer and Isabella, but it would detract from the prophetic role the speaker is taking on here, the poem's pretence that the regime has *not* fallen apart, but that Isabella should fear that outcome. Hence the reading in Royal 20 might be a later attempt to make sense of something which had perhaps already become corrupted and incomprehensible in the Longleat manuscript.

62 A peculiarity of the title was that it was the first to lay claim to an imprecise expanse of the realm rather than a specific city or county; it might have appeared to contemporaries the more overweening as a result. The practice became commonplace, however, and culminates, in our time, in the creation of a royal earldom of Wessex – a fictive area.

63 Wright, *Political Songs*, p. 212.

64 See further Haines, *Edward II*, pp. 217–18.

65 Thomas Gray, *The Scalachronica: The Reigns of Edward I, Edward II and Edward III as Recorded by Sir Thomas Grey*, trans. Sir Herbert Maxwell (1907; Felinfach: Llanerch Publishers, 2000), p. 86.

66 For a full account of the affair, see Caroline Shenton, 'Edward III and the Coup of 1330', in J. S. Bothwell (ed.), *The Age of Edward III* (York: York Medieval Press, 2001), pp. 13–34.

67 Valente, 'Lament of Edward II', 434.

68 Referring to the deposition of Edward II, Gwilym Dodd notes not only that Edward's 'political legitimacy' – by contrast with that of Bolingbroke later in the century – 'rested on the unassailable fact of his direct royal lineage', but also that 'Edward III could afford for his succession to be associated with parliament because all contemporaries realised that it was not parliament that gave the king his political legitimacy, but his royal blood.' 'Parliament and Political Legitimacy in the Reign of Edward II', in Gwilym Dodd and Anthony Musson (eds.), *The Reign of Edward II: New Perspectives* (Woodbridge: York Medieval Press, 2006), pp. 165–89 (p. 169).

69 Michael Prestwich, *Plantagenet England 1225–1360* (Oxford University Press, 2005), p. 218.

70 These features, along with the poem's repeated emphasis on the vanity of worldly things and the bliss of heaven, strongly suggest clerical origin. If the poem originated in the circle of Edward III himself as Valente suggests, then one likely candidate for authorship is the bibliophile Richard de Bury, the cleric who was highest in Edward's favour at the right time, having

participated in the 1330 plot, by which time he was keeper of the privy seal. As the supposed author of a Latin work entitled *Philobiblon*, he also had some literary achievement. See on him N. Denholm-Young, 'Richard de Bury', *Transactions of the Royal Historical Society*, 4th ser. 20 (1937), 135–68, and W. J. Courtenay, 'Bury, Richard (1287–1345)', *ODNB*, www.oxforddnb. com/view/article/4153, accessed 18 April 2008.

71 Zettl (ed.), *Anonymous Short English Metrical Chronicle*, lines 2364–7; see also www.nls.uk/auchinleck/mss/smc.html.

72 W. M. Ormrod, *The Reign of Edward III: Crown and Political Society in England 1327–1377* (New Haven, Conn. and London: Yale University Press, 1990), p. 57.

4 THE DESTRUCTION OF ENGLAND

1 See Leonard E. Boyle, 'William of Pagula and the *Speculum Regis Edwardi III*', *Mediaeval Studies* 32 (1970), 329–36. The A version is in fact entitled, in manuscripts, the *Epistola ad Regem Edwardum III*. Boyle suggested that it be given this title and that it was only the slightly later B version that should be known as the *Speculum Regis Edwardi*. I follow, however, Nederman's translation, which gives both versions under the one title, the *Mirror of King Edward III*. Cary J. Nederman, *Political Thought in Early Fourteenth-Century England: Treatises by Walter of Milemete, William of Pagula, and William of Ockham* (Turnhout: Arizona Center for Medieval and Renaissance Studies in association with Brepols, 2002). See also Joseph Moisant (ed.), *De Speculo Regis Edward III* (Paris, 1891).

2 On the differences between the situation in 1341 and that forty years later which *did* produce rebellion, see J. R. Maddicott, *The English Peasantry and the Demands of the Crown, 1294–1341*, Past and Present Supplement 1 (Oxford: Past and Present Society, 1975), p. 65.

3 *Speculum Regis Edwardi III*, Version A, para. 39, in Nederman's translation in *Political Thought*. Further references parenthetically in the text. Bible translation is Nederman's, of William. Cp. Vulgate, 1 Kings 21.19: 'et loqueris ad eum dicens haec dicit Dominus occidisti insuper et possedisti et post haec addes haec dicit Dominus in loco hoc in quo linxerunt canes sanguinem Naboth lambent tuum quoque sanguinem'.

4 Maddicott, *The English Peasantry*, p. 34.

5 *Ibid.*, p. 5.

6 *Ibid.*, p. 24.

7 G. H. Martin (ed. and trans.), *Knighton's Chronicle 1337–1396* (Oxford: Clarendon Press, 1995), p. 7.

8 May McKisack, *The Fourteenth Century, 1307–1399* (Oxford: Clarendon Press, 1959), pp. 179–80. See also W. M. Ormrod, *The Reign of Edward III: Crown and Political Society in England 1327–1377* (New Haven, Conn. and London: Yale University Press, 1990), pp. 97–105.

9 Maddicott, *The English Peasantry*, p. 17.

10 McKisack, *The Fourteenth Century*, p. 180.

11 Maddicott, *The English Peasantry*, pp. 61–2.

12 Nederman, *Political Thought*, p. 68. For further reflections on the *Speculum* see also Nederman, 'Property and Protest: Political Theory and Subjective Rights in Fourteenth-Century England', *Review of Politics* 58 (1996), 323–44, which locates the work as an early example of the theory of 'subjective rights' typically more closely associated with the seventeenth century (323–4) and argues for William of Pagula as an advocate for a free market (336).

13 The attribution in some manuscripts to Archbishop Simon Islip (accepted in Moisant's edition), is clearly incorrect, as James Tait argues: 'On the Date and Authorship of the *Speculum Regis Edwardi*', *EHR* 16 (1901), 110–15. Boyle identified the author on the basis of several attributions made in the fourteenth and fifteenth centuries in his 'William of Pagula', 331. On William of Pagula see further Nederman, *Political Thought*, pp. 66–8 and 'Pagula, William (d. 1332?)', *ODNB*, www.oxforddnb.com/view/article/21127, accessed 20 Oct 2006.

14 Boyle, 'William of Pagula', p. 336.

15 Nederman, *Political Thought*, p. 70.

16 Concerning a tract on kingship with which Edward was presented (that by Walter of Milemete), Ormrod says that he 'was probably much more impressed with the sumptuous illustrations than with the implications of the text'. *Reign of Edward III*, p. 55.

17 Nederman finds it problematic that William of Pagula was writing at a time when purveyance was *not* particularly prominent (*Political Thought*, p. 68; Nederman's *ODNB* entry on William slightly amplifies this point). But the tenor of William's objections makes it perfectly clear that what was happening was purveyance on a local scale, affecting people in the district near Windsor. As William describes it, it was not strictly speaking purveyance at all, because the king's armies had nothing to do with it. It amounts, rather, to licensed theft. 'Whenever rumors are heard about your arrival', William writes, 'and one horn is heard, almost anyone who is in the village trembles. Presently your scout comes to the village and, seeing him, all are sorrowful and are filled with dread.' The scout will take oats, hay and demand stabling for the king's horses, William explains, and then another will take geese and hens, while yet another will want grain (p. 111).

18 Boyle, 'William of Pagula', 331.

19 Nederman, *Political Thought*, p. 68.

20 Maddicott writes, '[i]t is hard to be sure that the author of the *De Speculo Regis* was exaggerating when he wrote that purveyance had brought many to their deaths, or that the possibility of rebellion was not as real as the Ordinances twice stated it to be'. *The English Peasantry*, p. 34. On the other hand, Wendy Scase notes, of the *nonarum inquisitiones* records in Edward's reign, that 'it is tempting to interpret these complaints as the peasants' own strategic exploitation of the old tradition of "peasant lament"' and that 'Arguably, peasant plaint is so prevalent in the records because such traditional grievances were

what the clerks were primed to hear and record.' *Literature and Complaint in England, 1272–1553* (Oxford University Press, 2007), p. 14.

21 Nederman, 'Property and Protest', 340.

22 Scase, *Literature and Complaint*, p. 24.

23 Nederman, 'Property and Protest', suggests that '[a]t a time when advice books were still essentially litanies of public virtues', William was 'offering recommendations for the political administration and economic management of the realm' (339). This is not incompatible with address to a wider public rather than Edward himself; indeed, it could be viewed as more effective to circulate such ideas about how the king ought to act than to aim those ideas at the one man whose interests the ideas opposed.

24 For these texts see F. J. Child (ed.), *English and Scottish Ballads,* 8 vols. (Boston, Mass.: Little, Brown and Co., 1857), vol. v, pp. 67–87.

25 *NIMEV* 988. Partial edition in Wright, *Political Songs*, pp. 377–8; see also Walter Hoyt French and Charles Brockway Hale, *Middle English Metrical Romances* (New York: Prentice-Hall, 1930), pp. 947–85.

26 G. L. Brook (ed.), *The Harley Lyrics: The Middle English Lyrics of MS. Harley 2253*, 4th edn (Manchester University Press, 1968). This influential anthology – which focuses on lyrics of love rather than politics – first appeared in 1948.

27 Richard Firth Green, *A Crisis of Truth: Literature and Law in Ricardian England* (Philadelphia, Pa: University of Pennsylvania Press, 1999), p. 171.

28 Michael Prestwich, *Plantagenet England 1225–1360* (Oxford University Press, 2005), p. 518. For abuses of this system, see also Green, *Crisis of Truth*, pp. 173–5. There seems no reason to dispute Aspin's argument, accepted by Green, for dating this poem at the time of the commissions, near the end of the reign of Edward I.

29 Aspin, *ANPS*, pp. 67–78, lines 5–7; translations are hers.

30 *Ibid.*, p. 77.

31 Scase, *Literature and Complaint,* p. 48.

32 Green, *Crisis of Truth*, p. 171.

33 Aspin, *ANPS*, p. 63, lines 17–20. Further references parenthetically to the Auchinleck version, *NIMEV* 1857, in Aspin's edition.

34 Aspin seems to have regarded the second poem merely as a variation on the first; V.J. Scattergood argues that the differences in the second 'are deliberate authorial alterations'. 'Political Context, Date and Composition of *The Sayings of the Four Philosophers*', *Medium Ævum* 37 (1968), 157–65 (160). Laura Kendrick disputes the date of c.1305 given by Aspin and Scattergood to the earlier poem, and regards it as alluding, in its first stanza, to events in summer 1309 and Edward's repudiation of his own confirmation of *articuli super cartas* at a parliament in Stamford, before the poem leaps back to 1258 and the Provisions of Oxford in the second stanza. The later poem she regards, like Wright and Scattergood, as commenting on the repudiation of the 1311 Ordinances. In the first poem, 'the partisan poet intends to prod certain bishops and barons into taking a more uncompromising position of

opposition to Edward II'; in the second the poet, 'perhaps one of [archbishop of Canterbury] Winchelsea's clerical partisans, revised the earlier [poem] by altering a few lines in the opening macaronic section to broaden and secularize the issues of complaint and by adding a longer, Middle English section [i.e. *The Sayings of the Four Philosophers*] on the theme of misgovernment'. 'On Reading Medieval Political Verse: Two Partisan Poems from the Reign of Edward II', *Mediaevalia* 5 (1979), 183–204 (188, 190).

35 As Aspin edited only the preamble, I cite the *Sayings* here from Wright, *Political Songs*, p. 254.

36 Wright, *Political Songs*, pp. 254, 256. For a contemporary view of Edward's alleged predilections see Brie, *Brut*, p. 208.

37 See on this Thorlac Turville-Petre, *England the Nation: Language, Literature, and National Identity, 1290–1340* (Oxford: Clarendon Press, 1996), pp. 112–14, who believes 'that there was an editor who took responsibility not only for selecting and organizing the material, but also for reworking and adapting some texts, and perhaps even for composing works or commissioning their composition and translation' (p. 112). But it is not necessary to see this level of conscious intervention to account for the shape of the manuscript; one or more active scribe-compilers would explain many of the characteristics of texts in this manuscript.

38 Aspin, *ANPS* (Auchinleck version), p. 63, lines 4, 28.

39 Wright, *Political Songs*, p. 257.

40 *NIMEV* 4165. The poem exists in three versions, of which that in the Auchinleck manuscript of c.1330–40 is the earliest, best known, and most frequently edited; it has no ending, due to a missing manuscript leaf. The text in Oxford, Bodleian Library, Bodley MS 48 (c.1425–50?) is incomplete; the text in Cambridge, Peterhouse MS 104 (1375–1425), it has been convincingly argued, is a later revision, probably not far in date from its manuscript. There are major variations between the three versions; each has 'unique inclusions and unique omissions', according to Embree and Urquhart. 'The Simonie' is written in red ink immediately above the text in the Auchinleck manuscript (fol. 328r), though in a different hand from that in which the text is written. The text in the Bodleian manuscript concludes with the words 'Explicit Symonye and Covetise'. Though this is a better indicator of the poem's wider concerns, the Auchinleck title has stuck. Dan Embree and Elizabeth Urquhart (eds.), *The Simonie: A Parallel-Text Edition* (Heidelberg: Carl Winter Universitätsverlag, 1991), p. 7.

41 Embree and Urquhart argue for stronger connections than those seen by previous commentators. *The Simonie*, p. 22.

42 Elizabeth Salter, *English and International: Studies in the Literature, Art and Patronage of Medieval England*, ed. Derek Pearsall and Nicolette Zeeman (Cambridge University Press, 1988), pp. 159, 163–4.

43 Embree and Urquhart (eds.), *The Simonie*, p. 19.

44 Turville-Petre, *England the Nation*, p. 12.

45 *Ibid.*, p. 134.

46 James M. Dean (ed.), *The Simonie*, in *Medieval English Political Writings*, TEAMS Middle English Texts (Kalamazoo, Mich.: Medieval Institute Publications, 1996), lines 313–14, 319–20.

47 These stanza divisions are clearly signalled in the Auchinleck manuscript, with the bob appearing in the otherwise blank space to the right of the fourth line of the quatrain, and the first line of each stanza marked by a symbol in red ink. See the transcript and accompanying digitised images of the manuscript at www.nls.uk/auchinleck/mss/simonie.html.

48 Embree and Urquhart (eds.), *The Simonie*, pp. 28, 29.

49 Translation is mine, but heavily indebted to Dean's notes to lines 115–20; Dean suggests that the difficult first line has the sense 'that the "wantoune prestes" mock prelates, with perhaps an allusion to Christ's crown of thorns' (line 115, note).

50 Janet Coleman, *English Literature in History: 1350–1400, Medieval Readers and Writers* (London: Hutchinson, 1981), p. 64.

51 Embree and Urquhart (eds.), *The Simonie*, p. 34.

52 G. R. Owst, *Literature and Pulpit in Medieval England: A Neglected Chapter in the History of English Letters & of the English People*, 2nd edn (Oxford: Basil Blackwell, 1961), p. 220.

53 Stephen Knight, 'The Voice of Labour in Fourteenth-Century English Literature' in James Bothwell, P. J. P. Goldberg and W. M. Ormrod (eds.), *The Problem of Labour in Fourteenth-Century England* (Woodbridge: York Medieval Press in association with Boydell & Brewer, 2000), pp. 101–22 (p. 108).

54 Embree and Urquhart (eds.), *The Simonie*, p. 34.

55 *MED* ransaken (v., (a), (b), (c)).

56 R. R. Davies, *The First English Empire: Power and Identities in the British Isles 1093–1343* (Oxford University Press, 2000), p. 80.

57 Knight, 'Voice of Labour', pp. 115–16.

58 Coleman, *English Literature in History*, p. 64.

59 George Kane, 'Some Fourteenth-Century "Political" Poems', in Gregory Kratzmann and James Simpson (eds.), *Medieval English Religious and Ethical Literature: Essays in Honour of G. H. Russell* (Cambridge: D.S. Brewer, 1986), pp. 82–91.

60 *NIMEV* 1320.5; lines 1–4; all citations from the edition in Dean (ed.), *Medieval English Political Writings*; glosses based on Dean's. Dating this poem is difficult as it fits several contexts. It used to be thought of as belonging to the reign of Edward I; Maddicott placed it c.1300 (*The English Peasantry*, p. 13). But the reference in the closing lines to bad weather ruining harvests fits better with the famine years of 1315–17, while other aspects recall the discontent of the 1330s. Maddicott later changed his mind, placing the poem around 1340, in 'Poems of Social Protest in Early Fourteenth-Century England', in W. M. Ormrod (ed.), *England in the Fourteenth Century: Proceedings of the 1985 Harlaxton Symposium* (Woodbridge: Boydell,

1986), pp. 130–44 (p. 132); Peter Coss concurs. *Thomas Wright's Political Songs of England: From the Reign of John to that of Edward II*, with a new intro. by Peter Coss (Cambridge University Press, 1996), p. lii. Richard Newhauser proposes 1320–40, which is perhaps the best that can be said. 'Historicity and Complaint in *Song of the Husbandman*', in Susanna Fein (ed.), *Studies in the Harley Manuscript: The Scribes, Contents, and Social Contexts of British Library MS Harley 2253* (Kalamazoo, Mich. : Medieval Institute Publications, 2000), pp. 203–17.

61 Knight, 'The Voice of Labour', p. 117.

62 Newhauser, 'Historicity and Complaint in *Song of the Husbandman*', pp. 216–17. A similar point is made by Scase, *Literature and Complaint*, p. 39.

63 '[D]ie Reichen reissen [alles] an sich, ohne das Recht [dazu zu haben].' Elisabeth Danninger, *Sieben Politische Gedichte der HS. B.L. Harley 2253: Textausgabe und Kommentar* (Würzburg: Konigshausen & Neumann, 1980), p. 52; so too A. Brandl and O. Zippel, *Mittelenglische Sprach- und Literaturproben*, 2nd edn (New York: Chelsea, 1949), pp. 134–5. '[T]he sense is', Dean suggests, '"steal from me."' Dean (ed.), 'Song of the Husbandman', *Medieval English Political Writings,* note to line 26.

64 Kane, 'Some Fourteenth-Century "Political" Poems', p. 86; Scase, *Literature and Complaint*, p. 36.

65 *MED* wele (n. (1)). For the citation from 'Man haue hit' (*NIMEV* 2054), see 1.(a).

66 Turville-Petre makes a similar point to this in his 'Political Lyrics', in Thomas G. Duncan (ed.), *A Companion to the Middle English Lyric* (Woodbridge: D.S. Brewer, 2005), pp. 171–88 (p. 171).

67 Dean (ed.), 'Song of the Husbandman', *Medieval English Political Writings,* note to line 38.

68 Steven Justice, *Writing and Rebellion: England in 1381* (Berkeley, Calif. and London: University of California Press, 1994), p. 135.

69 Maddicott, *The English Peasantry*, p. 69.

70 Newhauser, 'Historicity and Complaint in *Song of the Husbandman*', pp. 208, 210.

71 Scase (*Literature and Complaint*, p. 30) notes that while historians have usually taken the poem as reflecting a popular viewpoint, there are 'similarities' between it and 'the appropriation of peasant plaint in texts that defend the Church'. Judith Ferster states that although the writer was 'clearly learned' he 'has sympathy with the poor'. *Fictions of Advice: The Literature and Politics of Counsel in Late Medieval England* (Philadelphia, Pa: University of Pennsylvania Press, 1996), p. 18.

72 Aspin, *ANPS*, p. 108, lines 1–5; her translations.

73 Scase, *Literature and Complaint*, p. 32–3.

74 Aspin, *ANPS*, p. 114 n. 7.

75 Aspin remarks that 'a hostile party was active against him [Stratford], and this remark – perhaps also the covert allusion in line 4 – may be part of a campaign of slander directed against him'. *ANPS*, p. 115 n. 37.

76 On the presence of clergy in the commons in the first half of the fourteenth century, see S. H. Rigby, *English Society in the Later Middle Ages: Class, Status and Gender* (Basingstoke: Macmillan, 1995), p. 223.

77 See further, on the involvement of peasants in the struggles of 1258–67, D. A. Carpenter, 'English Peasants in Politics, 1258–1267', *The Reign of Henry III* (London and Rio Grande, Oh.: Hambledon, 1996), pp. 309–48.

78 Maddicott, *The English Peasantry*, p. 67.

79 Michael Prestwich remarks, however, that there are no records of *peasants* profiting from war. *Plantagenet England*, p. 464.

5 LOVE LETTERS TO EDWARD III

1 Thomas Gray, *The Scalachronica: The Reigns of Edward I, Edward II and Edward III as Recorded by Sir Thomas Grey*, trans. Sir Herbert Maxwell (1907; Felinfach: Llanerch Publishers, 2000), p. 102.

2 Salisbury: William Montagu; Suffolk: Robert Ufford; Huntingdon: William Clinton; Northampton: William Bohun; Gloucester: Hugh Audley. Of these, Montagu, Ufford, Clinton, and Audley could be regarded as 'new men' in that they came from the middle-ranking baronage at best rather than important magnate families (the Bohuns were a prominent Marcher family). All were members of the conspiracy of 1330 except Audley and Bohun, whose brother Edward had been involved but was by then deceased. Henry of Grosmont, made earl of Derby, presents a slightly different case, as he was already heir to one earldom (Lancaster) and simply took another, already existing earldom, one of his father's lesser inheritances, at the same time as the new creations. On his father's death he became earl of Lancaster (later to become duke, as will be discussed below). On the 1337 creations, see J. S. Bothwell, 'Edward III, The English Peerage, and the 1337 Earls: Estate Redistribution in Fourteenth-Century England', in James Bothwell (ed.), *The Age of Edward III* (York: York Medieval Press, 2001), pp. 35–52.

3 Chris Given-Wilson and Michael Prestwich, 'Introduction', Bothwell (ed.), *Age of Edward III*, pp. 1–11 (p. 7).

4 Michael Prestwich, *Plantagenet England 1225–1360*, New Oxford History of England (Oxford University Press, 2005), p. 572.

5 W. M. Ormrod, *The Reign of Edward III: Crown and Political Society in England 1327–1377* (New Haven, Conn. and London: Yale University Press, 1990), p. 12; see also p. 58. Prestwich states that Edward 'was not a man to indulge in favourites' but 'had his friends, such as William Montague'. *Plantagenet England*, p. 290. The difficult question, though, is that of when a friend (as the favourite, Gaveston, undoubtedly was) becomes a favourite (as the king's friend Montagu also was). As Steve Rigby has suggested to me, a favourite is a friend that *somebody else* objects to.

6 Ormrod, *Reign of Edward III*, p. 7.

7 For Ardis Butterfield, the war was the most important reason for the 'vital and complex questions about what we have subsequently come to call

"national" identity' in the later Middle Ages. 'Nationhood', in Steve Ellis (ed.), *Chaucer: An Oxford Guide* (Oxford University Press, 2005), pp. 50–65 (p. 50). See further Ardis Butterfield, *The Familiar Enemy: Chaucer, Language, and Nation in the Hundred Years War* (Oxford University Press, 2009); at time of writing, I had not seen a copy of this book. See also Frederick Hertz, 'War and the Formation of National Traditions', in C. Leon Tipton (ed.), *Nationalism in the Middle Ages* (New York: Holt, Rinehart and Winston, 1972), pp. 54–8; reprinted from his *Nationality in History and Politics* (New York: Humanities Press, 1944), pp. 217–23.

8 On Caen see Sir John Froissart, *Chronicles of England, France, Spain … * trans. Thomas Johnes, 2 vols. (London: William Smith, 1842), vol. I, pp. 155–7; Jonathan Sumption, *The Hundred Years War I: Trial by Battle* (Philadelphia, Pa: University of Pennsylvania Press, 1999), pp. 507–11.

9 Various suggestions have been made, beginning with Ritson's idea that Minot was a monk: [Joseph Ritson (ed.)], *Poems on Interesting Events in the Reign of King Edward III* (London, 1795), p. xiii. He has also been seen as a 'a camp-following minstrel': Janet Coleman, *English Literature in History: 1350–1400, Medieval Readers and Writers* (London: Hutchinson, 1981), p. 73; see also R. H. Robbins, 'Poems Dealing with Contemporary Conditions', *Manual*, vol. V (1975), p. 1412. Thomas Beaumont James and John Simons' suggestion of Minot as a kind of court poet is discussed below. See James and Simons (eds.), *The Poems of Laurence Minot 1333–1352* (University of Exeter, 1989), p. 10; on this idea see also Douglas C. Stedman, *The War Ballads of Laurence Minot* (Dublin: Hodges, Figgis; London: Simpkin, Marshall, Hamilton, Kent, 1917), p. xi. Richard H. Osberg's location of Minot among the county gentry seems to me the most likely; Osberg suggests that he was 'a gentleman-poet' who perhaps 'should be thought of, at least in his youth, as a versifying esquire like the knight's son in Chaucer'. Osberg (ed.), *The Poems of Laurence Minot 1333–1352*, TEAMS Middle English Texts (Kalamazoo, Mich.: Medieval Institute Publications, 1996), p. 5.

10 Robbins, *Manual*, vol. V (1975), p. 1413.

11 David Wallace, *Premodern Places: Calais to Surinam, Chaucer to Aphra Behn* (Oxford University Press, 2004), p. 48.

12 Poem 2, lines 7–12 (*NIMEV* 3080). Minot's verse is cited by poem and line number from the edition of Richard Osberg.

13 By Wilhelm Scholle in 1884, Joseph Hall three times between 1887 and 1914, and Stedman in 1917. In addition, teaching anthologies usually included two or three of Minot's poems: for example, Eduard Mätzner, *Altenglische Sprachproben* (Berlin: Weidmann'sche Buchhandlung, 1867); Richard Paul Wülcker, *Altenglisches Lesebuch*, vol. I (Halle: Max Niemeyer, 1874); Richard Morris and Walter W. Skeat (eds.), *Specimens of Early English*, new and rev. edn (Oxford: Clarendon Press, 1882); Kenneth Sisam (ed.), *Fourteenth Century Verse and Prose* (1921; Oxford: Clarendon Press, 1962). I have written at greater length about the reception of Minot's poems in an article, 'Laurence Minot, Edward III, and Nationalism', *Viator* 38 (2007), 269–88.

14 Sisam (ed.), *Fourteenth Century Verse and Prose*, p. 151. McKisack writes off Minot's verse as 'crudely patriotic'; Sumption calls him a 'patriotic poetaster' and most recently, Michael Prestwich refers to his 'bombastic patriotic poetry … perhaps some of the worst to be produced in that undistinguished genre'. May McKisack, *The Fourteenth Century, 1307–1399* (Oxford: Clarendon Press, 1959), p. 150; Sumption, *Hundred Years War I*, p. 132; Prestwich, *Plantagenet England*, p. 563.

15 Thorlac Turville-Petre, 'Political Lyrics', in Thomas G. Duncan (ed.), *A Companion to the Middle English Lyric* (Woodbridge: D.S. Brewer, 2005), pp. 171–88 (p. 182).

16 Turville-Petre, 'Political Lyrics', pp. 185, 183–4.

17 See Sumption, *Hundred Years War I*, p. 581. Stanley notes that a contemporary French chronicle exists in London, British Library, Harley MS 4690, in which the motif of the intercessory queen, made famous by Le Bel and Froissart, is absent. E. G. Stanley, 'Laurence Minot's "Ten Lyrick Poems, of singular merit, upon the principal events of the reign of the then monarch, king Edward the third"', *Poetica* 67 (2007), 1–18 (4–5, 15 n.10).

18 Pierre Macherey, *A Theory of Literary Production*, trans. Geoffrey Wall (London: Routledge, 1978), p. 87.

19 Paul Strohm, 'What Can We Know About Chaucer That He Didn't Know About Himself?' in *Theory and the Premodern Text* (Minneapolis, Minn. and London: University of Minnesota Press, 2000), pp. 165–81 (p. 165; emphasis added).

20 Macherey, *Theory of Literary Production*, p. 80.

21 Derek Pearsall, *Old English and Middle English Poetry* (London: Routledge & Kegan Paul, 1977), p. 122.

22 For this conclusion, and a summary of critical positions, see Helen Phillips, *An Introduction to The Canterbury Tales: Reading, Fiction, Context* (London: Macmillan, 2000), p. 164.

23 Judson Boyce Allen, 'Grammar, Poetic Form, and the Lyric Ego: A Medieval *A Priori*', in Lois Ebin (ed.), *Vernacular Poetics in the Middle Ages* (Kalamazoo, Mich.: Medieval Institute Publications, 1984), pp. 199–226 (p. 208).

24 Gregory B. Stone, *The Death of the Troubadour: The Late Medieval Resistance to the Renaissance* (Philadelphia, Pa: University of Pennsylvania Press, 1994), pp. 5–6.

25 J. A. W. Bennett, *Middle English Literature*, ed. and completed by Douglas Gray (Oxford: Clarendon Press, 1990), p. 395.

26 James and Simons (eds.), *Poems of Laurence Minot*, pp. 7–8; see Osberg's comment, *Poems of Laurence Minot*, p. 2. Equally well, however, Minot's verse could have been reproduced as a celebration of fresh victories against the French in the reign of Henry V.

27 James and Simons, *Poems of Laurence Minot*, p. 10; Douglas Gray, 'Minot, Laurence (fl. early 14th cent.)', *ODNB*, www.oxforddnb.com/view/article/18812, accessed 8 May 2008. A Laurence Minot is recorded as having purchased land in Ponthieu which belonged to Isabella before it reverted to

Edward (who remitted part of the payment) in 1331. As Gray adds, however, 'there is little hard evidence' about patronage.

28 All three were French speakers. Edward, in Ormrod's opinion, was not bookish. Though he is now seen as having been 'the patron of some of the finest artistic achievements of the day', these were principally in building works. Ormrod, 'Image and Personality' in his 'Edward III (1312–1377)', *ODNB*, www.oxforddnb.com/view/article/8519, accessed 8 May 2008. See also his *Reign of Edward III*, p. 43. Isabella and Philippa, like many queens, seem to have been readers and patrons of books – but the likelihood is, unsurprisingly, that they read works in French. See Katherine Gretchen Allocco, 'Intercessor, Rebel, Regent: The Political Life of Isabella of France (1292/6–1358)', unpublished PhD thesis, University of Texas at Austin (2004), p. 345; see also, on Isabella's education, p. 36; and Juliet Vale, 'Cultural Interests and Patronage' in her 'Philippa (1310x15?–1369)', *ODNB*, www.oxforddnb.com/view/article/22110, accessed 8 May 2008.

29 In demonstrating this Osberg shows, against earlier opinion, that Minot's alliterative formulae have no 'special debt' to the romances or the poems of the so-called alliterative revival. *Poems of Laurence Minot*, pp. 17–18.

30 Ormrod, *Reign of Edward III*, p. 7.

31 Ormrod, 'Posthumous Reputation', in 'Edward III', *ODNB*. Prestwich, similarly, notes Edward's preference for the cults of English saints, suggesting that 'Consciously or unconsciously, he was bolstering not only the crown, but also a sense of English identity.' *Plantagenet England*, p. 31.

32 See, on contemporaneous composition, Joseph Hall (ed.), *Poems of Laurence Minot*, 3rd edn (Oxford: Clarendon Press, 1914), p. xiii; Robbins, *Manual*, vol. v (1975), p. 1412. The last event Minot refers to occurred in 1352 and it is usually assumed that he ended there, probably dying soon after (he would scarcely have declined to write about the victory at Poitiers four years later, this argument assumes). Two pieces of historical evidence are usually regarded as keys: Minot refers to Henry of Lancaster as 'duc', a title which Henry was only given in 1351 (5.41). By contrast, he also implies that Edward can still succeed at the 1340 siege of Tournai, which in fact Edward was forced to give up with nothing achieved (6.35–6). Ritson, however, noting the detail about Lancaster, concluded that the poems were only *composed* after 1352 (*Poems on Interesting Events*, p. xi). *Duc* is an alliterating word, which might suggest it was the original word choice and hence evidence in favour of Ritson's assumption. The detail about Tournai, by contrast, argues for *contemporaneous* composition with later revision at a time when Lancaster's 1351 elevation could be included. It has never been sufficiently recognised, however, that the two details about Lancaster and Tournai contradict one another: if Minot updated Lancaster's title (anachronistically) in 1352, why did he at the same time leave out the knowledge he by then must have had about the failure of the Tournai siege? Clearly, whether he composed at the time or later, Minot simply ignores the failure at Tournai; he writes of what *ought* to have been, in a way parallel with the work of those chroniclers

who made excuses for Edward's failure at this point. Both Minot and the chroniclers ignored inconvenient truths that did not suit their narratives. See further Kelly DeVries, 'Contemporary Views of Edward III's Failure at the Siege of Tournai, 1340', *Nottingham Medieval Studies* 39 (1995), 70–105.

33 A. S. G. Edwards argues that the poems are not necessarily all by Minot; he proposes that the most obvious way of explaining changes in the layout of the poems in the manuscript is through a change of exemplar in Poem 9. This would suggest that the material we attribute to Minot did not originally come from a single source, but that somewhere in the textual tradition, different texts were merged, so that the poems we call Minot's 'may reflect a process of assemblage made not on authorial but on topical grounds through which various poems on the martial achievements of Edward III were yoked together over time'. 'The Authorship of the Poems of Laurence Minot: A Reconsideration', *Florilegium* 23 (2006), 145–53 (151). The main impact of his argument on mine is to suggest that there were more writers doing what I currently impute to Minot alone. I am grateful to Professor Edwards for showing me a copy of his article before publication.

34 James and Simons, *Poems of Laurence Minot*, p. 13. The importance of Minot's affinity with romance has been convincingly disputed by Osberg, but the suggestion of a more unified work still stands. See above, note 29.

35 As I argue more fully in 'Laurence Minot', the rubrics need not always be read as marking the end of one poem and the beginning of another but in some cases seem only to punctuate the narrative, most obviously for example in the case of the transition between Poems 7 and 8. In what follows, this point is not essential to the argument, but it seems to me likely that Minot *composed* in or after 1352, attempting to create an embryonic biography-panegyric, which might be called Minot's *Edward*.

36 'Song of the Husbandman', line 57 in James M. Dean (ed.), *Medieval English Political Writings*, TEAMS Middle English Texts (Kalamazoo, Mich.: Medieval Institute Publications, 1996); Minot, 9.21–2. The image also appears in *Havelok* (line 1994), to describe Havelok's pursuit of his enemies.

37 Even the Scottish defeat at Dupplin Moor in 1332 is equivocal, as Edward III was not present at this treaty-violating venture which relaunched the war with Scotland suspended by Mortimer's *turpis pax* in 1328. Osberg takes the first four lines of Poem 9 as referring to Dupplin Moor: 'Sir David the Bruse . was at distance / when Edward the Baliolfe . rade with his lance; / the north end of Ingland . teched him to daunce / when he was met on the more . with mekill mischance' (*Poems of Laurence Minot*, p. 15). Minot makes no other mention of it.

38 For an extended, and generally positive, analysis of Minot's verse forms see Stanley, 'Laurence Minot's "Ten Lyric Poems"', 5–12.

39 He says almost nothing about the 'appalling' damage done to Southampton, which led to the cessation of commerce 'almost entirely for a year'. Portsmouth had been burnt earlier in the same year. Sumption, *Hundred Years War I*, p. 248.

40 In the manuscript, the first line of this section is marked out by a decorated capital in which a capital 'A' appears as an animal head. It is perhaps intended to be a boar, though if so, the likeness is not good. As I have suggested in 'Laurence Minot', this opening, with its reference to Merlin, its self-naming and its inception of a narrative of a series of victories has the appearance of a beginning; did Minot start here, before prefacing it with the poems on events in the 1330s? An alternative explanation is Edwards' proposal that different poems have been merged; see above, note 33.

41 Benedict Anderson, *Imagined Communities: Reflections on the Origins and Spread of Nationalism*, rev. edn (London and New York: Verso, 1991), p. 36. For fuller discussion of the arguments for and against medieval nationalism, see the Introduction, pp. 18–28.

42 See 3.41–2, 4.55–61, 88, 5.7, 7.88–92.

43 As has been seen above, he praises certain English nobles. There is also praise for such lesser figures as John Badding, apparently a galley master of the Cinque Ports whom earlier editors conjecture to have been a friend of Minot. See Osberg (ed.), *Poems of Laurence Minot,* note to 5.59.

44 Anderson, *Imagined Communities*, p. 7.

45 Making the case against medieval nationalism, Anthony D. Smith states that nationalism is not constituted simply in 'resistance to cultural and political outsiders'; were it to be defined in this way, then 'nationalism can be found in every era and continent'. *National Identity* (London: Penguin, 1991), p. 46. While this appears to constitute a significant mitigation of the case for Minot's nationalism – which arguably consists precisely in his resistance to cultural and political outsiders – what is important is the constitution of *insider*dom that goes along with the resistance to outsiders.

46 R. R. Davies, *The First English Empire: Power and Identities in the British Isles 1093–1343* (Oxford University Press, 2000), p. 80.

47 See Jonathan Sumption, 'Mauny, Sir Walter (c.1310–1372)', *ODNB*, www.oxforddnb.com/view/article/17985, accessed 13 May 2008.

ENVOY

1 Geoffrey Chaucer, *Canterbury Tales* IV.15–19, in Larry D. Benson, gen. ed. *The Riverside Chaucer* (Oxford University Press, 1988).

2 Though it has been thought to have dwindled in importance after mid-century, Gwilym Dodd argues that petitioning continued into the reign of Richard II, but became hidden from view for a number of reasons. 'The Hidden Presence: Parliament and the Private Petition in the Fourteenth Century', in Anthony Musson (ed.), *Expectations of the Law in the Middle Ages* (Woodbridge: Boydell, 2001), pp. 135–49, esp. 137–47. Concerning the reign of Edward III, W. M. Ormrod states that '[t]he widespread belief that requests could only be satisfied if they reached the king's person meant that Edward was constantly and relentlessly pursued'. *The Reign of Edward*

III: Crown and Political Society in England 1327–1377 (New Haven, Conn. and London: Yale University Press, 1990), p. 57.

3 James M. Dean (ed.), *Richard the Redeless and Mum and the Sothsegger* (Kalamazoo, Mich.: Medieval Institute Publications, 2000), lines 15, 31–42.

4 In his recent article, David R. Carlson suggests that there is no secure reference to 'any event postdating the summer of 1399 by more than a few weeks'. 'English Poetry, July–October 1399, and Lancastrian Crime', *Studies in the Age of Chaucer* 29 (2007), 375–418 (380). However, Helen Barr argues for composition after January 1400 in 'The Dates of *Richard the Redeless* and *Mum and the Sothsegger*', *Notes and Queries* 37 (1990), 270–5 (271).

5 On the more general 'petitionary intention' of much fourteenth- and fifteenth-century autobiographical verse and the fictionalizing of that intention as a narrative strategy see J. A. Burrow, 'The Poet as Petitioner', *Studies in the Age of Chaucer* 3 (1981), 61–75.

6 James Simpson, *Oxford English Literary History, Vol. 2: Reform and Cultural Revolution* (Oxford University Press, 2002), p. 2; Simpson's history covers 1350–1547; David Wallace (ed.), *The Cambridge History of Medieval English Literature* (Cambridge University Press, 1999), while more compendious in going back to early Middle English, also takes its account up to 1547. I have discussed what I argue is a new periodisation – in such works as Robert J. Meyer-Lee's *Poets and Power from Chaucer to Wyatt* (Cambridge University Press, 2007) and Wendy Scase's *Literature and Complaint in England, 1272–1553* (Oxford University Press, 2007) – at greater length in my 'Analytical Survey: The Medieval Invasion of Early-Modern England', *New Medieval Literatures* 10 (2008), 227–48.

7 Nicholas Watson, 'Response to the New Chaucer Society Conference, New York, July 27–31, 2006', *The New Chaucer Society Newsletter* 28.2 (Fall 2006), 1–5 (5).

8 On the fifteenth-century stance of abjection, see Seth Lerer, *Chaucer and His Readers: Imagining the Author in Late-Medieval England* (Princeton University Press, 1993); for a bibliography on this point see the Preface, note 3; see also, on the more obscure reaches of the fifteenth century, Paul Strohm, *Politique: Languages of Statecraft between Chaucer and Shakespeare* (Notre Dame, Ind.: University of Notre Dame Press, 2005).

9 Richard H. Osberg (ed.), *The Poems of Laurence Minot 1333–1352* (Kalamazoo, Mich.: Medieval Institute Publications, 1996), pp. 17, 24. Minot might be the only poet combining alliteration and end-rhyme whose *name* we have, but the mingling of the two techniques is abundantly clear in the Harley Lyrics, written down c. 1340.

10 Michael Prestwich, *Plantagenet England 1225–1360* (Oxford: Clarendon Press, 2005), p. 563.

11 Meyer-Lee, *Poets and Power*, p. 29, referring to Leo Spitzer, 'Note on the Poetic and the Empirical "I" in Medieval Authors', *Traditio* 4 (1946), 414–22.

Bibliography

Agamben, Giorgio, *Homo Sacer: Sovereign Power and Bare Life*, trans. Daniel Heller-Roazen (Stanford University Press, 1998)

Allen, Judson Boyce, 'Grammar, Poetic Form, and the Lyric Ego: A Medieval *A Priori*', in Lois Ebin (ed.), *Vernacular Poetics in the Middle Ages* (Kalamazoo, Mich.: Medieval Institute Publications, 1984), pp. 199–226

Allocco, Katherine Gretchen, 'Intercessor, Rebel, Regent: The Political Life of Isabella of France (1292/6–1358)', unpublished PhD thesis, University of Texas at Austin, 2004

Anderson, Benedict, *Imagined Communities: Reflections on the Origins and Spread of Nationalism* rev. edn (London and New York: Verso, 1991)

Ashe, Laura, *Fiction and History in England, 1066–1200* (Cambridge University Press, 2007)

Aspin, Isabel (ed.), *Anglo-Norman Political Songs* (Oxford: Anglo-Norman Text Society, 1953)

Barr, Helen, 'The Dates of *Richard the Redeless* and *Mum and the Sothsegger*', *Notes and Queries* 37 (1990), 270–5

Barrow, G. W., *Robert Bruce and the Community of the Realm of Scotland*, 3rd edn (Edinburgh University Press, 1988)

Bennett, J. A. W., *Middle English Literature*, ed. and completed by Douglas Gray (Oxford: Clarendon Press, 1990)

Bhabha, Homi K., *The Location of Culture* (London: Routledge, 1994)

Bloch, Marc, *Feudal Society*, trans. L. A. Manyon (London: Routledge & Kegan Paul, 1961)

Böddeker, K., *Altenglische Dichtungen des MS. Harley 2253* (Berlin, 1878)

Bothwell, J. S., 'Edward III, The English Peerage, and the 1337 Earls: Estate Redistribution in Fourteenth-Century England', in Bothwell (ed.), *The Age of Edward III*, pp. 35–52

  (ed.), *The Age of Edward III* (York: York Medieval Press, 2001)

Boulton, Maureen Barry McCann, *The Song in the Story: Lyric Insertions in French Narrative Fiction, 1200–1400* (Philadelphia, Pa: University of Pennsylvania Press, 1993)

Boyle, Leonard E., 'William of Pagula and the *Speculum Regis Edwardi III*', *Mediaeval Studies* 32 (1970), 329–36

Brand, Paul, 'Petitions and Parliament in the Reign of Edward I', in Linda Clark
    (ed.), *Parchment and People: Parliament in the Middle Ages*, Parliamentary
    History special issue (Edinburgh University Press, 2004), pp. 14–38
Brandl, A., and O. Zippel, *Mittelenglische Sprach- und Literaturproben*, 2nd edn
    (New York: Chelsea, 1949)
Brie, Friedrich W. D. (ed.), *The Brut or the Chronicles of England*, 2 parts, EETS
    o.s. 131, 136 (Oxford University Press, 1906–8)
Brook, G. L. (ed.), *The Harley Lyrics: The Middle English Lyrics of MS. Harley
    2253*, 4th edn (Manchester University Press, 1968)
    and R.F. Leslie (eds.), *Laȝamon: Brut*, 2 vols, EETS o.s. 250, 277 (Oxford
    University Press for the EETS, 1963, 1978)
Brown, Carleton (ed.), *English Lyrics of the XIIIth Century* (Oxford: Clarendon
    Press, 1932)
Burrow, J. A., 'The Poet as Petitioner', *Studies in the Age of Chaucer* 3 (1981),
    61–75
Butterfield, Ardis, 'Nationhood', in Steve Ellis (ed.), *Chaucer: An Oxford Guide*
    (Oxford University Press, 2005), pp. 50–65
    The Familiar Enemy: Chaucer, Language, and Nation in the Hundred Years War
    (Oxford University Press, 2009)
Calin, William, *The French Tradition and the Literature of Medieval England*
    (Toronto University Press, 1994)
Cannon, Christopher, *The Making of Chaucer's English: A Study of Words*
    (Cambridge University Press, 1998)
    The Grounds of English Literature (Oxford University Press, 2003)
Carlson, David R., 'English Poetry, July–October 1399, and Lancastrian Crime',
    Studies in the Age of Chaucer 29 (2007), 375–418
Carpenter, D.A., *The Battles of Lewes and Evesham, 1264/65* (Keele: Mercia, 1987)
    The Reign of Henry III (London and Rio Grande, Oh.: Hambledon, 1996)
Cerquiglini, Bernard, *In Praise of the Variant: A Critical History of Philology*,
    trans. Betsy Wing (Baltimore, Md and London: Johns Hopkins University
    Press, 1999)
Certeau, Michel de, *The Practice of Everyday Life*, trans. Steven Rendall (Berkeley,
    Calif.: University of California Press, 1984)
Chaucer, Geoffrey, *The Canterbury Tales*, in Larry Benson (gen. ed.), *The
    Riverside Chaucer* (Oxford University Press, 1988)
Child, F. J. (ed.), English and Scottish Ballads. 8 vols. (Boston, Mass.: Little,
    Brown and Co., 1857)
Childs, W. R., '"Welcome, my Brother": Edward II, John of Powderham and the
    Chronicles, 1318', in Ian Wood and G. A. Loud (eds.), *Church and Chronicle
    in the Middle Ages: Essays Presented to John Taylor* (London: Hambledon
    Press, 1991), pp. 149–63
Childs, Wendy (ed. and trans.), *Vita Edwardi Secundi: The Life of Edward the
    Second* (Oxford: Clarendon Press, 2005)
Clanchy, Michael, *From Memory to Written Record: England 1066–1307*, 2nd edn
    (Oxford: Blackwell, 1993)

England and Its Rulers: 1066–1307, 3rd edn (Oxford: Blackwell, 2006)

Cohen, Jeffrey Jerome, *Of Giants: Sex, Monsters, and the Middle Ages* (Minneapolis, Minn.: University of Minnesota Press, 1999)

Coleman, Janet, *English Literature in History: 1350–1400, Medieval Readers and Writers* (London: Hutchinson, 1981)

Danninger, Elizabeth, *Sieben Politische Gedichte der HS. B.L. Harley 2253: Textausgabe und Kommentar* (Würzburg: Konigshausen & Neumann, 1980)

Davies, R. G. and J. H. Denton (eds.), *The English Parliament in the Middle Ages* (Manchester University Press, 1981)

Davies, R. R., *The First English Empire: Power and Identities in the British Isles 1093–1343* (Oxford University Press, 2000)

Davis, Kathleen, 'National Writing in the Ninth Century: A Reminder for Postcolonial Thinking about the Nation', *Journal of Medieval and Early Modern Studies* 28 (1998), 611–37

De Laborderie, Olivier, J. R. Maddicott and D. A. Carpenter, 'The Last Hours of Simon de Montfort: A New Account', *EHR* 115.461 (2000), 378–412

De Wilde, Geert, 'The Stanza Form of the Middle English *Lament for the Death of Edward I*: A Reconstruction', *Anglia* 123.2 (2005), 230–45

Dean, James M. (ed.), *Medieval English Political Writings*, TEAMS Middle English Texts (Kalamazoo, Mich.: Medieval Institute Publications, 1996)

(ed.), *Richard the Redeless and Mum and the Sothsegger* (Kalamazoo, Mich.: Medieval Institute Publications, 2000)

Denholm-Young, N., 'Richard de Bury', *Transactions of the Royal Historical Society*, 4th ser. 20 (1937), 135–68

Richard of Cornwall (Oxford: Basil Blackwell, 1947)

DeVries, Kelly, 'Contemporary Views of Edward III's Failure at the Siege of Tournai, 1340', *Nottingham Medieval Studies* 39 (1995), 70–105

Dickins, Bruce, and R.M. Wilson (eds.), *Early Middle English Texts* (London: Bowes & Bowes, 1951)

Dodd, Gwilym, 'The Hidden Presence: Parliament and the Private Petition in the Fourteenth Century', in Anthony Musson (ed.), *Expectations of the Law in the Middle Ages* (Woodbridge: Boydell, 2001), pp. 135–49

and Anthony Musson (eds.), *The Reign of Edward II: New Perspectives* (Woodbridge: York Medieval Press, 2006)

Eckhardt, Caroline D. (ed.), *Castleford's Chronicle or The Boke of Brut*, 2 vols., EETS 305, 306 (Oxford University Press for the EETS, 1996)

Edwards, A. S. G., 'The Authorship of the Poems of Laurence Minot: A Reconsideration', *Florilegium* 23 (2006), 145–53

Embree, Dan, and Elizabeth Urquhart (eds.), *The Simonie: A Parallel-Text Edition* (Heidelberg: Carl Winter Universitätsverlag, 1991)

Emerson, Oliver Farrar, *A Middle English Reader* (London: Macmillan, 1915)

Fabyan, Robert, *Newe Cronycles of Englande and of Fraunce* (London: Pynson, 1516)

Fein, Susanna (ed.), *Studies in the Harley Manuscript: The Scribes, Contents, and Social Contexts of British Library MS Harley 2253* (Kalamazoo, Mich.: Medieval Institute Publications, 2000)

Ferster, Judith, *Fictions of Advice: The Literature and Politics of Counsel in Late Medieval England* (Philadelphia, Pa: University of Pennsylvania Press, 1996)

Foucault, Michel, *Discipline and Punish: The Birth of the Prison*, trans. Alan Sheridan (New York: Vintage Books, 1979)

Freedman, Paul, *Images of the Medieval Peasant* (Stanford, Calif.: Stanford University Press, 1999)

French, Walter Hoyt, and Charles Brockway Hale, *Middle English Metrical Romances* (New York: Prentice-Hall, 1930)

Froissart, Sir John, *Chronicles of England, France, Spain ...* trans. Thomas Johnes, 2 vols. (London: William Smith, 1842)

Geary, Patrick, *Phantoms of Remembrance: Memory and Oblivion at the End of the First Millennium* (Princeton University Press, 1994)

   The Myth of Nations: The Medieval Origins of Europe (Princeton University Press, 2002)

Geoffrey of Monmouth, *The History of the Kings of Britain*, trans. Lewis Thorpe (London: Penguin, 1966)

   The Historia Regum Britannie of Geoffrey of Monmouth I: Bern, Burgerbibliothek, MS. 568, ed. Neil Wright (Cambridge: D.S. Brewer, 1985)

Gertz, SunHee Kim, *Chaucer to Shakespeare, 1337–1580* (Basingstoke: Palgrave, 2000)

Giancarlo, Matthew, *Parliament and Literature in Late Medieval England* (Cambridge and New York: Cambridge University Press, 2007)

Gillingham, John, *The English in the Twelfth Century: Imperialism, National Identity, and Political Values* (Woodbridge: Boydell, 2000)

Gransden, Antonia, *Historical Writing in England, c.550 to c.1307* (London: Routledge and Kegan Paul, 1974)

   'Propaganda in English Medieval Historiography', *Journal of Medieval History* 1 (1975), 363–82

   Historical Writing in England, c.1307 to the Early Sixteenth Century (London: Routledge & Kegan Paul, 1982)

Gray, Thomas, *Scalachronica: The Reigns of Edward I, Edward II and Edward III as Recorded by Sir Thomas Grey*, trans. Herbert Maxwell (1907; Felinfach: Llanerch Publishers, 2000)

Green, Richard Firth, *A Crisis of Truth: Literature and Law in Ricardian England* (Philadelphia, Pa: University of Pennsylvania, 1999)

Haines, Roy Martin, *King Edward II: Edward of Caernarfon, His Life, His Reign, and Its Aftermath, 1284–1330* (Montreal–Kingston: McGill-Queen's University Press, 2003)

Hall, Joseph (ed.), *Poems of Laurence Minot*, 3rd edn (Oxford: Clarendon Press, 1914)

Halliwell, James Orchard (ed.), *The Chronicle of William de Rishanger, of the Barons' Wars; The Miracles of Simon de Montfort* (London: Camden Society, 1840)

Harding, Alan, 'Plaints and Bills in the History of English Law, Mainly in the Period 1250–1330', in Dafydd Jenkins (ed.), *Legal History Studies 1972: Papers*

Presented to the Legal History Conference Aberystwyth, 18–21 July 1972 (Cardiff: University of Wales Press, 1975), pp. 65–86

Harriss, G.L., 'The Formation of Parliament 1272–1377', in Davies and Denton (eds.), *The English Parliament*, pp. 29–60

Hastings, Adrian, *The Construction of Nationhood: Ethnicity, Religion and Nationalism* (Cambridge University Press, 1997)

Henry, Archdeacon of Huntingdon, *Historia Anglorum: The History of the English People*, ed. and trans. Diana Greenway (Oxford: Clarendon Press, 1996)

Hertz, Frederick, *Nationality in History and Politics* (New York: Humanities Press, 1944)

Herzman, Ronald B., Graham Drake, and Eve Salisbury (eds.), *Four Romances of England* (Kalamazoo, Mich.: Medieval Institute Publications, 1999)

Hewitt, H. J., *The Organisation of War Under Edward III* (Manchester University Press, 1966)

Hoyt, Robert S., 'The Coronation Oath of 1308', *EHR* 71.280 (Jul., 1956), 393–83

Huizinga, Johan, *Men and Ideas: History, the Middle Ages, the Renaissance*, trans. James S. Holmes and Hans van Marle (London: Eyre & Spottiswoode, 1960)

Ingham, Patricia Clare, *Sovereign Fantasies: Arthurian Romance and the Making of Britain* (Philadelphia, Pa: University of Pennsylvania Press, 2001)

Jahn, Johanna, *Die mittelenglische spielmannsballade von Simon Fraser* (Bonn: Peter Hanstein, 1921)

James, Thomas Beaumont, and John Simons (eds.), *The Poems of Laurence Minot 1333–1352* (University of Exeter, 1989)

Justice, Steven, *Writing and Rebellion: England in 1381* (Berkeley, Calif. and London: University of California Press, 1994)

Kaeuper, Richard W., *War, Justice, and Public Order: England and France in the Later Middle Ages* (Oxford: Clarendon Press, 1988)

Kane, George, 'Some Fourteenth-Century "Political" Poems', in Gregory Kratzmann and James Simpson (eds.), *Medieval English Religious and Ethical Literature: Essays in Honour of G. H. Russell* (Cambridge: D.S. Brewer, 1986), pp. 82–91

Kantorowicz, Ernst H., *The King's Two Bodies: A Study in Mediaeval Political Theology* (Princeton University Press, 1957)

Keeney, Barnaby C., 'Military Service and the Development of Nationalism in England, 1272–1327', *Speculum* 22 (1947), 534–49

Kendrick, Laura, 'On Reading Medieval Political Verse: Two Partisan Poems from the Reign of Edward II', *Mediaevalia* 5 (1979), 183–204

Kingsford, C. L. (ed. and trans.), *The Song of Lewes* (Oxford: Clarendon Press, 1890)

Knapp, Ethan, *The Bureaucratic Muse: Thomas Hoccleve and the Literature of Late Medieval England* (University Park, Pa: Pennsylvania State University Press, 2001)

Knight, Stephen, 'The Voice of Labour in Fourteenth-Century English Literature' in James Bothwell, P. J. P. Goldberg and W. M. Ormrod (eds.),

The Problem of Labour in Fourteenth-Century England (Woodbridge: York Medieval Press in association with Boydell & Brewer, 2000), pp. 101–22

and Thomas H. Ohlgren (eds.), *Robin Hood and Other Outlaw Tales* (Kalamazoo, Mich.: Medieval Institute Publications, 1997)

Kohn, Hans, *The Idea of Nationalism: A Study of its Origins and Background* (New York: Macmillan, 1944)

Lavezzo, Kathy (ed.), *Imagining a Medieval English Nation* (Minneapolis, Minn.: University of Minnesota Press, 2003)

Legge, M. Dominica, *Anglo-Norman in the Cloister* (Edinburgh University Press, 1950)

Anglo-Norman Literature and its Background (Oxford: Clarendon, 1963)

Lerer, Seth, *Chaucer and His Readers: Imagining the Author in Late-Medieval England* (Princeton University Press, 1993)

Loomis, R. S., 'Edward I, Arthurian Enthusiast', *Speculum* 28 (1953), 114–27

Luard, Henry Richards (ed.), *Matthaei Parisiensis, Monachi Sancti Albani, Chronica Majora*, 7 vols. RS 57 (London: Longman & Co, Trübner & Co., 1872–83)

(ed.), *Flores Historiarum*, 3 vols. RS 95 (London: HMSO, 1890)

Lumby, J. Rawson (ed.), *Bernardus de cura rei famuliaris, with Early Scottish Prophecies*, EETS o.s. 42 (London: Trübner, 1870)

Machan, Tim William, *English in the Middle Ages* (Oxford University Press, 2003)

Macherey, Pierre, *A Theory of Literary Production*, trans. Geoffrey Wall (London: Routledge, 1978)

Maddicott, J. R., *Thomas of Lancaster 1307–1322: A Study in the Reign of Edward II* (Oxford University Press, 1970)

The English Peasantry and the Demands of the Crown, 1294–1341, Past and Present Society Supplement 1 (Oxford: Past and Present Society, 1975)

'Parliament and the Constituencies, 1272–1377', in Davies and Denton (eds.), *The English Parliament in the Middle Ages*, pp. 61–87

'Poems of Social Protest in Early Fourteenth-Century England', in Ormrod (ed.), *England in the Fourteenth Century*, pp. 130–44

Simon de Montfort (Cambridge University Press, 1994)

Maitland, Frederic, 'A Song on the Death of Simon de Montfort', in H. A. L. Fisher (ed.), *The Collected Papers of Frederic William Maitland*, 3 vols. (Cambridge University Press, 1911), vol. III, pp. 43–9

Martin, G.H. (ed. and trans.), *Knighton's Chronicle 1337–1396* (Oxford: Clarendon Press, 1995)

Masschaele, James, 'The Public Space of the Marketplace in Medieval England', *Speculum* 77 (2002), 383–421

Matthews, David, *The Invention of Middle English: An Anthology of Sources* (Turnhout: Brepols, 2000)

'Laurence Minot, Edward III, and Nationalism', *Viator* 38 (2007), 269–88

'Analytical Survey: The Medieval Invasion of Early-Modern England', *New Medieval Literatures* 10 (2008), 227–48

Mätzner, Eduard, *Altenglische Sprachproben* (Berlin: Weidmann'sche Buchhandlung, 1867)

Maxwell, Herbert (trans.), *The Chronicle of Lanercost 1272–1346* (Glasgow: J. MacLehose, 1913)

McKisack, May, *The Fourteenth Century, 1307–1399* (Oxford: Clarendon Press, 1959)

Merback, Mitchell B., *The Thief, the Cross and the Wheel: Pain and the Spectacle of Punishment in Medieval and Renaissance Europe* (London: Reaktion Books, 1999)

Meyer-Lee, Robert J., *Poets and Power from Chaucer to Wyatt* (Cambridge University Press, 2007)

Moffat, Douglas, 'Sin, Conquest, Servitude: English Self-Image in the Chronicles of the Early Fourteenth Century', in Allen J. Frantzen and Douglas Moffat (eds.), *The Work of Work: Servitude, Slavery, and Labor in Medieval England* (Glasgow: Cruithne Press, 1994), pp. 148–68

Moisant, Joseph (ed.), *De Speculo Regis Edward III* (Paris, 1891)

Morris, Richard, and Walter W. Skeat (eds.), *Specimens of Early English*, new and rev. edn (Oxford: Clarendon Press, 1882)

Nederman, Cary J., 'Property and Protest: Political Theory and Subjective Rights in Fourteenth-Century England', *Review of Politics* 58 (1996), 323–44

  Political Thought in Early Fourteenth-Century England: Treatises by Walter of Milemete, William of Pagula, and William of Ockham (Turnhout: Arizona Center for Medieval and Renaissance Studies in association with Brepols, 2002)

Newhauser, Richard, 'Historicity and Complaint in Song of the Husbandman', in Fein (ed.), *Studies in the Harley Manuscript*, pp. 203–17

Nolan, Maura, *John Lydgate and the Making of Public Culture* (Cambridge University Press, 2005)

Ormrod, W. M. (ed.), *England in the Fourteenth Century: Proceedings of the 1985 Harlaxton Symposium* (Woodbridge: Boydell, 1986)

  The Reign of Edward III: Crown and Political Society in England 1327–1377 (New Haven, Conn. and London: Yale University Press, 1990)

  'Robin Hood and Public Record: The Authority of Writing in the Medieval Outlaw Tradition', in Ruth Evans, Helen Fulton, and David Matthews (eds.), *Medieval Cultural Studies: Essays in Honour of Stephen Knight* (Cardiff: University of Wales Press, 2006), pp. 57–74

Osberg, Richard H. (ed.), *The Poems of Laurence Minot 1333–1352* (Kalamazoo, Mich.: Medieval Institute Publications, 1996)

Owst, G. R., *Literature and Pulpit in Medieval England: A Neglected Chapter in the History of English Letters & of the English People* (1933; 2nd edn Oxford: Basil Blackwell, 1961)

Palgrave, Sir Francis, *Documents and Records Illustrating the History of Scotland and the Transactions between the Crowns of Scotland and England, Preserved in the Treasury of Her Majesty's Exchequer* ([London]: Record Commission, 1837)

Pearsall, Derek, *Old English and Middle English Poetry* (London: Routledge & Kegan Paul, 1977)

Perkins, Nicholas, *Hoccleve's 'Regiment of Princes': Counsel and Constraint* (Cambridge University Press, 2001)

Phillips, Helen, *An Introduction to The Canterbury Tales* (London: Macmillan, 2000)

Post, Gaines, 'Two Notes on Nationalism in the Middle Ages', *Traditio* 9 (1953), 281–320

Powicke, Sir Maurice, *The Thirteenth Century, 1216–1307* (Oxford: Clarendon Press, 1953)

Prestwich, Michael, *Edward I* (New Haven, Conn. and London: Yale University Press, 1997)

  Plantagenet England 1225–1360, New Oxford History of England (Oxford University Press, 2005)

Pritchard, V., *English Medieval Graffiti* (Cambridge University Press, 1967)

Prothero, George Walter, *The Life of Simon de Montfort* (London: Longmans, Green, 1877)

Reynolds, Susan, *Kingdoms and Communities in Western Europe, 900–1300*, 2nd edn (Oxford: Clarendon Press, 1997)

Ridgeway, Huw, 'King Henry III and the "Aliens", 1236–1272', *Thirteenth Century England* 2 (1987), 81–92

Rigby, S. H., *English Society in the Later Middle Ages: Class, Status and Gender* (Basingstoke: Macmillan, 1995)

Rigg, A. G., *A History of Anglo-Latin Literature 1066–1422* (Cambridge University Press, 1992)

Riley, Henry Thomas (ed.), *Willelmi Rishanger, quondam Monachi S. Albani ... Cronica et annales (A.D. 1259–1307) ...* RS 28.2 (London: Longman, Green, Longman, Roberts and Green, 1865)

  (ed.), *Johannis de Trokelowe, et Henrici de Blaneforde ... Chronica et Annales ...* RS 28.3 (London: Longman, Green, Reader and Dyer, 1866)

[Ritson, Joseph (ed.)], *Poems on Interesting Events in the Reign of King Edward III ... By Laurence Minot* (London, 1795)

Robbins, Rossell Hope, 'Middle English Poems of Protest', *Anglia* 78 (1960), 193–203

  (ed.), *Historical Poems of the XIVth and XVth Centuries* (New York: Columbia University Press, 1959)

Roche, T. W. E., *The King of Almayne* (London: John Murray, 1966)

Rothwell, Harry (ed.), *English Historical Documents, 1189–1327* (London: Eyre & Spottiswoode, 1975)

Royer, Katherine, 'The Body in Parts: Reading the Execution Ritual in Late Medieval England', *Historical Reflections* 29.2 (2003), 313–39

Salter, Elisabeth, *English and International: Studies in the Literature, Art and Patronage of Medieval England*, ed. Derek Pearsall and Nicolette Zeeman (Cambridge University Press, 1988)

Scanlon, Larry, *Narrative, Authority, and Power: The Medieval Exemplum and the Chaucerian Tradition* (Cambridge University Press, 1994) and James Simpson (eds.), *John Lydgate: Poetry, Culture, and Lancastrian England* (Notre Dame, Ind.: University of Notre Dame Press, 2006)

Scarry, Elaine, *The Body in Pain* (Oxford University Press, 1985)

Scase, Wendy, *Literature and Complaint in England, 1272–1553* (Oxford University Press, 2007)

Scattergood, John, 'Authority and Resistance: The Political Verse', in Fein (ed.), *Studies in the Harley Manuscript*, pp. 163–201

Scattergood, V. J., 'Political Context, Date and Composition of *The Sayings of the Four Philosophers*', *Medium Ævum* 37 (1968), 157–65

'Adam Davy's *Dreams* and Edward II', *Archiv für das Studium der Neueren Sprachen und Literaturen* 206 (1970), 253–60

Politics and Poetry in the Fifteenth Century (London: Blandford, 1971)

Schulze, Hagen, *States, Nations and Nationalism: From the Middle Ages to the Present*, trans. William E. Yuill (Oxford: Blackwell, 1996)

Shafer, Boyd C., *Nationalism: Myth and Reality* (London: Victor Gollancz, 1955)

Shenton, Caroline, 'Edward III and the Coup of 1330', in Bothwell (ed.), *The Age of Edward III*, pp. 13–34

Simpson, James, *Oxford English Literary History, Vol. 2, 1350–1547: Reform and Cultural Revolution* (Oxford University Press, 2002)

Sisam, Kenneth (ed.), *Fourteenth Century Verse and Prose* (1921; Oxford: Clarendon Press, 1962)

Smallwood, T. M., 'The Lament of Edward II', *Modern Language Review* 68 (1973), 521–9

Smith, Anthony D., *National Identity* (London: Penguin, 1991)

Sperber, Hilmar, *Historisch-politische Gedichte im England Edwards I: Untersuchungen zu mittelenglischen, anglonormannischen und anglolateinischen Texten aus den Jahren 1261 bis 1308*, Series Anglistische Forschungen 178 (Heidelberg: Carl Winter Universitätsverlag, 1985)

Spierenburg, Pieter, *The Spectacle of Suffering: Executions and the Evolution of Repression: From a Preindustrial Metropolis to the European Experience* (Cambridge University Press, 1984)

Spitzer, Leo, 'Note on the Poetic and Empirical "I" in Medieval Authors', *Traditio* 4 (1946), 414–22

Stanley, E. G., 'Laurence Minot's "Ten Lyrick Poems, of singular merit, upon the principal events of the reign of the then monarch, king Edward the third"', *Poetica* 67 (2007), 1–18

Stedman, Douglas C., *The War Ballads of Laurence Minot* (Dublin: Hodges, Figgis; London: Simpkin, Marshall, Hamilton, Kent, 1917)

Steiner, Emily, *Documentary Culture and the Making of Medieval English Literature* (Cambridge University Press, 2003)

Stone, Gregory B., *The Death of the Troubadour: The Late Medieval Resistance to the Renaissance* (Philadelphia, Pa: University of Pennsylvania Press, 1994)

Stones, E. L. G., 'The Anglo-Scottish Negotiations of 1327', *Scottish Historical Review* 30 (1951), 49–54 and Grant G. Simpson, *Edward I and the Throne of Scotland, 1290–1296*, 2 vols. (Oxford University Press, 1978)

'English Chroniclers and the Affairs of Scotland, 1286–1296', in R. H. C. Davis, and J. M. Wallace-Hadrill (eds.), *The Writing of History in the Middle Ages: Essays Presented to Richard William Southern* (Oxford: Clarendon Press, 1981), pp. 323–48

Strohm, Paul, *Hochon's Arrow: The Social Imagination of Fourteenth-Century Texts* (Princeton University Press, 1992)

England's Empty Throne: Usurpation and the Language of Legitimation, 1399–1422 (New Haven, Conn. and London: Yale University Press, 1998)

Theory and the Premodern Text (Minneapolis, Minn. and London: University of Minnesota Press, 2000)

Politique: Languages of Statecraft between Chaucer and Shakespeare (Notre Dame, Ind.: University of Notre Dame Press, 2005)

Stubbs, William, *Select Charters and Other Illustrations of English Constitutional History*, 8th edn (Oxford: Clarendon Press, 1905)

(ed.), *Chronicles of the Reigns of Edward I and Edward II*, 2 vols., RS 76 (London: Longman, 1882–83)

Studer, Paul, 'An Anglo-Norman Poem', *Modern Language Review* 16 (1921), 34–46

Sullens, Idelle (ed.), *Robert Mannyng of Brunne: The Chronicle*, MRTS 153 (Binghamton, NY: MRTS, 1996)

Summerfield, Thea, 'The Context and Genesis of Pierre de Langtoft's *Chronicle*', in Donald Maddox and Sarah Sturm-Maddox (eds.), *Literary Aspects of Courtly Culture* (Cambridge: D.S. Brewer, 1994), pp. 321–32

'The Political Songs in the *Chronicles* of Pierre de Langtoft and Robert Mannyng', in Evelyn Mullally and John Thompson (eds.), *The Court and Cultural Diversity* (Woodbridge: D.S. Brewer, 1997), pp. 139–48

The Matter of King's Lives: The Design of Past and Present in the Early Fourteenth-Century Verse Chronicles by Pierre de Langtoft and Robert Mannyng (Amsterdam and Atlanta, Ga.: Rodopi, 1998)

'The Testimony of Writing: Pierre de Langtoft and the Appeals to History, 1291–1306', in Rhiannon Purdie and Nicola Royan (eds.), *The Scots and Medieval Arthurian Legend* (Woodbridge: D.S. Brewer, 2005), pp. 25–41

Sumption, Jonathan, *The Hundred Years War I: Trial by Battle* (Philadelphia, Pa: University of Pennsylvania Press, 1999)

Tait, James, 'On the Date and Authorship of the *Speculum Regis Edwardi*', EHR 16 (1901), 110–15

Thiolier, Jean Claude, *Édition Critique et Commentée de Pierre de Langtoft: Le Règne d'Édouard Ier* (Créteil: CELIMA Université de Paris, 1989)

'Pierre de Langtoft: Historiographe d'Edouard Ier Plantagenêt', in Ian Short (ed.), *Anglo-Norman Anniversary Essays,* Anglo-Norman Text Society occasional publications series, 2 (London: Anglo-Norman Text Society, 1993), pp. 379–94

Thorne, Samuel E. (trans.), *Bracton on the Laws and Customs of England*, 3 vols. (Cambridge: Belknap Press in association with the Selden Society, 1968–77)

Tipton, C. Leon (ed.), *Nationalism in the Middle Ages* (New York: Holt, Rinehart and Winston, 1972)

Tout, T. F., 'The Captivity and Death of Edward of Carnarvon', *Bulletin of the John Rylands Library* 6 (1921), 69–114

Turville-Petre, Thorlac, 'Politics and Poetry in the Early Fourteenth Century: The Case of Robert Mannyng's *Chronicle*', *Review of English Studies* 39 (1988), 1–28

    'The "Nation" in English Writings of the Early Fourteenth Century', in N. Rogers (ed.), *England in the Fourteenth Century* (Stamford: Paul Watkins, 1993), pp. 128–39

    England the Nation: Language, Literature, and National Identity, 1290–1340 (Oxford: Clarendon Press, 1996)

    'Political Lyrics', in Thomas G. Duncan (ed.), *A Companion to the Middle English Lyric* (Woodbridge: D.S. Brewer, 2005), pp. 171–88

Valente, Claire, 'The "Lament of Edward II": Religious Lyric, Political Propaganda', *Speculum* 77 (2002), 422–39

    The Theory and Practice of Revolt in Medieval England (Aldershot: Ashgate, 2003)

Wallace, David, *Premodern Places: Calais to Surinam, Chaucer to Aphra Behn* (Oxford University Press, 2004)

    (ed.), *The Cambridge History of Medieval English Literature* (Cambridge University Press, 1999)

Warren, Michelle R., *History on the Edge: Excalibur and the Borders of Britain, 1100–1300* (Minneapolis, Minn.: University of Minnesota Press, 2000)

Watson, Nicholas, 'Response to the New Chaucer Society Conference, New York, July 27–31, 2006', *The New Chaucer Society Newsletter* 28.2 (Fall 2006), 1–5

Wilde, Fergus, 'History and Legend in the Chronicle of Peter of Langtoft', unpublished PhD Thesis, University of Manchester, 1997

Wilson, R. M., *The Lost Literature of Medieval England* (London: Methuen, 1952)

Wogan-Browne, Jocelyn, Nicholas Watson, Andrew Taylor and Ruth Evans (eds.), *The Idea of the Vernacular: An Anthology of Middle English Literary Theory, 1280–1520* (University Park Pa: Pennsylvania State University Press, 1999)

Woodbine, George E. (ed.), *De legibus et consuetudinibus Angliae*, 4 vols. (New Haven, Conn.: Yale University Press, 1915–42)

Wright, Thomas (ed. and trans.), *The Political Songs of England: From the Reign of John to that of Edward II* (London: Camden Society, 1839)

    (ed.), *Political Poems and Songs Relating to English History*, RS 14.2 (London: Longman, Green, Longman and Roberts, 1861) (ed.), *The Chronicle of Pierre de Langtoft*, 2 vols., RS 47 (London: Longmans, Green, Reader, and Dyer, 1866–8)

(ed.), *Thomas Wright's Political Songs of England: From the Reign of John to that of Edward II*, with a new intro. by Peter Coss (Cambridge University Press, 1996)

Wright, William Aldis (ed.), *The Metrical Chronicle of Robert of Gloucester*, 2 vols., RS 86 (London: HMSO, 1887)

Wülcker, Richard Paul, *Altenglisches Lesebuch* (Halle: Max Niemeyer, 1874)

Young, Robert, *White Mythologies: Writing History and the West* (London: Routledge, 1990)

Zettl, Ewald (ed.), *An Anonymous Short English Metrical Chronicle*, EETS o.s. 196 (Oxford University Press for EETS, 1935)

Zumthor, Paul, *Essai de poétique médiévale* (Paris: Seuil, 1972)

Index

CAMBRIDGE STUDIES IN MEDIEVAL LITERATURE